DISCRIMINATION, RETIREMENT AND PENSIONS

To Sushma, Sunny and Rishi

Discrimination, Retirement and Pensions

JAGDISH HANDA
McGill University

Avebury

Aldershot · Brookfield USA · Hong Kong · Singapore · Sydney

Published by
Avebury
Ashgate Publishing Limited
Gower House
Croft Road
Aldershot
Hants GU11 3HR
England

Ashgate Publishing Company
Old Post Road
Brookfield
Vermont 05036
USA

British Library Cataloguing in Publication Data

Handa, Jagdish
  Discrimination, Retirement and Pensions
  I. Title
  331.252
ISBN 1 85628 849 8

Library of Congress Cataloging-in-Publication Data

Handa, Jagdish
  Discrimination, retirement and pensions / Jagdish Handa
    p. cm.
  Includes bibliographical references.
  ISBN 1-85628-849 8
  1. Age discrimination in employment. 2. Retirement.
  3. Women--Employment. 4. Equal pay for equal work.
  I. Title.
  HD6279.H36 1994   94-15634
  331.25'2--dc20   CIP

Printed and Bound in Great Britain by
Athenaeum Press Ltd, Newcastle upon Tyne.

Contents

Preface   viii

1   Introduction   1
     1.1 The outline of the book   1
     1.2 The distinctiveness of the book   9
     1.3 Distinctive predictions   11

2   Characteristics and the Returns to General and Specific Skills   15
     2.1 General and specific skills and technologies   18
     2.2 Skills and characteristics in long run analysis   20
     2.3 The return to the worker's characteristics   22
     2.4 The return to the firm for its characteristics   23
     2.5 Sharing the return to general skills   24
     2.6 Sharing the return to firm-specific skills   25
     Conclusion   26

3   Optimal Ages of Hiring and Retirement: The Firm's Perspective   31
     3.1 The basic model   33
     3.2 The optimal number of jobs   41
     3.3 The optimal hiring and retirement ages for career workers   42
     3.4 The optimal hiring and retirement ages for casual workers   44
     3.5 The rental value of jobs   47
     3.6 A clarification   50
     3.7 Wage and occupational discrimination   53
     Conclusion   54

4	Wage and Occupational Differentiation by Sex	57
	4.1 Expected turnover as a basis for wage differences	63
	4.2 Wage discrimination and hiring and training costs	66
	4.3 A female-male sequence versus an all female sequence	67
	4.4 Differences in abilities and wage discrimination	68
	4.5 Turnover, abilities and occupational segregation	70
	4.6 Differentiation within male and female categories	73
	4.7 Wage discrimination and increased longevity	74
	4.8 Wage differentiation and innovations	75
	4.9 The duration of employment, labour supply and education	76
	Conclusion	77
	Appendix	81
5	Discrimination against Hiring Older Workers	87
	5.1 The optimal hiring age model	88
	5.2 The optimal hiring age for career workers	91
	5.3 The optimal hiring age for casual workers	93
	5.4 Skill acquisition costs	94
	5.5 The discrimination premium	97
	5.6 The optimal hiring age and discrimination	99
	5.7 Unemployment and underemployment among older job losers	102
	Conclusion	103
6	Optimal Retirement Policies: The Firm's Choices	106
	6.1 The main existing approaches	112
	6.2 The basic model for decisions on retirement	117
	6.3 The optimal retirement ages for casual workers	122
	6.4 The optimal retirement age for career workers	123
	6.5 The optimal retirement age and innovations	124
	6.6 Retirement versus reductions in wages	127
	6.7 A diagrammatic illustration	132
	6.8 Team sports: an illustration	134
	6.9 Co-ordination of retirement ages	136
	6.10 Workers and mandatory retirement	137
	6.11 Some implications of our framework	138
	6.12 The elimination of mandatory retirement policies	141
	Conclusion	143

Contents

7	The Rental Value of a Job and Jobs as Dam Sites	151
	7.1 Jobs as dam sites	154
	7.2 The price and rental value of jobs:	
	jobs as a scarce resource	155
	7.3 Non-optimal classes of workers	162
	7.4 Job incumbents as job owners	163
	7.5 Severance payments and early retirement bonuses	166
	7.6 Reverse severance payments and vesting	169
	Conclusion	171
8	Retirement - The Worker's Choice	174
	8.1 Retirement: the worker's choice under certainty	175
	8.2 Uncertainty and stochastic dynamic analysis	
	of workers' choices	178
	8.3 The impact of the passage of time	185
	8.4 Policy-induced changes in retirement ages	189
	Conclusion	190
9	Retirement and Private Pension Plans	193
	9.1 Pensions and the divergence in the retirement ages	
	preferred by workers and firms	195
	9.2 Pensions and vesting: unvested pension funds	201
	9.3 Pensions as savings	204
	9.4 Pensions and the retirement age	205
	9.5 Some rough calculations	207
	Conclusion	208
10	Summary and Conclusions	213
	10.1 General and firm-specific skills	215
	10.2 The basic model	216
	10.3 Discrimination	217
	10.4 The firm's preferred retirement age	220
	10.5 The worker's preferred retirement age	222
	10.6 Pensions	223
	10.7 The rental value of a job position	224
	10.8 The impact of innovations	225
Bibliography		229

Preface

Discrimination against women and minorities, and in hiring older workers, are pervasive aspects of the European and North American economies, as well as of most other economies, cutting across geographical and cultural boundaries. Societal tolerance for them seems to have almost vanished, perhaps more so at the intellectual level than in practice, and often also at the legislative level. The actual extent of discrimination has also been decreasing, though not as fast as societal attitudes and legislation seem to want.

Changes have also been occurring in society's attitudes to firms' mandatory retirement schemes, and legislation to abolish these - just as legislation to abolish discrimination in jobs - has been put in place in many countries. Again, while such schemes may have been legally abolished, their existence, through firm-induced layoffs, does not seem to have decreased to the extent desired by popular intent and national or sub-national legislation.

Both discrimination and retirement are interesting topics to study at any time but are made even more interesting at the present time when there are fundamental changes in our views on their legitimacy, without corresponding decreases in their prevalence. This conflict between reality and legitimacy compels an examination of the fundamental determinants of the exercise of discriminatory practices by the firm and of its retirement policies. There are several theories in the literature explaining these determinants. However, in general, they treat discrimination and retirement as separate topics, with distinctive theories for each. This book argues that there are strong common elements affecting firms' policies regarding wage discrimination, discrimination in hiring and about retirement, and adds to the existing literature by presenting a more unified framework on these topics than currently exists.

The study of labour economics has been almost transformed in recent decades by applications to it of the human capital approach, starting with the contributions of Mincer, Oi, Schultz and, perhaps more than anyone else, of Becker. These applications have cut a wide swathe through the economics of the labour market, including the parts of it dealing with wage differentiation and discrimination, retirement and pensions.

The contributions of Oi, Becker and Okun, among others, had drawn a distinction between general and firm-specific skills, and their distinctive roles in the sharing of the worker's marginal product between the worker's wages and a rent or quasi-rent retained by the firm. This distinctiveness has often not been maintained in recent applications of the human capital approach to wage differentiation and discrimination, retirement and pensions. To illustrate, several recent theories of retirement would apply equally well to workers with purely general skills as to workers possessing also significant firm-specific skills. This book makes a contribution to labour economics by basing its analysis on the distinction between firm-specific and general skills and using this analysis as a unifying theme to explain several aspects of wage differentiation and discrimination, retirement and pensions. The core of this analysis is a theory of the optimal hiring and retirement ages of workers.

The theories of wage determination, hiring and retirement currently prevalent in labour economics also do not generally take into account the replacement of workers over time in a given job. This is so even though by far the dominant case in practice for a firm when retiring or laying off a worker is not to eliminate the job but to hire another worker to fill it. This book rectifies this omission in the literature by incorporating the replacement of workers in a given job throughout its analysis.

A still another aspect of the current state of labour economics seems to be its quite separate theories or models for wage and occupational discrimination against women, for wage and occupational discrimination in hiring against older male and female job applicants and for retirement. This book shows that the analysis of firm-specific skills within a worker replacement model surprisingly provides a unifying framework for explaining certain facets of all of these, and, as such, provides new testable hypotheses spanning these fields.

Parts of this book have been presented in various conferences and seminars in the past few years. Chapters 2, 4 and 5 in earlier forms were published in:

"Labour characteristics and the return to general and specific skills", *Eastern Economic Journal*, vol. XIII, no. 2, April-June 1987, pp. 99 - 106.

"Wage and occupational discrimination against women: A labour rents analysis", *Anvasek*, vol. 17, no.1, June 1987, pp. 1-25.

"The optimal hiring age and discrimination by age", in Edgar Ortiz, ed., *Public Administration, Economics and Finance, Current Issues in the North American and Caribbean Countries*, 1988-89, pp. 384 - 401.

I am grateful to the publishers of the above materials for their reuse in this book.

I am also grateful to many individuals for their comments and suggestions over the years and especially to Venkatesh Bala, Tony Deutsch and John Galbraith for their suggestions and help. I am especially grateful to Paul Davenport for his encouragement.

I wish to thank Maria Orsini-Marcheschi, Linda Holtzman and Janet Martone for their assistance in typing this manuscript. I also owe a considerable debt of gratitude to Donald Sedgewick and Joseph Vacirca for their assistance with the computer programs.

I dedicate this book to my wife, *Sushma*, and sons, *Sunny* and *Rishi*, in appreciation of their love and support over the years.

1 Introduction

1.1 The outline of the book

Oi (1962) and Becker (1962, 1975), among others, categorized workers' skills as general or firm-specific. These skills are partly learnt in specialized institutions - such as schools, universities or training courses - or learnt on the job, as a by-product of experience. The acquisition of skills is a major determinant of the workers' productivity (Topel, 1991). Of the two types of skills, the firm-specific skills are more likely to be acquired by learning on the job over a period of time in a given firm, rather than in educational institutions, though the latter do seem to provide the infra-structure of general knowledge and skills facilitating the acquisition and productivity of firm-specific skills. From another perspective, with firm-specific skills acquired by experience on the job, the job's characteristics may be seen as generating the ability to acquire firm-specific skills and as determining their productivity. In reality, it is the combination of the worker's abilities and knowledge, combined with the nature of the job and the environment within the firm, which determines both the acquisition and the productivity of firm-specific skills.

Workers/jobs can, therefore, be distinguished on the basis of whether they possess/require only general skills or whether they also possess/require some firm-specific skills. Following Okun (1981), the former can be designated as casual workers/jobs, and the latter as career ones. In reality, every job involves some firm-specificity. However, minor forms of firm-specificity which require very short periods of learning do not seem to have significant implications and might be ignored. With this *caveat*, casual jobs may well be more numerous than career jobs in the economy, though both

1

are quite common.

The acquisition of firm-specific skills may require the incurring of an explicit cost, such as in training courses; an implicit cost, such as in output foregone while time is taken out for learning on the job; or through an almost costless process, mainly involving being on the job. While human capital theory has attributed many of its results on job attachment to the learning of firm-specific skills at a significant cost, a considerable part of the acquisition of firm-specific skills occurs almost costlessly through the workers performing or observing the performance of the relevant career job. The appropriate term for such acquisition of skills may then be 'development' rather than training or learning of skills. We envisage this developmental form of the acquisition of skills over a significant period while on the job, to be the more important case, though our analysis and implications in this book apply equally well to both costless and at cost cases. While our analysis does take some account of hiring and training costs, they are not the main focus of our analysis. Further, we deliberately choose to ignore search and search costs though they are often elements of the usual treatment of firm-specific skills.

The 'career' - that is, the employment path - of a career worker is envisaged to include promotions, when such promotions are part of an internal progression of jobs within the firm. Each promotion may involve the acquisition of new firm-specific skills, so that the development of such skills may be a discontinuous process over the worker's career.

The acquisition of firm-specific skills makes workers more productive to the firm. This gain in productivity is the return to such skills. From another perspective, workers possessing firm-specific skills have a higher productivity in the given firm in which their job utilizing those skills is located rather than in other firms. This productivity difference is in the form of a rent or quasi-rent since it is lost if the worker moves to another firm. In competitive markets, the minimum wage the given firm has to pay to retain the career worker equals his productivity - and wage - in other firms, so that the firm can retain the whole of the rent generated by the worker on the job utilizing his firm-specific skills. In practice, as Okun emphasized, the rent is likely to be shared between the firm and the worker. This can be justified as improving the worker's morale and productivity, an argument that leads to an efficiency wage model (Akerlof, 1984). It can also be justified in a more neoclassical manner, as we will discuss below in the remarks on chapter 2.

The sharing of the rents between the firm and the worker in a job utilizing firm-specific skills, and given a significant acquisition period for

2

such skills, creates an incentive for the worker to stay with the firm, and for the firm to retain him, for a long period. Such an interest does not exist in the case of casual workers doing casual jobs, since such workers can receive the same wage in other firms and since the firm can hire other workers with the same net return or rents, so that replacing a casual worker by another will not change the firm's profits. Long term job attachment is thus a consequence of significant firm-specific skills with significant acquisition periods. By comparison, casual workers in casual jobs will not have long term job attachment, in so far as the nature of their skills and jobs is concerned.

The productivity of firm-specific skills arises out of the interaction of workers' ability, strength and other characteristics with the nature of the job. Since the former vary with the worker's age, the optimal beginning/hiring and end (through a quit, firing or retirement) points of the job attachment period depend upon the worker's life cycle of characteristics. The firm would, therefore, prefer to hire the worker at some age and fire/retire him at another, depending upon his rent generating function. The worker, on the basis of his own preferences and constraints, would have his own preferred ages for joining the firm and leaving it. There is no reason to assume that the firm's preferred ages for hiring and for retirement would match those preferred by the worker for joining and for leaving the firm. This likely conflict creates the potential for discrimination in wages and occupations between otherwise equally qualified workers. To illustrate, if the firm finds it profit-maximizing to hire workers at age 25 (in years), it would only hire older and younger workers than this age at lower wages than for the optimal age group. A manifestation of this is wage discrimination against hiring older workers. And if female workers are not expected to stay with the firm until the firm's preferred retirement age, while male workers are, the firm increases its profits by employing only male workers, unless it can pay sufficiently lower wages to female workers, with the resulting wage discrimination against female workers. Further, wage discrimination, under certain circumstances such as a penalty to the firm for practising such discrimination or in the context of efficiency wages, leads to occupational discrimination.

Firm-specific skills lead to long term job attachment, and job attachment often makes it attractive for workers to leave part of their compensation as savings with the firm, to be paid later as pensions. Therefore, firm-administered private pension schemes are likely to occur for firm-specific workers. The potential conflict between the firm's and the worker's preferred retirement ages leads to the institution of actuarially unfair pension plans, early retirement bonuses etc.

Firm-specific skills are a more or less significant aspect of many jobs in the economy. Consequently, we find that their accompaniments in the form of long term job attachment, discrimination against women and older workers, retirement policies and pensions etc. are pervasive in the economy. This book is an investigation into these implications of firm-specific skills.

The major alternative models in the literature on long-term job attachment assume an implicit contract which the worker and the firm honour over the term of the contract, even though the contract is not legally binding. This term of the contract may be several decades, since it is from hiring to retirement. These implicit contracts can be based on mutual interest over very long periods by the firm in the worker and by the worker in the firm. Such trust is especially one of the cornerstones of the wage-deferral incentives models (Becker and Stigler, 1974, Lazear 1979; Lazear and Moore, 1984; Viscusi, 1980, among others) which imply that in the early years on the job, the worker will be willing to receive only part of his current marginal product in current wages, with the remainder accumulated in an *unvested* fund in the firm's hands for payment to the worker later in his career. We do not believe that workers in general can trust the firm enough over long periods to agree to such a payment scheme. Firms fire, and not merely lay off, workers for a variety of reasons, including changes in demand, changes in personal preferences arising from changes in managers, etc. Few industrial workers seem to feel that they have long term security in their jobs, but tend to believe that the civil service and academia are the sectors with such security. And even in the case of universities, such security of employment is explicit, not implicit, through the established concept of tenure.

Empirical evidence on this question of trust and deferral of compensation varies. Among other studies, while Medoff and Abraham (1980, 1981) presented conclusions that seniority related earnings growth need not wholly come from productivity growth, Abraham and Farber (1987) found no evidence of earnings deferral as an important force in labour markets, justifying our assumption that workers may not trust firms sufficiently to agree to wage deferral over long periods. Further, wage deferral schemes are not the only - or the simplest - methods of encouraging effort and absence of shirking on the job. Among other factors encouraging effort is that jobs consist of promotion possibilities, with those putting in greater effort being rewarded by promotions and higher wages, so that compensation varies with effort (Fama, 1980). The labour market also enforces discipline on workers since those caught shirking and laid off find it difficult to find jobs, with heavy search costs and often at reduced wages. Further, workers being laid off or quitting also tend to lose seniority rights which confer monetary and nonmonetary rewards. Hence, wage deferral schemes are only one way of enforcing greater effort and are supplementary to factors which exist automatically in the very fact of being employed and in promotion possibilities.

Alternative models to the incentive based wage deferral schemes have also been proposed by Hashimoto (1981) and Carmichael (1983), though their model relies on a contract under which junior workers would be promoted to jobs held by senior workers if the latter were laid off by the firm. Therefore, the *firm* will not have an incentive to cheat since the junior workers rather than the firm gains by such layoffs. The replacement workers in our model serve as a type of 'junior' workers in Carmichael's model.

As against the above, we tend to rely on the shared interest of the *firm* and the *worker* in the rents generated by the already accumulated firm-specific skills, with *both* suffering a loss of these from a job separation.

Given our lack of reliance on incentives based wage deferral ideas or on an implicit insurance scheme, long-term job tenure in our model is an *ex post* phenomena resulting from the *continuing self-interest* of workers and firms: each earns firm-specific rents through continued employment so that each would be worse off by a quit/dismissal. However, if this self-interest changes sufficiently to make a quit or dismissal attractive enough, job separation would result. Thus, changes in demand, technology, compatibility requirements (e.g., with new foremen and managers), etc., may persuade a firm to opt for a change in employees. Changes in personal factors, such as new job offers, marriage, birth of children and relocation of a spouse, personality conflicts with other employees and managers, health factors, etc. may induce workers to quit an existing job. Therefore, in our theory, there is no *ex ante* implicit contract for long term job attachment, though there is *ex post* evidence of long duration of employment with the same firm. Given the prevalence in the literature of models espousing implicit and incentives based contracts, the preceding statement may seem heretical. However, while there is plenty of evidence of long duration of employment with the same firm in certain types of occupations, the evidence of the existence of *ex ante* implicit contracts is quite weak.

In our approach, workers and firms stay together for long periods, not because of *past* commitments and past benefits received, but because each expects net benefits over the *present and future* from the continuation of employment. These net benefits arise from the rents generated by the accumulated firm-specific skills. Clearly, more accumulated skills generate

5

more rents and benefits for each party than less accumulated ones, so that job layoffs and quits will fall with seniority until other factors such as skill obsolescence, physical and mental slow-down and poor health with advanced age come into play.

Several recent models, especially in the implicit contract approach, assume that the firm takes its workers' interests into account in formulating its own layoff and retirement policies. Thus in the incentives approach to retirements, the firm adopts a retirement age consistent with the worker's preferences. Our analysis eschews such harmonization. Our analysis for the retirement ages preferred by the firm (in chapter 6) and that by the worker (in chapter 8) are distinct ones, with uncertainty and incomplete markets playing a major role. This distinctiveness leads to imposed mandatory retirement policies (chapter 6) and/or the use of pension plans and early retirement bonuses as harmonization tools (chapter 9).

Chapter 2 looks at the implications of worker and job characteristics for wages, especially from a long-term perspective. It argues that the distinction between general and firm-specific skills is based on the rigidities in skills after they have been acquired. As such, it is incongruous with the general tenor of Becker's analysis and of human capital theory generally since they deal with the *ex ante* decisions on the acquisition of skills. This *ex ante* perspective has to be from a point in time before the skills are acquired and before the rigidities introduced by firm-specific skills enter into the picture. What is pertinent at this *ab initio* point in time are the abilities and the prior knowledge of workers, as well as the facilities provided by the firm for acquiring such skills. The general thrust of long-run neoclassical analysis has to be on these abilities, prior knowledge and facilities. Chapter 2 focuses on these factors and the returns to them - and through them on the returns to general and firm-specific skills - in an analysis based on Lancaster's distinction between characteristics and activities (Lancaster, 1966a, 1966b).

Much, if not most, of the human capital literature has focused on the *worker's* acquisition of such capital and its implications. The part of this literature that has focused on the *firm's* decisions - especially in the incentives models (Lazear, 1979) or in applications of the human capital model to mandatory retirement decisions (Blinder, 1981) - has done so in models ignoring the replacement of workers over time in a given job, even though empirical studies on the layoff or retirement of older workers usually do mention the firm's desire to replace them with younger workers (for example, see Kleiler, 1978, p.76; Gee and McDaniel, 1991). That is, the former have ignored the factors that come into play in the firm's decision on when to replace one worker by another in a given job. Chapter 3 focuses on these factors and lays out the unifying framework for chapters 4 to 7 of this book. Chapters 4 and 5 use such a replacement model to explain elements of the discrimination in wages and hiring by sex and age. Chapter 6 uses a similar model to explain the preferred retirement policies of firms, including firms' desire to impose a mandatory retirement age on their workers. Such discrimination and mandatory retirement policies are aspects of a unified framework yielding the optimal hiring and retirement decisions by firms, as analyzed in chapter 3.

The common definition of wage discrimination is unequal wages for equally productive workers. Such discrimination is a common occurrence. Sloane (1985), Hamermesh and Rees (1988), Ragan and Tremblay (1988), Gunderson (1989), Fuchs (1989) and Lazear (1990), Lazear and Rosen (1990), and Loprest (1992), among many others, present recent forms of the analysis and empirical evidence on discrimination. Chapters 4 and 5 use the firm-specific human capital model of chapter 3 to establish that one of the grounds for wage differentiation by profit maximizing, competitive firms are different expected periods of employment with the firm. Firms retain part of the rents generated by firm-specific skills. The longer the period of employment, the larger will be the present expected value of the firm's share of these rents in a given job position in the firm. Firms will maximize this expected value. Therefore, workers with the longest expected stay with the firm will get the job, unless workers with a shorter expected stay make up the expected value of rents required by the firm by accepting lower wage rates. This is so even if two workers, say a man from the former group and a woman from the latter one, are equally able and *equally productive* during their common years on the job, providing that the woman has a shorter expected stay than the man with the firm. The notion of 'equally productive' in the definition of discrimination must then be over the period of employment of the *longest* employed worker, not over annual periods, as often used in the literature on discrimination. Discrimination against women, assumed to have a shorter expected stay with the firm, is discussed in chapter 4. Discrimination in hiring against older workers - that is, older than the optimal hiring age - is discussed in chapter 5.

The literature on mandatory retirement has used a non-replacement model with the assumption that the worker and the firm arrive at a mutually beneficial retirement date, with the firm's decisions based on an incentives model (Lazear, 1979), a human capital model (Blinder, 1981) or an insurance one (Lapp, 1985). Chapter 6 on the optimal retirement age from the firm's viewpoint questions the appropriateness of a non-replacement assumption in this context. It uses a replacement model to assign critical roles to ageing and to shifts in skills and productivity among generations. This emphasis on age and replacement explains why mandatory retirement occurs at very different ages in various occupations and why it occurs at relatively early ages in professional physical sports. The emphasis on replacement also explains why firms are willing to bribe workers with 'golden handshakes' or 'sweeteners' in early retirement plans.

Chapter 7 focuses on the concept of the rental value of the job, first derived in passing in chapters 2 and 3. A job is a technological opportunity with promotion possibilities (Lazear and Rosen, 1990). It requires certain levels of education, abilities and skills and offers opportunities for learning additional skills and promotions. The rental value of the job is the value of the rents that the firm can earn in perfect competition as its due from its ownership of a job generating and utilizing firm-specific skills. The returns to the firm's contribution to such skills, as a characteristic generated by the firm through its production activities, are analyzed in chapter 2. The expression for these in the context of our basic replacement model is derived in chapter 3. Chapter 7 develops these ideas further and relates them to Akerlof's (1984, ch. 6) concept of jobs as dam sites, with the rental value of the job corresponding to the rental value of the dam site.

Chapter 8 analyzes the worker's preferred retirement age under certainty and under uncertainty as to the wage path. The worker is assumed to maximize an intertemporal utility function with his lifetime consumption and leisure, in the form of the retirement years, as its arguments. The analysis under the certainty assumption follows the standard application of economic theory to the worker's choice between consumption and leisure (see, for example, Burbidge and Robb, 1980; Fields and Mitchell, 1984) and derives the usual income and substitution effects for the optimal retirement age.

The focus of chapter 8 lies in its analysis of the worker's preferred retirement age under uncertainty of the wage path. The worker, early in his career, cannot predict with certainty his wage path and therefore his lifetime income, and cannot predict the income and assets close to the retirement years. Therefore, he would not in early or mid-career be willing to specify his desired retirement age to the firm and would want to keep his options open. Similarly, he would not want the firm to have a mandatory retirement policy at a fixed age for its workers. This implication of our analysis runs counter to the implications of the certainty analysis and to the recent literature on mandatory retirement built on the human capital model (Blinder, 1981) or the incentives model (Lazear, 1979).

Chapters 6 and 8 yield different determinants of the firm's and the worker's preferred retirement ages. It is, therefore, quite unlikely that the individual worker would want to retire at an age which maximizes the firm's profits. The firm, then, might try to force him into retirement through a layoff or through a mandatory retirement policy, and incur the costs of resentment generated by these. Or it might use its pension plan to induce the worker to voluntarily change his preferred retirement age. This is the subject of chapter 9.

Chapter 10 presents the summary and conclusions.

1.2 The distinctiveness of the book

This book presents a *general theoretical approach* to explain several observed facets of labour market behaviour. Among these are aspects of discrimination against female workers, racial discrimination, discrimination in hiring older workers, firms' preference for mandatory retirement policies, and the occurrence of pensions, vesting etc. The framework used for this purpose is based on the existence of firm-specific skills in an intertemporal context where the firms are long-lived entities and their optimizing decision takes into account the replacement of workers in the job positions in the firm. Workers are of different types or classes distinguished by the firm by their expected period of stay with the firm. Firms and workers are taken to be separate entities whose interests are distinctive and who engage in separate optimizing frameworks.

The attempt at explaining several observed labour market phenomena within a common theoretical framework makes this book distinctive from most other books or other contributions on such topics in the literature. There are two dimensions of this distinctiveness. One is the emphasis on a more general framework than commonly presented. The other is the theoretical treatment as against a descriptive one of the subject. Most works on topics such as discrimination, retirement and pensions tend to be specific to the topic and to have a heavy emphasis on the empirical and descriptive aspects of the topic. This book stays away from such a treatment since its aim is to focus on the commonality of theoretical considerations underlying the observed phenomena, while accepting the major empirical findings on them. As such, the book does not present a new empirical study nor does it engage in extensive descriptions of the observed phenomena.

As mentioned above, this book attempts to explain discrimination against certain types of workers such as women and minorities, in hiring older workers, and retirement and pensions within a unified framework.

Existing theories do not do so and are usually specific to one of these phenomena. To illustrate, the dominant theory of discrimination against women and blacks in the USA is the Arrow-Becker one. It bases its explanation for such discrimination on a 'taste' or preference for employing - or working with or being served by - white male workers rather than by women or blacks, so that the firm's profit-maximizing/optimal solution when offering a job to such workers is to pay them less than the white male workers. This theory makes no attempt to explain the discrimination against hiring older white male workers against younger white male workers - or in hiring older female workers as against younger female workers etc. In fact, it would have great difficulty in claiming plausibility if it tried to explain the discrimination in hiring older male workers on the basis that firms and managers possess an innate preference for younger over older males, since most employers and managers tend to be older males themselves.

Further, the Arrow-Becker tastes' approach to discrimination does not attempt to explain - and cannot - explain firms' preference for the specific retirement ages incorporated in mandatory retirement policies.

Conversely, consider the currently dominant theory of mandatory retirement and its related theory of pensions. This is Lazear's incentives based wage deferral approach. It does not attempt to explain - and cannot - explain, discrimination against women and certain minorities. Its major element is a tendency for the workers to shirk unless an incentive scheme with a wage path in which workers receive less than their marginal product in their early years on the job and more than it in their later years, is put in place. We do not see any way in which this approach could be used, with or without modifications, to explain discrimination against female workers. It also cannot be used to explain discrimination in hiring against older versus younger workers of either sex.

This book ties in the unified treatment of discrimination and firm's preferred retirement dates with pensions through the recognition that firms and workers have differing interests and there may be no mutually optimizing solution for their distinctive interests or there may not be sufficient trust between them to implement such a solution. The distinctiveness of the interests of economic agents is a *sine qua non* of economics, leading to differing demand and supply behaviour, and leaving it to the market to achieve a common trading point. This is fundamental to the theory of discrimination since there can be no mutually optimizing solution to the interests of the firm and the workers *being discriminated against* and *often not even being hired*. While the incentives theory of retirement alludes to higher marginal products and consequently higher wages through the prevention of shirking through incentives, the possibility that workers and firms do not trust each other sufficiently to maintain non-binding implicit arrangements extending over several decades, is sufficiently strong for us to look for other causes of firms' preferences for mandatory retirement provisions and pensions. Such a lack of trust is fundamental to the existence of unions, contracts, human rights commissions and lawsuits by workers against firms. This book therefore takes the view that while incentives do play some role in the worker-firm implicit contracts, the dominant factor is still one where each has optimizing behaviour which may be in conflict. This leads to the theory of pensions legally vested in the workers and to golden handshakes to encourage early retirement. Discrimination, retirement and pensions, and other related labour market phenomena, are thus tied into a unified framework. Such a unified framework is missing from other existing approaches.

The framework of this book is distinctive in other ways also. It treats different groups of workers as different 'categories' or 'classes', with differing expected periods of stay with the firm, or, in the case of older workers, with a differing marginal productivity path than of younger workers due to age related factors. Profit maximization by the firm implies that it would prefer employing workers from the class which has the more productive workers only, unless the less productive workers are paid sufficiently below those of the more productive class, thus providing the rationale for firms' wage and occupational differentiation among workers in the economy. As compared with this approach, its productivity based division among workers as the key element in wage and occupational discrimination is missing in the tastes based discrimination model and in the incentives based approach to mandatory retirement.

Another major departure from the existing approaches is that this book also differentiates among types of jobs. Here it draws upon the literature on general and firm-specific skills and especially Okun's analysis of them. This distinction leads to distinctive predictions for the existence of wage and occupational differentiation, and of firms' preferences for differing retirement and pensions policies, varying by the nature of the job. Again, existing approaches do not always distinguish between types of jobs and often fail to recognise that such labour market phenomena are not identical across types of jobs.

1.3 Distinctive predictions

Since the analytic approach of this book differs from the other more specific ones in the literature, its empirical predictions must also be somewhat different. These are interspersed in the book. Here we go through some on wage differentiation for illustration purposes.

We know from history that discrimination against female workers has existed for centuries and in virtually every industrialized society. It has existed in Europe, North and South America, India and Japan, among others. It must be taken to be both a long run phenomena and one cutting across societies. Yet the established theories cannot explain its existence in the long run, for competition will lead to the survival of firms which do not discriminate. Further, these theories rely upon a preference or taste for employing or working with male workers rather than with female ones. This explanation becomes suspect when one considers that the societies practising such discrimination over differing historical periods had widely differing customs and modes of societal patterns and organizations. It would rather seem that there were more fundamental, technological factors making for such discrimination.

This book draws upon 'technological factors' in its reliance on the distinction between general and career jobs, and the shorter expected uninterrupted stay of female workers with a given firm as compared with that of male workers of similar ages. The latter in turn is based on the high fertility rates of women until the invention of effective and cheap contraceptive devices and their need to stay at home necessitated by the expected numerous pregnancies and the care of several expected children in a woman's lifetime, along with the much greater incidence of disease and death among children. Historically, the likelihood of a woman bearing several children was high, and the duration for which she would be a mother of young children, tied down to the home by their needs for care and supervision, was a large part of a woman's life. In such societies, the firms' general expectation that a young woman would have a much shorter expected stay with the firm was technologically based. These factors were common to all industrialized societies until the last few decades, so that, according to the analytical framework of this book, discrimination would have occurred across societies and historical periods in the industrialized economies.

The analytical framework of this book also relies upon 'technological changes' broadly defined to explain why discrimination would be less against the next generation of female workers now entering the labour force than it was for earlier generations. The technological changes that have occurred are related to: the invention of cheap and effective contraceptives allowing pregnancies and family size to be controlled; the drastic reductions in death and disease, especially among young children, because of technological breakthroughs in medicine; the decrease in the length of the work week; the increasing availability of child care facilities; the technological changes in the work in the home, and changes in the nature of jobs, especially those related to the generally lower requirements of physical strength. There have also been many other changes affecting the nature of jobs and the ability of females to meet their requirements. These have led to a drastic increase in the expected uninterrupted stay in the labour force and also with a given firm of young female workers. This in turn implies in the context of our framework a drastic reduction in the wage and occupational differentiation among young male and female workers in this generation over those in previous generations. We believe that this explanation and prediction of drastic reductions in such differentiation because of fundamental technological changes is better than one which relies upon changes in tastes or preferences for discrimination. Would the latter have occurred without the former? Can the latter explain the decrease in the tendencies to discriminate if the former had not occurred? We doubt these.

Consider another prediction on discrimination. Discrimination occurs against both female workers and in hiring older workers. Technological changes have lengthened expected lifetimes and improved the health of older people. But these would benefit *both* younger and older workers in terms of lengthening the expected duration and productivity of their employment periods. Consequently, such changes have not drastically benefited older workers seeking a job over younger workers, and definitely not as much as technological changes have benefited young female workers vis-a-vis young male workers. Consequently, our model predicts that discrimination in hiring older workers would not decrease as significantly as in hiring young female workers, legislation to the contrary notwithstanding.

As another, and final, example presented here of the distinctive differences in the predictions of our model, consider the approach of this book and of Lazear's incentives model to issues of mandatory retirement. In ours, young workers at the beginning of their careers face uncertainty about their incomes, wealth and the career levels they will eventually attain. Further, there do not exist adequate insurance mechanisms in the economy or through arrangements with the firms for these young workers to buy appropriate insurance against risks thirty or forty years into the future. The insurance markets are sufficiently incomplete for uncertainty not to be eliminated. Hence, the optimization of a worker's choices at the start of his career does not define a unique optimal age which he would prefer over all others for retirement. The optimal retirement age is then state dependent -

and the states likely to occur far in the future are vague and difficult to define with any degree of confidence - and thus not uniquely defined by workers until close to the general retirement ages. As these approach and workers define their preferred retirement ages, they would resent any mandatory retirement age imposed by the firm if this happened to be earlier than their own preferred one. That is, workers would indicate a lack of concern or interest in specifying at the beginning of their careers their preferred retirement age and any lack of resentment over the firm's specification of one since their own - some thirty years or so in the future - is going to vary depending upon their health, achievements, wages and wealth. But they would later in life develop resentments over firm-imposed mandatory retirement if they find that they would prefer to retire at a later age than the firm wants them to do so. More compactly, the predictions would be: workers at the beginning of their careers refuse to define their optimal retirement ages and do not bother to show resentment against the firm's declared retirement age; close to the retirement ages, some but not all - since some workers would find that their preferred retirement ages are less than the firm's one - workers would show resentment at being forced to retire, unless induced to do so voluntarily through some kind of compensation. Further, some workers would find their preferred retirement ages to be earlier than the firm's imposed one and would retire earlier than the mandatory retirement age, without needing inducements to do so.

By comparison, the incentives model implies that the firm and its workers enter into an implicit contract at the beginning of the workers' careers to retire at an age which is optimal for both. There is no *ex ante* divergence between the firm's and the workers' preferred retirement ages, and no resentment by workers of the imposed mandatory retirement ages except as an *ex post* instance of sour grapes. There also would not exist earlier retirement than the agreed upon age, except as an *ex post* deviation from *ex ante* optimality. Our approach does not have to rely upon the deviation of *ex post* from *ex ante* optimal choices to explain observed behaviour. This is a questionable *deux ex machina* to explain the divergence between the predictions of the theory and observed behaviour: such repeated divergence would lead rational workers as a group to change their behaviour and the kind of contracts they would be willing to enter into with the firms. By comparison, the *ex ante* behaviour in our theory explains the observed behaviour - definitely making ours a more desirable approach.

This section has only pointed out a few of the distinctive predictions of our approach. We leave it to the main chapters of the book to specify others.

2 Characteristics and the Returns to General and Specific Skills

The preceding chapter had distinguished between workers' general skills and firm-specific skills. The former are ones which raise the worker's productivity in any firm, at least in the same industry and possibly in other industries as well. The latter only raise the worker's productivity in the firm in which they were acquired. We have also pointed out that there are few workers who would not possess some of each of these skills, and it is for reasons of analytical convenience that we will categorize some workers as possessing firm-specific skills and others as not doing so. Workers possessing some of these skills were denoted as career workers and those without any such skills were denoted as casual ones. Both types of workers will possess some general skills.

We also denoted jobs in a similar manner to workers' skills. Career jobs were defined as ones which require some firm-specific skills to perform so that possession of these by a worker increases his productivity in that job. Casual jobs were defined as ones on which the possession of any firm-specific skills does not increase productivity. In general, we can expect that holding a career job allows the workers to acquire some of the firm-specific - and general - skills relevant to that job. The extent of such acquisition would depend upon the abilities and education of the worker relative to the needs and other characteristics of the job.

The human capital literature normally deals only with the returns to the general and firm-specific skills possessed by workers. This chapter uses long run neoclassical analysis to specify the demand and supply functions for the determinants of firm-specific and general elements of workers' skills and of jobs, and to analyze their returns. The framework used is that proposed by Lancaster (1966a; 1966b) for the analysis of the demand for commodities. Adapting this analysis, this chapter assumes that firms use the 'activities' of general and firm-specific skills, among others, to produce output. These activities are in turn produced by workers' characteristics, such as aptitudes, schooling and experience, and by the environment provided by the firm for the use of workers' characteristics. It is also assumed that workers are sufficiently heterogeneous in the possession of their characteristics to allow firms to buy any combinations of characteristics and to use the cost-minimizing combinations to generate the opportunity cost of the activities.

This chapter assumes that workers wish to maximize their lifetime utility. As a simplification, this will be taken to mean that they wish to maximize their lifetime earnings. A worker with given characteristics or aptitudes for learning general and firm-specific skills, upon entering the labour force for the first time, will wish to join that firm where he expects these earnings to be maximized. In a competitive framework with full and symmetric information, these earnings will include the scarcity return to his characteristics. If he already possesses or acquires general skills while on the job, he will obtain the scarcity value of his characteristics contributing to such skills. He may also acquire firm-specific-skills in the course of his employment or training for it. Again, he will get the scarcity return to those of his characteristics which contribute to such skills.

Once a worker has acquired firm-specific skills, he operates in a short run in which he can only move to another firm by foregoing any return to these skills. In this, such skills share the property of specialized assets which *ex post* generate quasi-returns, though, barring unexpected changes, these are part of their *ex ante* returns (Dow, 1993). That is, since the acquisition of such skills is often a very gradual process occurring over a considerable period of time, a switch to another firm could mean a considerable reduction in earnings while the worker sets about gradually acquiring the specific skills relevant to the new firm. Thus a part of the return to the characteristics which led to the acquisition of the original specific skills becomes a quasi-rent in the original firm, which the firm could try to retain out of the worker's earnings (Becker, 1975; Okun, 1981).

From one perspective, Becker's and Okun's results on the firm-specific skills flow from a short run partial equilibrium analysis with *ex post* fixities. In particular, this analysis does not focus on the point of decision-making, when the worker has to decide in which firm he should work and acquire his skills and what type of skills to acquire. At the moment of decision-making, the worker only has the abilities to acquire such skills; he has not yet acquired them and thus does not suffer from the implications of

16

the fixity imposed by already-acquired skills. Focusing on this point shifts the analysis from that of firm-specific skills and the quasi-rents generated by them to the demand for and supply of such abilities and the opportunities for acquiring the skills. These demands and supplies then get to determine the *ex ante* returns to these abilities and opportunities, and hence to what will *ex post* emerge as a rent to firm-specific skills.

From another perspective, Becker's path-breaking analysis, focusing as it did on firm's choices, can be enhanced by also examining workers' choices and the role of information in the model. Under perfect symmetric information by workers and firms on workers' abilities and costs of training, and on firms' contributions to the acquisition of worker's skills, the marginal workers would receive the market rate of return to their characteristics but the intra-marginal workers would earn a rent, in addition to the market return, to their intra-marginal superior abilities (including intelligence, aptitudes, emotions, 'right connections' etc.). Similarly, the marginal firm would get the market rate of return to its inputs while the firm with superior management characteristics will earn an additional rent for this superiority. Whether the firm's and the worker's inputs translate after the learning and training process into general or firm-specific skills does not affect this conclusion.

Under asymmetric information, with firms possessing superior information on workers' abilities, the costs of training and the eventual degree of skills and productivity achieved, the firm could capture some of the return that would have accrued to workers for their characteristics under perfect information in the long run. Such superior knowledge by a firm is especially likely to occur in the context of firm-specific skills rather than in the context of general skills where the information is common among many firms and, thus, more easily available to workers also. In this case, Becker's conclusions are more likely to hold and the firm could more easily retain the whole or part of the intra-marginal returns to workers' special abilities in acquiring firm-specific skills.

Becker's analysis can be further enhanced by considering the firm's role in the worker's acquisition of skills while he is employed. The human capital literature has generally focused on training and other learning processes which impose a cost on such acquisition (Schultz, 1961, 1963; Becker, 1975; Ben-Porath, 1970). However, much of the acquisition of skills within a firm occurs from "familiarity with the physical environment" (Doeringer and Piore, 1971; p. 15), by "'osmosis', 'exposure', 'experience', or 'working one's way up through promotion'"(p. 18), in the process of production. Workers may be moulded to jobs more commonly than vice-versa (Ryan, 1981, p. 11). At least some of this acquisition of skills may be costless (Doeringer and Piore, 1971, ch. 2; Blaug, 1976). Further, such skills learned on a job may be general or firm-specific.

Workers' skills are, therefore, a joint product of the worker's characteristics such as abilities, education, etc. and the characteristics provided by the firm. The latter are related to the nature of production processes, equipment, other employees, training procedures, etc. (Okun, 1981, p. 184). The return to the worker's skills must, under competition, be shared between the worker, as a return to his characteristics, and the firm, as a return to its provision of characteristics. This is the subject of this chapter.

Our analysis in this chapter is set in a static, single-period format. The general pattern of the discussion on returns to general and firm-specific skills is usually an intertemporal one, often over the worker's work-life. The worker's concern, then, is with the life-time return to the characteristics that he possesses. Another way of modifying our analysis would be to mould it into an intertemporal format, taking explicit account of the evolution of skills as learning occurs and experience accumulates. This seems to us a cumbersome method, especially since we suspect that the long run qualitative results we would get from this analysis would be no different from those we derived earlier in this section.

This chapter does not deal with training costs, who pays for them and, therefore, with who receives the market return to them, as this issue is peripheral to our analysis. Our concern is really with the net return - that is net of training costs and the market return to them - to general and specific skills and this chapter should be read with this in mind.

2.1 General and specific skills and technologies

We have earlier in this chapter and in chapter 1 referred to the distinction between general and firm-specific skills and the contributions made in the human capital approach (for example, see Becker, 1975; Oi, 1962; Schultz, 1961, 1963; Mincer, 1974, among others) and in the dual or sequential market approach (for example, see Doeringer and Piore, 1971), among others. In our context, we deal with workers possessing firm-specific skills or general ones, and jobs requiring firm-specific characteristics or only general ones. We amplify below on these descriptions from Akerlof (1984, ch. 6).

Akerlof distinguishes between the 'specific' and 'general' *human capital* possessed by workers and 'specific' and 'general' *technology* supplied by a firm. He defines firm-specific technology as one specific to a firm, and general technology as one freely available to all firms. A job may have firm-specific technology and the worker holding the job may have firm-specific skills. If such a worker leaves the firm and is replaced on the given job by a worker with only general skills, the firm's output will decrease, with the decrease being the rent generated by the worker's firm-specific skills. If the output of the firm does not fall, then only the technology is firm-specific. (Akerlof, 1984, p. 108).

According to Akerlof, specific technology consists of fixed job descriptions which establish the relationships among the actual employees and how they perform the economic goals of the firm. It also includes specific knowledge of production processes. Akerlof calls the latter as a type of 'hardware', while the specific technology governing human interactions is termed as 'software'. This software consists of job descriptions, knowledge by the employees of how the firm operates and functions, and the social customs and interactions among the firm's employees. If this knowledge can be acquired by many workers through learning on the job, as a costless pursuit of the job, then this knowledge is classified by Akerlof as specific technology owned by the firm rather than firm-specific knowledge owned by the workers.

Akerlof cited Pattern (1976) to illustrate the relative importance of the software form of firm-specific technology. Pattern had pointed out that productivity per worker was about 50% greater in the U.S. plants of multinational firms compared to their British plants. However, output per worker in all manufacturing was about 116% greater in the U.S. than in Britain. The much smaller difference between the productivity per worker in the plants of the multinational firms was explained as being partly due to the greater skills and the greater physical capital per worker in the British plants of such firms, relative to all plants, and partly to the use in Britain by the multinational firms of their specific technology (Akerlof, 1984, p. 109).

Akerlof's term 'specific technology' is analogous to our concept of firm-specific environment, just as his concept of a general technology is analogous to our concept of a general environment. Of the two types of technology/environment, the more dominant form would seem to be the general one. This would consist of commonly known and commonly practised technology, job descriptions and employee and customer interactions. There is, therefore, both a 'hardware' as well as a 'software' component to general technology/environment as well as to firm-specific technology/environment. While some forms of both of these may be produced costlessly by the firm, most forms of them would seem to require knowledge, organization and time. They are then likely to have a positive cost to produce and to be more or less scarce.

2.2 Skills and characteristics in long run analysis

We adopt Lancaster's (1966a, 1966b) schema for this section. The firm will be assumed to produce an output Q, using inputs which are designated as 'activities'. These activities will be taken to be the services of the firm's stocks of firm-specific skills and general skills and its physical capital stock. Assuming the last item to be fixed for our analysis, we will ignore it henceforth. The firm-specific and general skills activities will, in turn, be taken to be produced by 'characteristics'. The five characteristics considered in this paper are the workers' aptitudes, schooling and experience, the specific environment - unique to the firm - and the general environment common among firms. The latter two are provided by the firm.

Characteristics are not directly marketed. They are produced by either workers or firms. Of the five characteristics, aptitudes, schooling and experience are produced by workers. The workers are assumed to be sufficiently heterogeneous in the possession of these characteristics to produce any combination of aptitudes, schooling and experience that the firm wishes to employ. The remaining two characteristics of the general and specific environments are provided by the firm and are determined by its size, policies and practices in terms of industrial relations, capital equipment, etc. We will consider these as given, largely because of the problems of measuring them. With these as given, the return to these characteristics will be a quasi-rent, rather than being determined by marginal productivity analysis.

The firm is taken to employ workers with different aptitudes, schooling and experience, paying them wages corresponding to their levels of aptitudes, schooling and experience. These differing wage rates are assumed to be determined in competitive markets and are given to the firm. For given levels of characteristics, the firm can find its cost-minimizing set of workers. It can also derive the minimum cost of obtaining additional units of each of these characteristics in question.[1]

The above arguments yield the formal framework as one where the firm faces a technology

$$Q = Q(Z_1, Z_2) \tag{1}$$

where
$$Z_1 = Z_1(X_1, X_2, X_3, X_4)$$

$$Z_2 = Z_2(X_1, X_2, X_3, X_4, X_5)$$

$$X_i = X_i(N_1, N_2, \ldots) \qquad\qquad i = 1,2,3$$

$$N_k = N_k(X_{1k}, X_{2k}, X_{3k}) \qquad\qquad k = 1,\ldots,n$$

where

Q   output
Activities (j = 1,2)
Z_1 general skills
Z_2 firm-specific skills
Characteristics (i = 1,2,3)
X_1 Amount of aptitudes
X_2 Amount of schooling
X_3 Amount of experience
X_4 Amount of general environment
X_5 Amount of firm-specific environment
X_{ik} Amount of characteristic i provided by the kth worker
Traded goods/inputs (k = 1,...,n)
N_k kth worker

$$Q \geq 0,\ Z_j \geq 0,\ X_i \geq 0,\ X_{ik} \geq 0 \text{ for all } i,j,k$$

Each of the above functions is assumed to be twice differentiable. Each of the respective first-order partial derivatives in these functions is assumed to be positive. Each of the second order partial derivatives is assumed to be negative. Assume that $Z_2(.) = 0$ for $X_5 = 0$ - that is, a firm without a firm-specific environment does not use firm-specific skills.

Designate the market rental cost per unit of the hired characteristics X_1, X_2 and X_3 as V_1, V_2 and V_3 respectively. The firm's decision problem can then be stated as: the firm maximizes

$$P.Q(Z_1(X_1, X_2, X_3, X_4), Z_2(X_1, X_2, X_3, X_4, X_5))$$

$$- \Sigma_{i=1}^{3} V_i X_i \tag{2}$$

with respect to the hired characteristics X_1, X_2 and X_3. P is the price of the firm's product, assumed to equal the general price level and V_i is the nominal price of the ith input. Let v_i (= V_i/P) be the real rental cost of the ith characteristic. Maximization of (2) with respect to the hired characteristics yields the first order conditions as,

$$\Sigma^2_{j=1} \; Q_j Z_{ji} = v_i \qquad\qquad i = 1,2,3. \qquad\qquad (3)$$

where,

$$Q_j = \partial Q/\partial Z_j \text{ and } Z_{ji} = \partial Z_j/\partial X_i \; .$$

(3) is the set of the familiar profit-maximizing conditions and specifies that each characteristic will be employed up to the point where its marginal product equals its real cost. We assume that the second-order conditions required for a maximum are satisfied by the solution to (3).

2.3 The return to the worker's characteristics

Our concern is with the division of the wage rate into compensation for the worker's general skills and for his specific skills. What the worker contributes to these skills are his aptitudes, schooling and experience. He receives a return to each of these. Designate the kth worker as $k(X_{1k}, X_{2k}, X_{3k})$ where X_{ik} is the level of X_i possessed by the kth worker. In the long run under perfect competition, the kth worker would receive a real wage w_k which equals the sum of the payments to his characteristics. Hence,

$$w_k = \Sigma^3_{i=1} \; v_i X_{ik} \qquad\qquad (4)$$

From (3) and (4),

$$w_k = \Sigma^2_{j=1} \Sigma^3_{i=1} \; Q_j Z_{ji} X_{ik} \qquad\qquad (5)$$

When the firm hires an additional worker, say the kth one, its use of the various characteristics increases and so does its output. These increases are given by the partial derivative of output with respect to its number of workers, with the additional worker specified to be the kth one. This gives, from (1):

$$Q_k = \Sigma^2_{j=1} \Sigma^3_{i=1} \; Q_j Z_{ji} \; X_{ik} \qquad\qquad (6)$$

where Q_k is the increase in the firm's output upon hiring the kth worker. X_{ik} is the partial derivative of X_i with respect to workers of the kth type. Hence from (5) and (6),

$$Q_k = w_k \qquad\qquad (7)$$

Equation (7) is the usual optimization condition equating the kth worker's marginal product, given by Q_k, to his real wage w_k.

2.4 The return to the firm for its characteristics

The total real wage bill of the firm is $\Sigma_k w_k$, $k = 1,...,n$, where n is the number of workers employed by the firm. Therefore, from (6) and (7), the firm's rent R due to its provision of the general and specific environment is,

$$R = Q - \Sigma_k w_k \qquad\qquad k = 1,...,n$$

$$= Q - \Sigma_k \, \Sigma_{j=1}^2 \, \Sigma_{i=1}^3 \, Q_j Z_{ji} X_{ik} \qquad\qquad (8)$$

Given diminishing returns to characteristics in (1), $R > 0$. This rent can be divided into amounts due to the firm's provisions of the specific and general environments. This can be done if either of these has a market price. Of the two, it is the general environment which is likely to have such a price. General environment, by definition, is that which is provided by many firms and a competitive system will provide a market return to the firm for this provision. This return will be reflected in the firm's profits, after payments for labour and capital. Assuming the return to the firm's provision of the general environment to be known, subtraction of this amount from the total rent R will give the rent due to the firm's provision of the specific environment.

The market return to the general environment will be zero if its provision was costless or if it was surplus in the economy. One can imagine a wide variety of types of general environment, homogeneous among firms in the same lines of business, but which take careful planning and execution to inculcate among the workers. Hence, there would be a cost to bringing it about. Given this cost, it is unlikely to be a surplus good in the economy. From another perspective, if the worker could himself engage in production and generate the same marginal product as when he works in (other) firms, his wage would equal this marginal product and the return to the general environment would be zero. Note that in this case, each worker can be taken as able to replicate the general environment just by setting up in production, so that the general environment must be in surplus; hence, its return would be zero. In the likely case, managerial skills are needed to run a firm and

23

these are scarce. Consequently, there is no reason to assume a zero-cost or surplus general environment as the most likely possibility.

2.5 Sharing the return to general skills

The worker's own characteristics and the firm's provision of the general environment produce general skills. The productivity of and the return to these skills is thus shared between the worker and the firm. The payment to a worker for his exercise of such skills must thus be less than the productivity of such skills. To see this formally, assume that the general environment is a variable. Then, assuming the specific environment and specific skills to be zero, and looking at the additional kth worker's contribution to output when the firm increases its provision of the general environment in the appropriate amount dX_4, equation (1) implies that

$$dQ = (\Sigma_{i=1}^3 Q_1 Z_{1i} X_{ik}) + Q_1 Z_{14} dX_4 = w_k + Q_1 Z_{14} dX_4 \qquad (9)$$

In (9), the increase in output, dQ, is divided between the worker's wage and a return to the firm for providing the general environment.[2] The return to general skills, therefore, does not accrue totally to workers exercising those skills. This conclusion differs somewhat from that of Becker (1975). Becker had concluded that in the case of general skills, the worker will be paid the marginal product (net of training costs) of such skills. Our analysis refines this conclusion: equation (9) shows that the worker will not receive the full marginal product of such skills but will share this marginal product with the firm.

To take an extreme case with conclusions differing from Becker's, consider a particular type of general skill for which the firms' aggregate demand is limited relative to the workers' total supply of characteristics for it. Since this type of skill would be in surplus, the workers will not receive a net return for it and hence will not receive any return for the characteristics that produce it, assuming that those characteristics cannot be used in any other activity. In such a case, the firms will retain the whole of the net return to the type of general skill being considered. It will not matter who pays initially for the acquisition of the skill, though, given that the same skill can be used in many firms, it is likely that the worker will pay this initial cost and be reimbursed for it by his employers in the course of his career.

2.6 Sharing the return to firm-specific skills

The return to the firm-specific environment can be treated in the same manner as that to the general environment. In the short run, with the levels of these given, the return to both of these is a quasi-rent. This rent is also likely to be positive for both types of environments. In the long run when these are variable, the returns to them will depend on their respective marginal products, which, in turn, depend upon their scarcity or cost of providing them. In both cases, the worker and the firm will receive the marginal product of the characteristics or environment that they supply.

Our result refines Becker's (1975) conclusions on the returns to firm-specific skills. Becker had concluded that the worker with firm-specific skills will receive less than his marginal product, with the firm capturing some or most - if not all - of the return to the firm-specific skills in the short run due to the specificity of such skills. The difference in results arises from Becker's emphasis on the fixity to the firm - that is, non-transferability to other firms - of such skills while, in our analysis, these skills are partly dependent upon the worker's characteristics (aptitudes, schooling and experience) which *ex ante* can be transferred to other firms, but their exercise needs the environment provided by the firm. Therefore, our analysis goes further than Becker's by looking at the determinants of firm-specific skills and separating these determinants into the characteristics of workers and the specific environment of the firm. The worker gets the return to the former. The firm gets the return to the latter.

Becker's analysis does not allow a direct comparison between the wages of workers possessing firm-specific skills and those possessing mainly general skills, when both have the same innate characteristics and education. In fact, since the firm can retain a large part of the return to the skills of the former workers, but not those of the latter, there is a presumption from Becker's analysis that the former would have lower wages. For our analytical framework, assume that all workers are identical but that there are two types of firms, with both producing the same good. One type uses only general skill occupations, contributing a general type of environment to them. The other type of firm uses only specific skills occupations, contributing a specific type of environment to them. Given perfect competition in the labour market, the present value of the two wage streams must be identical for both types of firms. Then the workers will receive the same return to their characteristics, no matter which type of firm and occupation they work in. If firms were free to move between the two types of occupations and have no particular advantage in providing general or specific environments, they must earn the same rents and profits in both types of occupations. Consequently, under the assumptions above, the return to general and firm-specific skills must be identical, with firms and workers sharing this return in an identical manner, irrespective of whether they choose to specialize in general or in firm-specific skills.

The returns to general and firm-specific skills can, and probably do, differ in the economy. This difference must arise from differences in the relative cost of generating them and the scarcity of the characteristics that produce them relative to the demand for such skills. There is no reason to assume that each pattern of production in the economy requires the same types of skills or that the aptitudes etc. possessed by the population are equally suitable for producing general and specific skills. The returns to these skills would then differ. The wages of workers would differ on the basis of their differences in characteristics and differences in the returns to these.

The demand, the productivity and the return to characteristics would depend not only on technological factors but also upon organizational ones. There are also likely to be non-linearities in the possession of characteristics and their productivity. Different industries and firms tend to use different technologies and have different organizational structures., so that the return to a given characteristic could vary among industries and firms. To illustrate, large firms tend to be more complex in their organizational structure so that successful completion of jobs requiring interaction and networking with other employees may require more of the appropriate characteristics and reward these by larger payments. Hence, workers in larger firms with such characteristics would be paid higher wages than in smaller firms. Wages for essentially similar levels of educations on similar jobs could then vary among industries and firms, with self selection by workers of jobs most suited to their characteristics. Given such variation in wages, there is also the possibility of barriers to perfect competition and to the freedom of choice of which firm to join. This topic belongs to the theories of labour market segmentation and is outside the scope of this book.

Conclusion

This chapter has extended the existing analysis of the returns to workers' general and firm-specific skills by looking at both their determinants and of those related to jobs. This extension assigns greater importance to jobs and their nature - including their provision of an environment in which workers with initially only general skills can learn the appropriate firm-specific skills - than is common in the human capital literature. This recognizes the emphasis of several other studies on the relevance of jobs in labour market analysis. We have already cited Akerlof's work on this and will return to his work again in chapter 7. This shift in focus towards jobs occurs even more strongly in chapter 3, where we deal with firms' decisions on the optimal number of jobs.

Lancaster's format using activities and characteristics provided an appropriate framework for our analysis in this chapter. In this framework, workers possess characteristics and, in the long run, receive the *ex ante* return to these depending upon their scarcity value. This focus on the long run determinants of wages, under symmetrical information between workers and firms, eschews any consideration of the short run non-transferability of workers' firm-specific skills among firms.

The *ex post* short run fixity of firm-specific skills introduces its own implications. These are of the type analyzed by Becker (1975) and by Okun (1981, ch. 2). They modify the applicability of our results to the short run. In particular, in the case of firm-specific skills, firms willing to ignore long run considerations and the consequences of such violations, could take advantage of the non-transferability between firms of such skills to pay workers less than what is due to them for their characteristics: the firm uses its short run power to keep back some part of the quasi-rent due to its workers for their firm-specific skill characteristics.

On the issue of who can appropriate the short run quasi-rents, we have assumed in the above analysis that the firm is owned by the suppliers of capital. However, the analysis of firm-specific human and physical capital can be used to analyze the question of who - the suppliers of capital or the workers - owns and manages the firm and keeps its residual. Dow (1993) addresses this issue, basically relating such ownership to whether physical or human capital has greater *ex post* specificity. This issue belongs to the larger one of the political structure of the firm. This topic is outside the scope of this book. A recent review of it is presented in Rebitzer (1993).

The above short run result allowing firms (owned by the suppliers of capital) to retain all or most of quasi-rents - and therefore renege on the long run division - is, however, subject to several limitations. One of these is that if the firm wishes to hire new workers with similar characteristics, these workers would wish to evaluate the firm's policies with respect to its existing workers, as Okun (1981) had emphasized. If they see the firm appropriating the quasi-rent to the workers' characteristics, while other firms do not, they will not join the firm. The firm's desire to hire additional workers may, then, force it to honour the preceding long run solution in which the worker gets the net return to his characteristics. This factor is especially relevant to our analytical framework in this book since our model is a replacement model: when a vacancy occurs on a job through a quit or firing, the firm is taken to fill the job with another worker and the firm's reputation would be an element in the new worker's decisions. An additional factor emerges from this emphasis on the replacement of workers on the job. If the worker is sufficiently upset with the firm's reneging on its long run division of the returns to firm-specific skills and leaves the firm, the firm loses its share of the rents from the higher productivity of the experienced worker while the replacement is still acquiring such skills. This is shown in the next chapter.

A further factor making for the convergence of the short run sharing of the rents to the long run solution, emerges from the dependence of the worker's productivity on his commitment and morale. A disgruntled worker, who is not paid the quasi-rent to his characteristics embodied in the firm-specific skill while workers in other firms are, might be able to reduce his productivity sufficiently to eliminate the quasi-rent without being fired. For these and other reasons, the firm could find it in its interest to stick close to the long run solution and pay the worker the net return to his characteristics even in the short run.

Our model in this book is a rent-sharing model. Rebitzer (1993, p. 1418) requires of such models that they show why the firm would share these rents with its workers, even when they are nonunionized and presumably have little political power over the firm. Explanations of this in the literature include the sociological theories based on social norms, mutual obligations and fair play, and monitoring models where the worker or/and the firm can shirk on their commitments on effort and the sharing of rents. Such factors can and do exist in the real world. However, this chapter has adduced another factor. This is the long run determination of the returns to each of the characteristics, with workers possessing some and firms possessing others of the characteristics that go into producing general and firm-specific skills, and with various factors - such as the morale of workers, the firm's reputation and the rotation of workers on jobs, etc. - acting to persuade firms to stay close to the long run division of returns to skills.

Our introduction of characteristics into the analysis allows a tie-up of the return to skills with what many analysts consider to be the basic determinants of life-time earnings, such as aptitudes, social practices regarding the division of work at home, family background and sex (in the presence of discrimination), etc. The maximization of the lifetime returns to these characteristics would channel individual workers into differing combinations of general and specific skills. To illustrate, the greater uncertainty among young females, as compared with young males, about the duration of their labour force stay and its intermittency may make it optimal for them to go more into the acquisition of general rather than firm-specific skills. A strong preference on the part of a considerable proportion of the population for general rather than firm-specific skills could drive down the relative net return to general skills. If such a preference disappears over time due to changing social factors or if it was itself endogenous to the economic process, the net returns to the workers' characteristics producing the two types of skills could tend toward equality in the long run, though only if these characteristics were equally scarce relative to the demand for them or if they were perfect substitutes, though both of these seem doubtful.

The assumptions and conclusions of this chapter are quite common in the human capital literature. We illustrate this here by only a few references, other than those already mentioned in this chapter. Paglin and Rufolo (1990) point out that different occupations require different types of characteristics. Workers possess different initial abilities which produce the characteristics required by jobs to different degrees. Such abilities are scarce, and individuals choose occupations in which they maximize their earnings. In equilibrium, the returns to individual abilities and characteristics, even if they are not traded separately in markets, will be equalized across occupations. Therefore, the return to education includes an implicit return to the worker's initial abilities/characteristics and their relative scarcity. Paglin and Rufolo test these implications with respect to the mathematical and verbal abilities of male and female students and find that these characteristics are important in determining occupational choices and that job compensation varies with the extent to which jobs require different amounts of these characteristics.

Workers' characteristics are an element in their acquisition of firm-specific skills. Such characteristics, if they are scarce, are entitled to a return in equilibrium, but the firm-specific skills once they are acquired produce quasi-rents which the firm may be tempted to retain. Various factors have been adduced in the literature to enforce payment by the firm to the workers of their equilibrium return out of the quasi-rents. Becker and Okun had relied on implicit or explicit contracts and the reputation of the firm among new workers and the damage to this reputation if the firm does not pay the appropriate share to the worker. Hashimoto (1980) and Charmichael (1983) rely upon seniority rights and promotion ladders to make firms pay the appropriate amounts. In Hashimoto's model, firms do not benefit by firing workers with acquired firm-specific skills since, in cases of job separation, other workers would have to be promoted into their jobs and paid correspondingly. Chapter 3 below relies on this and on an additional element: firm-specific skills take time to learn, so that job separation would be suboptimal since the replacement worker - needing time to learn all the skills of the experienced worker subjected to the job separation - would not for some time generate as much for the firm's share of the quasi-rent as the original worker. From the perspective of the firm's profits, there is an optimal time for such layoffs and induced quits. We call this the optimal (from the firm's perspective) retirement age and analyze this in chapter 3.

FOOTNOTES

1. One procedure for finding these prices would be of the type popularized by Denison (1962) to evaluate the contribution of education, increased experience and better utilization of women workers, quality of man-hour's work due to shorter hours, etc.
2. We are not assuming that the general environment is a 'public good' such as defence, whose services expand costlessly to provide 'coverage' for an additional worker: it is usually more difficult to organize and deal with a larger number of workers than a smaller one.

3 Optimal Ages of Hiring and Retirement: The Firm's Perspective

Economic literature does not seem to have a unified perspective or explanation for wage and occupational discrimination against women and in hiring older male workers. Given that very similar economic phenomena are observed in the two cases, it seems reasonable to expect the existence of a single factor or framework which can explain some, though not necessarily all, facets of these two kinds of discrimination.

The literature on discrimination includes a number of explanations for the observed lower wages of female workers. Of these explanations, the one implied by the human capital approach is that female workers have lower wage rates because of their shorter expected period of employment with a given firm. This can result either from their attempting to join the firm after what it considers to be its optimal hiring age for workers or from an expectation that they will leave before its optimal retirement age, or both. The usual explanation of the wage discrimination against female workers in the human capital approach focuses on the latter: that is, such workers are expected to leave the firm earlier than male workers. Such an explanation of wage discrimination against female workers is clearly an aspect of the theory of the optimal hiring and (expected) *retirement* ages for a firm's workers.

Discrimination by a firm against older workers in its hiring practices is also often explained in the human capital approach in terms of their age; that is, they are not hired because they are older than the firm's optimal hiring age. Such discrimination is, thus, also an aspect of the theory of the optimal *hiring* and (expected) retirement ages for the firm's workers.

Hence, a theory of the optimal hiring and (expected) retirement ages seems to provide a general unifying perspective in terms of the human capital approach on both discrimination against female workers as well as in hiring older workers.

Further, looking at the (expected) retirement age by itself, a number of theories have been offered in recent years to explain the decisions of firms to retire their workers. Among these are the incentives model (Lazear, 1981), the human capital model (Blinder, 1981), and the insurance model (Lapp, 1985). A common feature of all these models is that the firm's decision on the retirement age is treated either in isolation or even as being independent of the firm's decisions on the hiring age of its workers.

Conversely, optimal theories of hiring rarely try to explain the retirement decisions of firms. The theories of hiring often arise in the discussions or analysis of discrimination against hiring older job applicants - that is, of a firm's decision not to hire older workers at the same wages as younger ones. The discussions of discrimination in hiring on the basis of age are generally in an applied context rather than in the context of a rigorous theory of the optimal age of hiring. These discussions often emphasize the fixed costs incurred by the firm in hiring and training a new worker, and that the firm can spread these costs over a longer employment period by hiring a younger rather than an older worker. In an analysis incorporating these costs, Hutchens (1985) has extended the Lazear incentives model to include a fixed cost element to explain hiring decisions on older workers.

Given that age is a common variable in retirement and hiring decisions, it seems quite plausible that if the firm has an optimal retirement age for its employees, it would also have an optimal hiring age, and that the two would be based, at least partly, on the same sort of considerations. However, there are few theories which integrate the two types of decisions in a single framework.

Another aspect of the theories of the optimal retirement age is that such theories often do not treat the firm's decision as a replacement decision. A replacement decision would make the hiring and retirement age of a given worker or generation of workers dependent upon the productivity and wages of the preceding and subsequent generations of workers. A non-replacement decision would indicate independence in this respect. The models of Lazear, Blinder, Lapp and Hutchens are examples of the latter type of models. Recognition of the relatedness of the hiring and retirement decisions tends to draw attention to the replacement of workers in a given job: the hiring of a new worker follows the retirement of a preceding one so that at least some of the determinants of the two decisions on the ages (hiring of one and retirement of the other) would be shared ones. This replacement of older workers by younger ones has occupied a prominent place in the of firms and une periodes in recent discussions on the abolition of mandatory retirement so that the theoreticaajor detis of the problem does n productto be justified in ignoring it. In fact, Gee and McDaniel (1991) conclude from their revtless, ahe literature for Canadawork done, or matimes the real reason behind the mandatory retirement provisions has been to replace older employees with younger, more profitable workers.

This chapter presents an integrated analysis of the optimal decisions on the hiring and retirement ages along with those on the optimal number of jobs, in a rotation or replacement model. Since the retirement age is in the future, the term 'retirement age' has to be interpreted as the expected retirement age, with the expectations formed at the time of hiring. The model presented in this chapter is a human capital model, with emphasis on the generation and possession of firm-specific skills. This model forms the basic unifying framework for chapter 4 on discrimination against women, chapter 5 on discrimination against older workers in hiring, chapter 6 on mandatory retirement policies and chapter 7 on the rental value of a job.

3.1 The basic model

As discussed in chapter 2, Becker (1975) differentiated between general skills and firm-specific ones. Following Okun (1981), we will call workers with only general skills as 'casual workers' and those with some firm-specific skills as 'career workers'. The jobs held by the former will be designated as 'casual jobs' and those held by the latter as 'career jobs'. These designations are clearly extreme ones and are meant for analytical convenience. Real world jobs would normally incorporate both general and career skill components. Career workers may acquire firm-specific skills in a variety of ways. One of these is in the form of training provided by firms at the beginning of the worker's career with the firm, with training requiring positive costs. Another form is the gradual acquisition of skills over a considerable part of the period of employment with the firm. The literature has established such acquisition to be a major determinant of the workers' productivity and wages over their worklife (Topel, 1991). This acquisition of skills may be costless, as an externality of the work done, or may be costly, where, for example, the worker has to take time out from his normal work to acquire additional skills.

Firm-specific skills have the property that the worker's marginal productivity is higher in his existing firm - that is, the one for which his firm-specific skills are the appropriate ones - than in other firms. This difference can be labelled as the rent generated by the worker with these

33

skills. Chapter 2 argued that this rent will be split between the firm and the worker, the former receiving it in profits and the latter in wages.

For a given type of worker, define m and w as the marginal product and wage respectively in the given firm and m' and w' as the highest marginal product and wage respectively in other firms. The presence of firm-specific skills ensures that m > m', with (m-m') as the quasi-rent - or, for short, the rent - generated by the firm-specific skills. Our arguments in chapter 2 indicate that part of the rent will be paid to the worker in wages, so that w > w'. The firm's share of the rent will be [(m-m') - (w-w')] or [(m-w) - (m'-w')]. Since (m'-w') is exogenously given to the firm, the firm's decisions on employment etc. will focus on (m-w) rather than on [(m-w) - (m'-w')]. Further, m' would equal w' in perfect competition since the worker can only transfer general skills to other firms, so that (m'- w') would be zero. In any case, (m-w) is the relevant variable of concern to the profit maximizing firm since it indicates the net profit the firm will make in employing the worker. For terminological convenience, we will call (m-w) the firm's share of the rent or quasi-rent.

Our specification of the firm's share of the rent is different from that in the literature on firm-specific skills. Under our definition, the rents arise for two reasons. One is due to the rents or quasi-rents arising from firm-specific skills. the other is the difference between the marginal product and the wage of the worker even in the absence of such skills. Thus, for intra-marginal workers without firm-specific skills, a firm with diminishing marginal product will have marginal product greater than the wage, so that the rent under our definition will be positive. We find our broader definition of rents to be the more convenient one for our analysis.

Assume that the given firm has a neoclassical production function and operates in a competitive framework. It maximizes the present discounted value of profits. It has, for simplification, a given capital stock and variable labour input. The latter varies in the number of workers, the skills and the ages - as a proxy for the maturity, strength and other relevant characteristics varying with age - of the employed workers. The level of skills would depend upon the abilities and the knowledge of the workers prior to joining the firm. They join the firm at the 'hiring age'. The level of skills would also depend upon the hiring age itself and the skills gained through experience, with experience proxied by years on the job.

The firm's share r of the rent from a job position j is, $r_j = m_j - w_j$, where m is the value of the marginal product, w is the wage rate and j refers to the job position, with j=1,...,n. For analytical convenience, all product prices have been set to unity. The job positions are numbered in a sequence with declining marginal product. To maximize profits, the firm will fill job positions up to the point n* where $r_j = O$, so that for the filled job positions, $r_j \geq O$, with intra-marginal positions having $r_j > O$.

In the case of *career* workers with *firm-specific skills*, since marginal productivity and wages are affected by maturity, strength and health, etc. determined by age, m_j is a function of the age of the worker occupying the job. However, our concern is not really with these factors but with their influence on the acquisition and exercise of firm-specific skills and through that influence on the worker's marginal product. At young ages, as the worker's strength and maturity grows, his ability to acquire and use the firm-specific skills tends to increase, so that his marginal product will increase with age. At old ages, the physical and mental slowdown tends to reduce the marginal product. We will therefore assume that the marginal product of a firm-specific worker is concave over his lifetime. Given our arguments on the sharing of the returns to such skills, the wage path is also concave, as is the path of the rents r_j ($= m_j - w_j$) retained by the firm from the jth job position. The latter will be a function of both the hiring age and the time interval the worker has had to acquire the firm-specific skills. This time interval will be approximated by the time the worker has already been working in the firm.

In the case of *casual* workers with *general skills* only, the acquisition and use of these skills is also likely to depend on the age - through its associated variables of strength, maturity etc. - of the worker, so that the worker's marginal product would also depend on the age of the worker. However, under perfect competition, this increase in marginal product due to the acquisition of the general skills would be matched by the increase in the worker's wage so that r_j, the firm's share of the rent from the jth job position held by the casual worker, would not depend on the worker's age. This would also hold for workers who first join some other firms and acquire some general skills in them, so that they would have a higher hiring age when joining the firm in question, a higher level of marginal product and a correspondingly higher wage. We will therefore assume for our analysis that for the case of casual workers, r_j is independent of the hiring age and the period of employment with the firm. These sum to the age of the worker so that, for casual workers, r_j will also be independent of the worker's age.

However, note that r_j, where j can be the marginal or intramarginal job, will not necessarily be zero even for casual workers. The value of r_j is determined by the path of marginal productivity in the absence of quasi-rents generated by firm-specific skills. Since marginal productivity has been assumed to diminish as the number of jobs increases, the intra-marginal jobs would have a higher marginal product than the marginal job, so that the rents from the former will be positive, while being zero for the latter. Therefore, since r_j can be non-zero even in the absence of firm-specific skills, the distinguishing feature of casual versus firm-specific skills is not that the former will always have zero rents - that is, $r_j = 0$ for all j - while the latter do not. The distinguishing feature is that for casual jobs, r_j is independent of the skills - and therefore of the experience, hiring age and duration of employment with the firm - of the casual workers. This is not so for career workers.

To summarize our conclusions on the determinants of the firm's share of the rents from the worker's employment, in the case of a casual worker with only general skills, the firm's share of the rent will be invariant with respect to the worker's hiring age, experience and current age. It will be a function of the number of workers employed by the firm. It will also not be a function of any other of the worker's characteristics which affect his productivity through the acquisition or productivity of his general skills. In the case of a career worker with some firm-specific skills, the firm's share of the rent will be a function of the worker's hiring age, the duration of employment over which the firm-specific skills have been acquired and of the current age. It will also be a function of the number of workers employed in the firm. Further, it will also indirectly be a function of any other of the worker's characteristics which influence the acquisition and productivity of the firm-specific skills.

The firm is assumed to maximize the present discounted value of its profits. With labour as the only input, this requires maximizing the present discounted value of its share of the rents V_j over all its job positions. All job positions are assumed to be identical so that the firm would have either career jobs or casual jobs. Dropping the subscript j for simplicity of notation, and assuming an infinite horizon, for each job position,

$$V = \int_{h_1}^{R_1} r \, e^{-i(t-h_1)} \, dt - c + \int_{h_2}^{R_2} r \, e^{-i(t+T_1-h_2)} \, dt - c \, e^{-iT_1}$$

$$+ \int_{h_3}^{R_3} r \, e^{-i(t+T_1+T_2-h_3)} \, dt - c \, e^{-i(T_1+T_2)} + \dots \qquad (1)$$

where

    V   Present value of the net rents accruing to the firm
    r   Firm's share of the rents from the job position
    i   Interest rate
    t   period
    T_k Duration of employment of the kth worker ($= R_k - h_k$)
    c   Hiring and training costs
    R_k Retirement age ($= h_k + T_k$) of the kth worker
    h_k Hiring age of the kth worker
    g   Age ($= h + t$)

(1) assumes that the hiring and training costs c(.) are only incurred at the time of hiring and are identical over all job positions.

Assuming all workers in the sequence over time to be identical in terms of education and abilities - that is, with identical r(.) and c(.) functions - and since the interest rate i is also being held constant, the optimal hiring and retirement ages must also be identical for all workers in the sequence of workers. That is,

$$h_k = h \qquad \text{for all k}$$

$$R_k = R \qquad \text{for all k}$$

Hence,

$$T_k = T \qquad \text{for all k}$$

Therefore, from (1),

$$V = \int_h^R r\, e^{-i(t-h)}\, dt - c + \int_h^R r\, e^{-i(t+T-h)}\, dt - c\, e^{-iT}$$

$$+ \int_h^R r\, e^{-i(t+2T-h)}\, dt - c\, e^{-i2T} + \ldots \qquad (2)$$

Therefore,

$$V = \int_h^R r \ e^{-i(t-h)} \ dt - c + \sum_{k=1}^{\infty} e^{-ikT} \ \{\int_h^R r \ e^{-i(t-h)} \ dt - c\}$$

$$= \{\int_h^R r \ e^{-i(t-h)} \ dt - c\} + \frac{1}{e^{iT}-1} \ \{\int_h^R r \ e^{-i(t-h)} \ dt - c\}$$

Hence,

$$V = \frac{e^{iT}}{e^{iT}-1} \ \{\int_h^R r \ e^{-i(t-h)} \ dt - c\}$$

$$= \frac{e^{iT}}{e^{iT}-1} \ A \qquad\qquad (1')$$

$$where \ A = \{\int_h^R r \ e^{-i(t-h)} \ dt - c\} \qquad\qquad (1'')$$

The firm's present discounted value of profits π over n jobs is given by,

$$\pi = \int_0^n V \ dx \qquad\qquad (2')$$

$$= \int_0^n \frac{e^{iT}}{e^{iT}-1} \ A \ dx \qquad\qquad (2'')$$

Assuming that the firm maximizes the present discounted value of profits, it maximizes (2") with respect to n, h and R. As argued earlier at various points, these variables are the endogenous arguments in the r(.) and c(.) functions. With a given neoclassical production function for the firm, with the wage rate w not varying with the number of workers employed by the firm in perfect competition, both m_j and r_j are decreasing functions of the number n of jobs filled by the firm. m(.), r(.) and c(.) are assumed to be continuous and twice differentiable functions of n, h, and g. The first order conditions for a maximum are:

38

The firm's hiring and retirement ages

$$\frac{\partial \pi}{\partial n} - \frac{e^{iT}}{e^{iT}-1} A = 0 \qquad (3A)$$

$$\frac{\partial \pi}{\partial h} - \int_0^n \frac{\partial V}{\partial h} dx = 0 \qquad (3B)$$

$$\frac{\partial \pi}{\partial R} - \int_0^n \frac{\partial V}{\partial R} dx = 0 \qquad (3C)$$

where,

$$\frac{e^{iT}}{e^{iT}-1} \neq 0 \qquad for \ i > 0$$

$$\frac{\partial V}{\partial h} - A \frac{\partial}{\partial h} \left(\frac{e^{iT}}{e^{iT}-1} \right) + \frac{e^{iT}}{e^{iT}-1} \frac{\partial A}{\partial h}$$

$$\frac{\partial V}{\partial R} - A \frac{\partial}{\partial R} \left(\frac{e^{iT}}{e^{iT}-1} \right) + \frac{e^{iT}}{e^{iT}-1} \frac{\partial A}{\partial R}$$

$$\frac{\partial T}{\partial h} = -1$$

$$\frac{\partial T}{\partial R} = 1$$

$$- \frac{\partial}{\partial h} \left(\frac{e^{iT}}{e^{iT}-1} \right) - \frac{\partial}{\partial R} \left(\frac{e^{iT}}{e^{iT}-1} \right) - \frac{ie^{iT}}{e^{iT}-1} - \frac{ie^{2iT}}{(e^{iT}-1)^2}$$

Hence,

$$\frac{\partial V}{\partial h} - -\frac{ie^{iT}}{e^{iT}-1} A + \frac{ie^{2iT}}{(e^{it}-1)^2} A + \frac{e^{it}}{e^{iT}-1} \frac{\partial A}{\partial h}$$

which simplifies to,

$$\frac{\partial V}{\partial h} = [i(V-A) + \frac{\partial A}{\partial h}](\frac{e^{iT}}{e^{iT}-1})$$

Similarly,

$$\frac{\partial V}{\partial R} = [-i(V-A) + \frac{\partial A}{\partial R}](\frac{e^{iT}}{e^{iT}-1})$$

Therefore, the first order conditions become,

$$A = 0 \tag{3A$'$}$$

$$\frac{\partial \pi}{\partial h} = \int_0^n \{i(V-A) + \frac{\partial A}{\partial h}\}(\frac{e^{iT}}{e^{iT}-1})\ dx = 0 \tag{3B$'$}$$

$$\frac{\partial \pi}{\partial R} = \int_0^n \{-i(V-A) + \frac{\partial A}{\partial R}\}(\frac{e^{iT}}{e^{iT}-1})\ dx = 0 \tag{3C$'$}$$

Given that both V and A are unspecified functions of the number of jobs and that it is difficult to solve the integrals in (3B') and (3C'), we will proceed further only with the special cases of (3B') and (3C') where the integrand is zero. Alternatively, we assume that (3A'), (3B") and (3C") are the solutions to the first order conditions above, where (3A") and (3B") are,

$$i(V-A) + \frac{\partial A}{\partial h} = 0 \tag{3B$''$}$$

$$-i(V-A) + \frac{\partial A}{\partial R} = 0 \tag{3C$''$}$$

The first order conditions for the maximum present discounted value of the firm's profits then become,

$$A = 0 \tag{4A}$$

$$\frac{\partial A}{\partial h} = -i(V-A) \tag{4B}$$

$$\frac{\partial A}{\partial R} = i(V-A) \tag{4C}$$

We assume without further specification that the second order conditions for a maximum are satisfied by the solution to (4A) to (4C). Note that (4A) specifies that A=0 for the optimal values n*, h* and R* of n, h, and R respectively, where n*, h*, and R* are the solutions to equations (4A) to (4C). That is, in the current sequence of workers, the present discounted value of the firm's share of the rent from the marginal worker, when n* workers are hired at the optimal hiring age h* and retired at the optimal retirement age R*, is zero. It will not pay the firm to hire an additional worker or delay the retirement of any worker.

3.2 The optimal number of jobs

In equations (4A) to (4C), A(n,h,R) is the discounted value, discounted to the time of hiring, of profits from each worker in the sequence of workers occupying over time the marginal (nth) job position when n job positions are filled. From (4A), the firm's profits are maximized when the number of jobs are such that the marginal worker yields a zero value of A, and hence does not contribute to profits over time: that is, for the marginal worker, the discounted value of the marginal product is exactly offset by the sum of the discounted values of wages and hiring and training costs. (4A) is thus the counterpart in our framework of the more familiar profit maximizing condition in one-period analysis: marginal product equals the wage rate so that the contribution to profits of the marginal worker is zero.

Equations (4A), (4B) and (4C) determine the optimal values n, h, and R as n*, h* and R*. n* is thus an endogenous variable determined jointly with h* and R*. Our analysis, therefore, does not assume that the number of jobs is fixed. It is worth noting this point since the rest of our analysis in this and other chapters focuses on the determination of the optimal hiring and retirement ages, and, to simplify the discussion, does not in general refer to the determination of the number of jobs.

From (4A), A(n*,h*,R*) = 0. Further, given that the workers' marginal product is assumed to be diminishing in n, our assumptions on the relationship between increases in the marginal product and the firm's share of the rent imply that the latter will be diminishing in n. Hence, in the neighbourhood of (n*, h*, R*),

$$\frac{\partial A}{\partial n} < 0$$

Therefore, for the jth job position, with job positions ordered in terms of declining marginal product, $A_j(n^*,h^*,R^*) > 0$ for $j < n^*$. $A_j(n^*,h^*,R^*)$ is to be interpreted as the present discounted value of the firm's share of the rents from the jth job position when $h = h^*$, $R = R^*$, $n = n^*$ and $j < n^*$. That is, the firm has n^* workers working from ages h^* to R^*, and the focus is on the intra-marginal job position j, $j < n^*$, which yields positive net discounted rents/profits to the firm.

3.3 The optimal hiring and retirement ages for career workers

Our concern in this section, as in this book, is really with the optimal period of employment and with the optimal hiring and retirement ages for career workers. It is not with the optimal number of jobs. We, therefore, proceed with the interpretation of the optimizing conditions (4B) and (4C) for a given job position j, $j \leq n^*$, even though we recognize that the complete set of optimizing conditions also includes (4A).

Equations (3A) to (3C) clearly indicate that employing the marginal worker - that is, in the marginal job position n^* - with the marginal hiring period and the marginal retirement period yields the firm a zero increase in the present discounted value π of profits from the marginal job position.

Since $A^* = A(n^*,h^*,R^*) = 0$, $V^* = V(n^*,h^*,R^*) = 0$. Therefore, from (4B) and (4C),

$$\frac{\partial}{\partial h} A(n*,h*,R*) = -i(V* - A*) = 0$$

$$\frac{\partial}{\partial R} A(n*,h*,R*) = i(V* - A*) = 0$$

That is, maximizing the present discounted value of profits over all jobs, with a sequence of workers over time for each job, also implies that the present discounted value of rents/profits from each sequence of workers, including the current one, are also being maximized when the marginal job is held by any given worker from h^* to R^*.

However, as argued above, at the intra-marginal job position j, $j < n^*$, $A_j(n^*,h^*,R^*) > 0$. Therefore, at $j < n^*$, $V_j(n^*, h^*, R^*) > 0$. Since $V_j > A_j$, for $i > 0$,

$$\frac{\partial}{\partial h} A_j(n*, h*, R*) = -i(V - A) < 0 \qquad\qquad j < n*$$

$$\frac{\partial}{\partial R} A_j(n*, h*, R*) = i(V - A) > 0 \qquad\qquad j < n*$$

where $[-\partial A/\partial h]$ is the *decrease* in the present discounted value of the firm's share of the rents from raising the hiring age and $\partial A/\partial R$ is the *increase* in the present discounted value of the firm's share of the rents from postponing retirement. They specify the marginal profits associated respectively with the hiring and retirement ages. The two amounts are identical in absolute terms.

Therefore, for the intra-marginal workers, the marginal profits with respect to an increase in the retirement age are positive. Keeping on the worker for an extra period will increase the firm's profits. It would then seem to be rational for the firm to keep that worker for the extra period and the worker could legitimately claim that his marginal product beyond the retirement age would exceed his wage even for some periods beyond R*. However, keeping on such a worker beyond R* would in fact decrease the present discounted value of the firm's profits *from the sequence of workers* if such a worker was employed beyond R*, so that doing so is not really a rational policy for the firm. The reason for this is as follows. Keeping a worker beyond R* in a given job position delays hiring another worker in that job position and the firm has more to gain by having the young replacement worker filling that job position than the old existing worker continuing in it. But then, could the firm not increase its profits by keeping the worker beyond R* and hiring the younger worker also? The answer to this is in the negative, since keeping the existing worker while hiring the new one would increase the number of job positions beyond n* and decrease the firm's profits. We elaborate on this argument in section 3.5 below.

To reiterate, keeping on a given worker in a given job for an additional period beyond R* would decrease the firm's present discounted value of profits. The reason for this is that keeping the worker beyond R* would mean that his replacement in his job cannot be hired until he vacates his job - and the replacement worker contributes more through his rents than does the existing worker holding onto the job for an additional period.

Looking at the marginal profits at the optimal hiring age h*, this amount also equals i(V-A), which is, as shown above, greater than zero. Raising the hiring age by one period reduces the firm's present value of profits by i(V-A). How can a newly hired worker who has no prior firm-specific skills and presumably acquires little of these in the first period, yield a positive share of rents to the firm? The answer to this lies in focusing on the last period of employment, i.e., at R*. Delaying the hiring age by one period reduces the duration of employment by one period and cuts out the rent of one period when the worker would have already acquired all his skills. The amount reduced is therefore approximated by - and in some cases equal to - the present discounted value of the firm's share of the rent generated during the last period R* of employment. The latter is given by $\partial A/\partial R$ evaluated at R = R*.

3.4 The optimal hiring and retirement ages for casual workers

For casual workers, it was argued above that r_j ($=m_j-w_j$) would depend upon n, the number of workers employed by the firm, but not upon the hiring age or the duration of employment with the firm. If such a worker has higher general skills than other workers, he would receive a correspondingly higher wage, so that the difference between the marginal product and the wage would be the same, no matter what the age of the worker, how long he has been with the firm or what his skill level is. Hence, $\partial V/\partial h = \partial V/\partial R = 0$ for all values of h and R.

The expression for V, the present discounted value of profits associated with a given job can then be simplified to:

$$V = \frac{e^{iT}}{e^{iT}-1} \{r \int_h^R e^{-i(t-h)} \, dt - c\}$$

$$= \frac{e^{iT}}{e^{iT}-1} \{\frac{r}{i} (1 - e^{-iT}) - c\}$$

$$= \frac{r}{i} - \frac{e^{iT}}{e^{iT}-1} c \tag{5}$$

$$Define \ Y = \frac{e^{iT}}{e^{iT}-1} \{\int_h^R r \ e^{-i(t-h)} \, dt\} \tag{6}$$

$$X = \frac{e^{iT}}{e^{iT}-1} c \tag{7}$$

$Hence \ V = Y - X$

For casual workers, the present discounted value Y of the firm's share of the rent from a given job position is specified by:

$$Y = r/i \qquad (8)$$

The explanation for (8) is that for a given casual job, the rents are constant with respect to the characteristics of the workers, so that such a job is a 'consol' yielding a coupon rate r in perpetuity. Therefore, from (8),

$$\partial Y/\partial h = \partial Y/\partial R = 0 \qquad (9)$$

Since c, the cost of hiring and training paid by the firm, was assumed to be a constant,

$$\frac{\partial X}{\partial h} = \frac{ie^{iT}}{(e^{iT}-1)^2} \, c$$

$$\frac{\partial X}{\partial R} = -\frac{ie^{iT}}{(e^{iT}-1)^2} \, c$$

Therefore, the first order conditions for maximizing π are:

$$\frac{\partial V}{\partial h} = -\frac{ie^{iT}}{(e^{iT}-1)^2} \, c = 0$$

$$\frac{\partial V}{\partial R} = \frac{ie^{iT}}{(e^{iT}-1)^2} \, c = 0$$

For i > 0, these conditions require that $T \rightarrow \infty$. Intuitively, in the case of casual workers, the firm maximizes profits by spreading the constant cost of hiring and training over the longest possible period. For finite lives, this period would be from birth to death. This is clearly unrealistic, so that a more realistic formulation of the cost function has to be specified. This would be taken up in chapter 5. Alternatively, the worker would have to pay the full cost of hiring and training him so that the amount c paid by the firm would be zero. This is in agreement with the literature on general skills.

For the remainder of this section, assume that the hiring and training costs paid by the firm are zero. Then, X = 0 and V = Y. Therefore, for casual workers, V = r/i. Hence, $\partial V/\partial h = 0$ and $\partial V/\partial R = 0$ for all values of n, h and R. Hence, equations (3A) to (3C), with A = A(n), reduce to:

$$\frac{\partial \pi}{\partial n} - \frac{e^{iT}}{e^{iT}-1} A = 0 \tag{10A}$$

$$\frac{\partial \pi}{\partial h} - \int_0^n \frac{\partial V}{\partial h} dx = 0 \qquad for\ all\ n,h,r \tag{10B}$$

$$\frac{\partial \pi}{\partial R} - \int_0^n \frac{\partial V}{\partial R} dx = 0 \qquad for\ all\ n,h,r \tag{10C}$$

Hence, for casual workers, the firm will have an optimal number of workers, but since the first order conditions are satisfied by any value of h and r, the firm will not have a specific optimal hiring or retirement age. The firm will be indifferent as to the age of the job applicant and as to the age at which its casual workers want to leave the firm.

We can simplify some of the equations above for casual workers. As shown above, in the case of *casual* workers, $\partial r/\partial h = \partial r/\partial R = 0$ for all h and k, so that $r = r(n)$. Further, if c(.) is also zero for all n, as when the workers pay the full cost of their hiring and training, $\partial V/\partial h = \partial V/\partial R = 0$ for all n. Furthermore,

$$A = (1 - e^{-iT}) \frac{r}{i} \tag{11A}$$

$$-\frac{\partial A}{\partial h} = e^{-iT} r \tag{11B}$$

$$\frac{\partial A}{\partial R} = e^{-iT} r \tag{11C}$$

Since $i > 0$, (10A) implies that $A(n) = 0$ for the marginal worker. Further, since $T > 0$ for an employed worker, (11A) requires that for the marginal worker $r(n) = 0$ and specifies the optimal number of jobs as n^*, with $r(n^*) = 0$. That is, the *marginal* job will yield zero rents to the firm, and will have marginal product equal to the wage rate. However, as noted earlier, for an intra-marginal job position j, $j < n$, $r_j(n^*) > 0$.

The explanation for equation (11B) is as follows. r is the firm's share of the rent from the first worker, say in job position j, so that delaying the hiring by one period will mean that the worker will work for $(T - 1)$ periods, thereby not yielding the firm the rent r during the Tth period. The present value of this is re^{-iT}. However, also note that the firm would hire the next worker in what would have been the first worker's period T and this worker would yield re^{-iT} in present value. The net loss to the firm would then be zero (i.e., $\partial V/\partial h = 0$).

Similar considerations apply to an increase in the retirement age. For a given job position, at age R, the existing employee would increase the present value of the rents for the firm by re^{-iT}. But keeping on the existing worker beyond the optimal retirement age would mean that the firm would not be able to hire his replacement and the loss from not hiring the replacement is also re^{-iT}. Therefore, the firm would be indifferent between retiring the existing employee and hiring the replacement as against keeping the former for another period and not hiring the replacement.

Hence, for casual workers, the firm is indifferent as to the age of hiring: it will be willing to hire workers at any age and pay them their marginal product. It will also not make any special effort to retain such workers: they can leave when they want. Conversely, they can continue in the job if they so wish. *For these workers, there will be 'casual' hiring and 'casual' layoff.* Factors other than wages and economic performance can then easily determine such hiring and firing. Among these can be personal appearance, personality, connections, etc. Further, as another implication for empirical tests, the similarity in equations (11B) and (11) implies that there will be similarity of behaviour towards both hiring and layoff or retirement of casual workers.

3.5 The rental value of jobs

The optimizing conditions (4B) and (4C) were,

$$- \frac{\partial A}{\partial h} = \frac{\partial A}{\partial R} = i(V - A) \tag{12}$$

where (V-A) is the present value of the job position flowing from workers after the first one in the sequence of workers filling the position and i(V-A) is the rental value per period of the position on the basis of the productivity and wages of workers subsequent to the first one. Intuitively, the first worker has to guarantee the firm this net rent per period in order to get the job or to continue holding on to the job. In the case of casual workers, equations (11A) and (11B) showed that the rental value simplified to re^{-iT}.

(12), then, states that the first worker, in order to keep the job one period longer through earlier hiring or through retirement postponed by one period, must yield the firm a rent for the marginal period equal to the rental value of the job position to subsequent workers. If the first worker cannot yield at least this much, the firm can clearly increase its profits by replacing him by another worker (who yields i(V-A) per period). If the first worker yields more than this amount, the firm increases its profits by keeping him at least one period longer.

From (12), since the marginal conditions are symmetrical for the two sets of ages, the firm would be equally choosy or equally casual about the two. What this implies for empirical testing is that *firms which tend to discriminate more against hiring older workers, will also tend to have more rigid retirement policies.*

If the analysis was performed in a non-replacement model, with the hiring and retirement decisions confined to a worker's own productivity and wages, the firm would maximize A - that is, the present value of its profits over only the first generation of workers - with respect to n,h and R. The first order conditions corresponding to (4A) to (4C) would then be:

$$A - 0 \qquad\qquad\qquad (13A)$$

$$\frac{\partial A}{\partial h} - 0 \qquad\qquad\qquad (13B)$$

$$\frac{\partial A}{\partial R} - 0 \qquad\qquad\qquad (13C)$$

(13A) is identical with (4A) so that the marginal worker with the optimal hiring and retirement ages would yield a zero present value of the firm's share of the rents. However, equation (13B) differs from (4B) and (13C) differs from (4C). Hence equations (13A) to (13C) would yield the optimal values n^*, h^* and R^*, different from those implied by (4A) to (4C). For $j \leq n^*$, (13) implies that the worker with a concave rent function with respect to age, will be hired as soon as his marginal rent (per period) becomes zero and retained until it again becomes zero. Comparing (12) and (13) in the context of the concave age-related $\partial A/\partial g$ function for a given job position, as shown by the X curve in Figure 3.1, (13) for the non-replacement model would in general imply that workers will be hired at earlier ages (age h_1) and retired at later ages (age R_1) than under the replacement model (age h_0 for hiring and R_0 for retirement). $\partial A/\partial g$ is the increase in A due to employment at age g.

As pointed out above, (12) has to be interpreted with caution. It does not require that a worker has to yield a positive net rent to the firm in his first period on the job. This amount would often be zero or negative. Since a worker on his first year on the job will not yet possess any firm-specific

48

skills, he will not generate any rents; that is, have a marginal productivity in the firm in question in excess of his marginal product in other firms. Further, following Becker, if the firm pays the worker the whole or part of his training cost in the first period, the firm would pay him more in wages and training costs than his marginal product.

What (12) requires is that the postponement of the hiring age must increase the firm's share of the present value of the worker's lifetime rents by the rental value of the job. Figure 3.1, therefore, graphed $\partial A/\partial g$ on the vertical axis rather than the more usual m or r functions. $\partial A/\partial g$ can be positive at the hiring age even though the net rents to the firm in the hiring period are zero or negative.

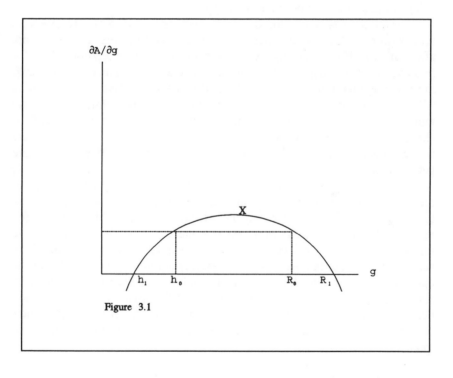

Figure 3.1

The availability and competence of the replacement workers will determine the net rents from them and hence their rental value. For given productivity and wage paths of the current generation or set of workers, the higher the rental value - because of greater productivity or lower wages of the replacement (incoming generation of) workers - the later will be the optimal hiring age and the earlier will be the optimal retirement age for the former set of workers: the working period will be shortened at both ends for the current generation of workers. If the current generation of workers have already been hired, the reduction in their optimal hiring age will no longer be relevant but their optimal retirement age will be reduced beyond what was expected at the time of hiring - increasing the tendency of firms to induce 'early retirement'. Improvements in technology between generations could cause such an effect by making 'younger' workers more productive by being 'in tune with the newer technology'.

Developments within the current generation can also clearly affect its retirement age. Unionization pushing up wages and lowering rents would not affect this age if these changes were permanent across generations. But if it pushed up wages temporarily over the current generation only, it would lower the optimal retirement age. Similarly, changes in health and longevity will delay the productivity decline. The impact of such shifts is taken up more explicitly in sections 4.7 and 4.8 of chapter 4 and section 6.5 of chapter 6. Their effect differs depending upon whether the changes were across generations or only over the current or only over the future generations.

Personal and sociological factors can also affect the optimal hiring and retirement ages. To illustrate, if increasing standards of living lead society to 'coddle' - that is to postpone the psychological maturity date for job responsibilities - its young ones, the $r(.)$ and $c(.)$ functions would shift to imply a delay in the optimal hiring age. Similarly, poorer consumption habits reducing the stamina to work, especially at older ages, could lower the optimal retirement age. Such an effect could operate even between the rich and the poor classes within a given society: if the 'rich' coddle their young but have consumption patterns leading to better health at older ages, their children will have a later hiring age and a later retirement age than the 'poor'.

3.6 A clarification

The preceding section envisages the firm as replacing one worker by another even while the employment of the former yields positive rents to the firm.

This follows from equation (12) where for an intra-marginal worker j with $A_j > 0$, the rent derived by the firm for the optimal retirement age/period is positive at i(V-A). That is, the former worker's marginal product m exceeds his wage w at the time of his retirement or layoff. This would seem to violate the usual profit-maximizing condition of m = w and raise the obvious question: would the firm not be able to increase its profits by keeping on the initial worker and hiring the new one as a net addition to the firm's work-force? This question has already been addressed in some of our earlier remarks. However, our result appears to be an unusual one and contrary to the common requirement in the literature that the wage exceed the marginal product as the condition for the firm to retire the worker. Therefore, we reformulate the explanation of our result in three different ways in order to provide more than one perspective on it.

We first present the formal justification for our conclusions. These are derived from the first order conditions for maximizing the firm's present discounted value of profits. These were equations (3A), (3B) and (3C). These yield the optimal values of n*, h* and R* - and also imply equation (12). For $j < n*$, $A_j > 0$ and the marginal retirement period yields a positive net contribution to the firm's profit equal to i(V-A). But keeping workers beyond the optimal retirement age R* will reduce the firm's present discounted value of its profits. Hence, even though continuing to employ the existing worker during the year (R*+1) could still yield positive rents, say somewhat below i(V-A), such employment will decrease the firm's present discounted value of profits. This happens because keeping the worker during the (R*+1) period prevents a new worker being hired as his replacement during (R*+1) where the new worker will yield i(V-A) on the same job during that period. Keeping both workers also will not increase the firm's present discounted value of profits since there is an optimal number of jobs n* and each job within this number has the optimal hiring age as h* and the optimal retirement as R*.

For the justification of our results from other, more intuitive, perspectives, we use one-period analysis and the concept of different classes of workers as an analogy.

Assuming diminishing marginal productivity (MP) of labour, figure 3.2 graphs MP against n, the number of workers employed by the firm. According to conventional theory, the profit-maximizing number of workers for a MP curve m and at a wage rate w_0 is $n*_0$. All workers except the marginal ones are of course, intra-marginal ones and yield the firm a net difference (m-w) which corresponds to the definition in this chapter of the rent retained by the firm. The firm is interested in making this difference,

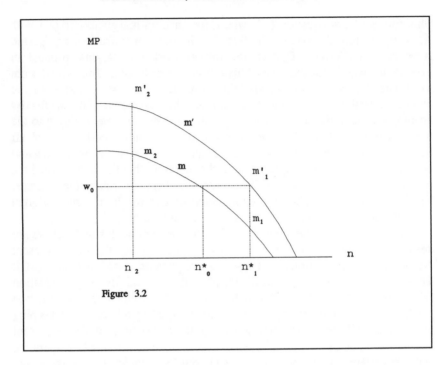

Figure 3.2

for any given n, as large as possible. That is, if superior workers were to become available and possess the MP curve shown as m' in figure 3.2, with m' > m for all n and with the wage rate still at w_0, the firm would employ the superior workers only, with their employment at n^*_1.

Since age is a characteristic of workers which affects their productivity, there is a set of workers who are superior - that is, have the optimal hiring age - to other workers - that is, those not having the optimal hiring age. Only these superior workers will be hired.

Looking at the intra-marginal job positions for $j < n^*_1$, the worker of the inferior type (with non-optimal hiring age) competing for the intra-marginal job position n_2 will not be hired even though his marginal product m_2 exceeds his wages w_0 since the superior worker will yield m'_2 and increase the firm's profit by more. Now, looking at the margin of profit maximization, where $j = n^*_1$, the superior worker would yield zero rents with marginal product equal to m'_1. The inferior worker will have marginal product equal to m_1 and will yield negative rents.

Therefore, the firm would only hire workers with the optimal hiring age and the optimal (expected) retirement age, even though other workers can yield positive net rents to the firm, as in the region $j < n^*_0$.

An extension of the preceding analysis and that of the preceding section arises if we were to also consider the firm's provision of firm-specific training and environment (in which such skills are accumulated) as a resource owned by the firm. We labelled this resource in chapter 2 as the firm-specific environment characteristic. As shown in that chapter, the net rent retained by the firm from the firm-specific skills of a worker can be considered to be the return to the firm for the provision to the worker of the firm-specific environment, with the worker's MP being the joint product of his own characteristics such as his aptitude, intelligence, schooling, age, etc., and the firm-specific environment. The MP attributable purely to the worker's own characteristics is (m-r) (= q), where m is the MP of the worker with firm-specific skills and r is the MP of the firm-specific environment. The profit-maximizing firm will then hire the number of workers to equate q to the wage rate, which is the cost to the firm of using the worker's characteristics for one period. At the margin, the optimal hiring age job applicant has w = q while the younger and older job applicants are less efficient by virtue of their age and have w > q. The profit maximizing firm will not, therefore, employ the latter unless their wage was lowered to match their lower productivity.

3.7 Wage and occupational discrimination

'Occupational discrimination' against both female workers and in hiring older workers can flow from both workers' and firms' choices in the context of our analysis. On the former, such workers may find that the wage - after ensuring the firm the rental value of the job - in more firm-specific jobs may be lower than in more casual jobs which have to ensure a lower rental value. Therefore, accepting the job with the highest wage would mean that such workers would shift into more casual jobs.

The greater the decline in rents for deviations from the optimal hiring and retirement ages for the more firm-specific jobs, the more would workers suffering from such a deviation in age shift to more casual jobs. And the greater the deviation in age, the more likely are the new jobs for such workers to be more casual than their former ones. This deviation in age will be greater, the older is the job applicant relative to the optimal hiring age of the given job. These considerations clearly have a bearing on the types of jobs offered to older - that is older than the optimal hiring age - job applicants, and are more explicitly treated in chapter 5. In the case of female workers, this deviation from the optimal retirement age will be greater the earlier the female worker is expected to leave or the later is the firm's optimal retirement age for the given job. This shifting of the workers from firm-specific jobs to more casual ones occurs, according to our arguments in this paragraph, at the volition of workers themselves, in their search for the highest paid jobs, though in the presence of wage differentiation by the firm for a given job.

Occupational discrimination will be imposed by the firm in our analysis if it faces any costs of wage discrimination. These costs may be imposed by law, by custom or may flow from one of the reasons given in the efficiency wage literature (Akerlof and Yellen, 1986). If there are higher costs to practising wage discrimination in firm-specific jobs, than to a refusal to hire, firms would find it optimal to refuse older job applicants and female workers entry to firm-specific jobs, forcing them into more casual ones in the economy.

Note that our analysis implies a double strike against female workers. Assuming that a given female worker has the optimal hiring age for firm-specific jobs at the time of initial entry into the labour force, she may not be hired into such jobs because firms expect her to leave before the optimal retirement age for these jobs. When, years later, she has established her long-term commitment to the job and employment generally, she cannot be re-employed into the more firm-specific jobs because she would by then be older than the optimal hiring age into these jobs. We would, therefore, observe more female workers in more casual jobs than their *ex post* observed long term stay with the firm justifies.

Conclusion

Our approach in this chapter has clearly been in the human capital tradition. However, this chapter in some ways shifts the focus from the treatment of characteristics of workers to that of jobs and as such may be interpreted as being closer to job-based theories. Among these would be Akerlof's (1984) treatment of jobs as dam sites. Another is the theory offered to explain the observed patterns of wage and occupational discrimination by Lazear and Rosen (1990). The latter argue that jobs are a set of technological opportunities, with certain promotion patterns, and that workers are categorized into jobs. Jobs with firm-specific skills and with limitations on the number of jobs to which promotion can take place are an element of the theory of Hashimoto (1980) and Carmichael (1983). Such theories have to assume a restriction on the number of available jobs. We have explained this restriction as coming from the optimal number of jobs.

The restriction on the number of jobs leads to the notion of different workers competing for the limited number of jobs. This is an element in Akerlof's approach and of Hashimoto and Carmichael. However, it is rarely translated into the concept of the replacement of workers on the given number of jobs over generations. We have done so in this chapter.

Examining the firm's hiring and retirement age decisions jointly in the context of a replacement model gives a different perspective on the firm's decisions from that obtained from models examining only one of these and especially from models without replacement. The preceding analysis showed the similarity of factors affecting both the hiring and retirement ages. In particular, the marginal contribution of each of these ages to the present value of the worker's stream of rents accruing to the firm must be equal.

Firm-specific skills are a very important element of workers' productivity (Topel, 1991). The rents or quasi-rents to such skills are shared between the firm and the worker. The notion of such skills yielding net rents as a return to the firm leads to the concept of the rental value of the job position, a concept relatively rare in the literature but a useful one in the context of firm-specific skills. This concept views the firm as owning an environment suitable for learning and exercising firm-specific skills. This environmental resource is scarce and the worker competing for a job position has to yield a return to the firm at least equal to what other workers can yield. Chapter 7 addresses this concept of the rental cost of jobs.

Workers with the optimal hiring and retirement ages - the optimal age workers - will yield the highest present value of the net rents to the firm. Workers with other ages in this respect will not be hired since the firm will lose by hiring them, unless such workers will accept an appropriately lower wage than paid to the optimal age workers. Hence, there will appear to be wage discrimination when hiring 'older' workers, or, if there are penalties to the firm of such wage discrimination, there will be occupational discrimination. Chapter 5 takes up this topic in detail. At the other end of the work-life, workers who are expected to retire from the given firm - that is, quit - 'too early' compared with the firm's optimal retirement age, will also be refused the job or suffer a wage reduction during their working years. Firms often tend to believe this to occur for young female workers more than for males, resulting in discrimination against female workers. Chapter 4 is devoted to this topic.

The unified analysis of hiring and retirement ages thus allows us to see discrimination against older workers and against female ones as reflecting similar forces, though for reasons operating at opposite ends of the employment period.

Given the length of the employment period in jobs with significant firm-specific skills, the uncertainties over this period, as well as the moral hazard implicit in the firm-worker relationship, insurance and principal-agent considerations would also be relevant to the analysis. The analyses of Lazear, Blinder, Lapp and others focusing on such factors is thus not irrelevant to the retirement decision in the real world. However, we believe that while these factors do shed light on the hiring-retirement decisions, they are not necessary for these decisions: the optimal hiring and retirement ages would exist even without them. We will return to the analysis of Lazear, Blinder and Lapp, and of mandatory retirement in detail in chapter 6.

We have not said much in this chapter on the hiring and retirement ages which are optimal for workers in terms of their preferences. We see the existence of widespread wage discrimination and job refusal to both female workers and older male ones as arguing for the independence of workers' and firms' decisions on the optimal hiring and retirement ages, with the strong possibility of divergence and conflict between the ages preferred by workers and those preferred by firms. This chapter has, therefore, presented the relevant analysis only for firms and, therefore, only for the demand, as if it were, for the optimal hiring and retirement ages. It is not a complete market analysis. The worker's side of these issues will be taken up in chapter 8.

4 Wage and Occupational Differentiation by Sex

This chapter examines the implications of the model in chapter 3 for the differentiation of wages and occupational segregation between male and female workers. To put our explanation in perspective relative to the wage and occupational differentiation that exists in the real world, the only part of real-world differentiation explained here is that due to differences in skills and productivity arising from differences in the expected period for which the worker would stay with the firm. Strictly speaking, we do not explain wage and occupational discrimination if this term was defined as differentiation in wages and occupations other than due to differences in hiring and training cost, due to differences in human capital and productivity *and due to differences in the firm's profits arising from differences in the expected period of stay with the firm.* Such a definition would force 'discrimination' to be either due to the tastes of employers, of other workers or of buyers of the product (as in Becker, 1971), due to monopsony or monopoly in labour markets(as in Madden, 1978), due to irrational behaviour from an economic viewpoint, or due to sociological and other considerations on the part of firms. These approaches are not dealt with here, so that we genuinely do not address the issue of discrimination as whole, especially *if* as term is defined above. However, the term 'discrimination' is also often used to refer to differences in the wages of workers whose *current* productivity is identical, or as differences in the wages of workers with equal abilities, education and seniority with the firm. We will generally follow these definitions of 'discrimination'.

The differentiation in wages and occupational structures by sex has been the focus of considerable theoretical and empirical research in recent years.

The extent of this differentiation has been documented in numerous studies. Among the numerous recent studies are Cannings (1988), Gunderson, (1989), Smith and Ward (1989), Ragan and Tremblay (1988), Fuchs (1989), Bergmann (1989) and Loprest (1992). The extent of wage differentiation across several industrialized countries is given in Gunderson (1989, p.47) and shows that women's earnings were lower than men's in his set of countries in both 1960 and 1980. In 1980, women's earnings as a ratio of men's were lowest in Japan (at 54%) and highest in Italy (83%), with those in Canada and USA being 64% and 66% respectively. Lazear (1989) reported average weekly wages of females to males in USA to be 0.58 in 1976, 0.59 in 1980 and 0.62 in 1986. Fuchs (1989) using somewhat different data reported that female wages were virtually stable until 1980 and then rose by 7% from 1980 to 1986. The increase in the female-male earnings ratio for full time workers is dramatic for Canada: this ratio was 63.87% in 1981, 65.8% in 1986 and 71.8% in 1992, with a steady increase each year from 1981 to 1992. The trend has been strongest since 1989: the ratio increased by only 2.1% from 1981 to 1989 but increased by 6.0% from 1989 to 1992 (Statistics Canada, *Earnings of Men and Women, 1992*). It seems clear that the relative wages of female to male workers have been rising very significantly in recent years, though they do definitely still remain lower.

Further, Smith and Ward (1989) argue that female workers have in fact done better in terms of wages *relative to trends in their average skills and productivity* than the data show and that there have been even more dramatic increases in the wages of younger professional women. For Canada, in terms of the changes by age, the female-male earnings of full time workers were: 77.5% in 1981 and 92.7% in 1992 for the 15-24 year age group; 69.5% in 1981 and 78.5% in 1992 for the 25-34 year age group; 61.4% in 1981 and 69.8% in 1992 for the 35-44 age group; and 57.0% in 1982 and 68.9% for the 45-54 age group. By marital status, the earnings ratio was 87.7% in 1981 versus 99.0% in 1992 for single (never married) women while it was 59.0% in 1981 versus 66.6% in 1992 for married women. By education, the female-male earnings ratio in 1991 was 71.1% for high school graduates while it was 74.4% for university graduates (Statistics Canada, *Earnings of Men and Women,1992*). The evidence is clear for Canada, and for most western industrialized countries that the female-male earnings ratios have been rising dramatically for all major categories, and especially for the young and for the females without family commitments.

Groschen (1991) and Lazear and Rosen (1990) point out that there is no significant differential between male and female wages in narrow job categories. Lazear and Rosen argue that any difference comes about because of differences in the types of jobs held by male and female workers or of their relative proportions in different job categories, with females workers being less likely to be promoted. Promotions of females require greater abilities than of males. Bergmann (1989) also points out the pervasive segregation of females by job title.

For each of the countries reported in Gunderson (1989), the female labour market participation rates were substantially lower than those of men in 1960 and in 1980, but the former did increase very significantly between these years. Using data given by Gunderson (1989, p.47) and excluding the former USSR, the highest female participation rate was at 76.9% in Sweden in 1980, with an increase from 51% in 1960. The next highest was Britain with 62.3% in 1980, up from 43.4% in 1960. The rates for USA were 51.3% in 1980 and 37.8% in 1960. For Canada, they were 50.4% in 1980 and 27.9% in 1960. The lifetime expected participation rates among *young* female workers entering the labour force appear to be even higher than these averages.

Occupational differentiation also exists in virtually all industrialized countries. Fuchs (1989, p.27) reports the Duncan indices of occupational segregation by sex and race for the United States for 1960 and 1980. His data shows that occupational segregation against women was rampant across all ages and educational levels and between whites and blacks.

The above very brief synopsis of wage and occupational differentiation, just as virtually every review in the literature, shows the long run persistence and intractability of both wage and occupational differentiation by sex. Of the two types of differentiation, occupational differentiation seems to be the more serious phenomena, and results in a considerable part of the observed wage differentiation (Gunderson, 1989, p. 67; Lazear and Rosen, 1990; Bergmann, 1989). Given the extent and tenacity of wage and occupational differentiation across countries and even within a specified country, it is likely that such differentiation is caused by a variety of factors rather than by a single one, so that we have to look for several different determinants or explanations for the total observed amounts.

Several explanations for wage and occupational differentiation have been suggested within the neo-classical paradigm. A major element of any such differentiation is likely to be due to differences in the characteristics such as abilities, aptitudes and schooling etc., of the workers at the time of entering the labour market. This is the main focus of many human capital models (e.g. see Mincer, 1970, 1974; Mincer and Polachek, 1974, 1978; Sandell and Shapiro, 1978). Discrimination theories tend to focus on the residual element after the contributions of these human capital factors have been eliminated from the data. However, there are conflicting viewpoints on how to arrive at these residuals. There are also disputes in the literature on the proper degree of reliance on human capital differences to explain the observed wage differentiation.

One set of the explanations for wage and occupation discrimination bases it on some form of discriminatory 'tastes' against women. This could be in the workplace by either firms, unions, or workers, or even prior to entering the labour force, in the home or in educational institutions (see, for example, Arrow, 1973; Becker, 1971; Madden, 1978; Zellner, 1975). However, Lazear and Rosen (1990, p. S106) argue that "only a tortured taste theory of discrimination can reconcile" the facts of the absence of significant wage discrimination in narrow wage categories, with discrimination in promotions and in higher paying jobs. If there is a taste for not working with female workers, its strongest impact should be within narrow job categories. The empirical study at the micro level by Ragan and Tremblay (1988) also rejects the tastes based model for discrimination in wages by sex, though they found some support for this model for the existence of wage discrimination by race.

Bergmann (1989) argues that human capital models also do not explain the large differences in wages between male and female workers. According to her, the observed wage differentiation largely results from job title segregation, which in turn is due to social customs. Lazear and Rosen (1990) also use discrimination in jobs and promotions as the main element of their approach.

Becker (1985) offers an alternative explanation of wage and occupational differentiation in terms of the housework and other family commitments that women have to perform, so that they have less energy and can devote less effort to their (market) jobs. This reduces their productivity and wages. Further, it leads them to seek less demanding jobs, inducing a further reduction in jobs and job segregation. Fuchs (1989) also refers to the stronger commitment of women versus men to the welfare of children and family needs and activities.

A quite different approach, also within the neo-classical paradigm, uses the lower labour force participation of women relative to men and the intermittency of this participation, as perceived by firms, to explain the wage and occupational differentiation between women and men. Women's lower labour force participation and its intermittency have been used in various human capital models (see, for example, Mincer and Polachek, 1974; Polachek, 1975) to show that the optimal investment in women in terms of schooling and post-schooling experience would tend to be less than in men.

Further, this investment would be in forms which have lower attrition rates during periods away from the job (Polachek, 1981). There is a considerable element of appeal in these ideas and empirical tests reported in the literature have sometimes been used to claim that most wage differentiation can be explained by the lower amounts of human capital acquired by women.

However, direct data on human capital other than schooling is often not available and many of the explanatory variables used in such tests are ones which represent the expected lower labour force participation rate of women and its intermittency. Thus, the proxies often used separately or in some combination, are the years of experience (often defined as age minus schooling minus six), years out of the labour force, sex, marital status, the number of hours worked in the year, etc. What these empirical studies establish, then, is that the pattern of labour force participation is a major determinant of wage differentiation. This pattern is explained by the human capital approach as affecting labour supply decisions in terms of the workers' acquisition of the quantity and type of human capital.

However, the expected lower labour force participation rate of women and its intermittency may affect not only the accumulation of human capital in the worker, but also the decision by the firm as to the wage the firm wants to pay the worker. Thus, Landes (1977) presents a model of firm behaviour in which the costs of investment by firms in workers' firm-specific skills depend upon labour force turnover. In his model, profit-maximization by firms yields a trade-off between wages and turnover which, along with the workers' corresponding trade-offs, implies the observed patterns of wage and occupational differentiation. Therefore, the expected male and female lifetime work participation patterns induce both labour supply and demand responses, each causing wage and occupational differentiation. Empirical studies do not generally separate these responses and thus do not resolve the identification problem involved in such estimation.[1] To illustrate, Polachek (1975) used years of potential experience, years out of the labour force and the number of hours worked per year, etc. as explanatory variables for explaining wage and occupational differentiation. Since he did not address the identification problem involved and there are clearly identification problems with the estimated equations, his estimates of the impact of the intermittency variables would encompass both labour supply (human capital) responses as well as labour demand ones: the estimated coefficients are likely to be reduced form ones rather than labour supply ones.

Standard human capital models of discrimination also often blur the distinction between general and firm-specific skills. The distinguishing feature of the latter, as Becker (1975) showed, is that firms do not have to pay workers wages equalling their marginal product. Human capital models do not take account of this feature of firm-specific skills. Nor does Landes (1977) in any satisfactory manner. This feature is critical to our analysis in this chapter.

We start with a brief review of the relevant arguments of the analysis in the preceding chapters. Chapters 1 and 3 had argued that the labour market can be envisaged as a continuum of career jobs/workers, approaching at one of its limits the casual jobs/workers and that the firm retains a share of the rent generated by its career workers. Chapter 3 had argued that the firm's share of the rent of a career worker increases its profits. Consequently, optimization requires that it would prefer to employ workers from whom it receives the largest rents during their stay with it. In fact, it will, in general, pay the firm to try to extend the length of this stay (Oi, 1962). Chapter 3 showed that the firm has an optimal number of workers and an optimal employment period for them, given their marginal productivity and wage patterns. Consequently, women who on average have shorter expected periods of stay with a given firm than this optimal period, will obtain lower wages and be in jobs with less firm specific training.

The analysis of this chapter is a special case of the basic model set out in chapter 3. The analyses there had derived the optimal number of jobs, the optimal hiring age and the optimal retirement age. In an application of the principle of Occam's razor to the concerns of this chapter, the model presented here starts with a number of simplifying assumptions. This model deals with a single job position, assuming the optimal number of jobs to be as determined in chapter 3. Further, the wage and the optimal duration of employment of male workers on the given job is assumed to be specified exogenously. The justification for this assumption is that the concern of this chapter is to show some of the major forces for the differentiation by firms of wages and for occupational segregation, not to analyze the duration of employment of the male workers.

In order to highlight its analysis and conclusions, this chapter also assumes the initial identity of human capital among different labour force participants. Thus sections 4.1 to 4.3 assume that workers are identical in their abilities and education, etc., at the time of joining the firm but differ in anticipated turnover rates. Section 4.4 allows for differentiation in abilities, a primitive element, without touching on the differentiation in the initial human capital. The intention here is not to deny the theoretical findings of the human capital approach but to take them as established and to present a distinct line of analysis focusing on the share of the rents retained by the firm.

Section 4.1 presents our basic analysis, while abstracting from the firm's *costs* of investment in firm-specific skills: these skills are taken to occur costlessly by learning on the job rather than result from costly on-the-job training, a distinction drawn by Blaug (1976). Section 4.2 show that the existence of these costs strengthens our conclusions. Section 4.3 analyzes the implications of a female-male sequence in the rotation of workers on the job, compared with only female workers in the sequence. Section 4.4 deals with wage differentiation arising from differences in abilities within the firm-specific skills model. Section 4.5 presents the implications of the model for occupational segregation. Section 4.6 briefly explores the topic of wage and occupational differentiation by race and sex.

This chapter does not take differences in effort - especially due to differences in commitments in the home - into account, a point emphasized by Becker (1985). We assume that all workers expend the same effort on the job.

4.1 Expected turnover as a basis for wage differences

This section assumes that all workers are identical in abilities, education and training *before* joining the firm.[2,3] It assumes, further, that a male worker will remain with the given firm for T' years (the optimal employment period from Chapter 3) while a female worker will remain with the firm for T" years, with T' > T".[4] The firm is taken to maximize profits in perfectly competitive markets, with the optimal number of jobs and the optimal hiring age as specified in chapter 3.[5]

The profit maximizing firm will be indifferent between employing a male worker or a sequence of T'/T" female workers in the given job position if it will receive the same present discounted value of the rents from the two alternatives; that is, over T' years, if

$$\sum_{t=1}^{T'} (m'_t - w'_t)\, a^t = \sum_{j=0}^{T'/T''-1} \sum_{t=1}^{T''} (m''_t - w''_t)\, a^{jT''+t} \qquad (1)$$

where

    m   marginal product
    w   real wage rate
    a   discount factor (= $1/(1 + \Phi)$)
    Φ interest rate

Primes stand for men and double primes stand for women. The number of female employees in the sequence, per male employee, is T'/T". In (1) j, j=0,1,2,...,T'/T", is the sequence of women employees. Thus, j is 0 for the periods 1, ..., T"; it equals 1 for the periods T"+1, ...,2T"; it equals 2 for the periods 2T"+1, ...,3T"; and so on. It is assumed, for simplification, that T'/T" is an integer.

In (1), the left hand side is the present discounted value of the firm's share of the rents from employing a male worker over T' years. The right hand side is the present discounted value of the firm's share of the rents from employing T'/(T"-1) female workers over the same T' years. Assume for the present that there are zero training costs, with the acquisition of skills occurring from costless learning-on-the-job. Rewrite (1) as:

$$- \sum_{t=1}^{T''} (m'_t - w'_t)\, a^t + \sum_{t=1}^{T''} (m''_t - w''_t)\, a^t$$

$$= [\, \sum_{t=T''+1}^{2T''} (m'_t - w'_t)\, a^t$$

$$- \sum_{t=1}^{T''} (m''_t - w''_t)\, a^{T''+t}] + \ldots$$

$$+ [\sum_{t=nT''+1}^{T'} (m'_t - w'_t)\, a^t$$

$$- \sum_{t=1}^{T''} (m''_t - w''_t)\, a^{nT''+t}] \qquad (2)$$

where n=((T'/T")-1). Since all workers are assumed to be identical in terms of their initial characteristics such as aptitudes, education, etc., their marginal products in the tth year of their being on the job in the firm will be identical. That is,

$$m'_t = m''_{jT''+t} \qquad t = 1,\ldots,T''$$

Hence, (2) can be restated as,

$$\sum_{t=1}^{T''} (w'_t - w''_t)\, a^t = [\sum_{t=1}^{T''} (m'_{T''+t} - w'_{T''+t})\, a^{T''+t}$$

$$- \sum_{t=1}^{T''} (m''_t - w''_t)\, a^{T''+t}] + \ldots$$

$$+ [\sum_{t=1}^{T''} (m'_{nT''+t} - w'_{nT''+t})\, a^{nT''+t}$$

$$- \sum_{t=1}^{T''} (m''_t - w''_t)\, a^{nT''+t}] \qquad (3)$$

Two broad cases can be isolated from (3). In the first case, *for the*

category of casual workers - that is, workers possessing only general skills -
the marginal product of the worker in the given firm will equal his marginal
product in other firms. The latter will equal the wage under perfect
competition. Consequently, each of the terms on the right hand side of
equation (3) is zero, so that the left hand side will equal zero. Further, since
casual workers can move among firms without any loss in wages, T" can
take any value from zero to the period women do stay in the labour force.
Hence, for casual workers, from (3), $w_t' = w''_t$ for all t. That is, differences
in labour turnover rates do not cause differences in wages. If the latter do
exist, they must be due to other factors, such as variations in ability, etc.

In the second case, for the category of *career workers*, assume that the
learning period over which skills are acquired and perfected is T, $T > 0$.[6]
Then $m_{t+i} > m_t$, for $t < T$, and $i > 0$. The firm's share of a career
worker's rent is $r_t = (m_t - w_t)$. As in chapter 3, the following analysis
assumes that:

$$\frac{\partial r}{\partial m} > 0 \qquad (4)$$

The rationale for assuming (4) is: as the worker acquires more firm-specific
skills and his productivity rises, the firm and the worker share the increase
in this productivity and his wage rises, but so does the amount retained by
the firm from this productivity.[7] This is the general conclusion of various
studies on the returns generated by firm-specific skills (Becker, 1975, p. 31;
Okun, 1981, p. 86).

From (4), with $T > 0$ and $a > 0$,

$$\sum_{t=1}^{T''} [\, (m'_{i+t} - w'_{i+t}) - (m''_t - w''_t)\,]\, a^{i+t} > 0 \qquad (5)$$

where $i = T'', 2T'', \ldots, nT''$. (5) specifies that each of the bracketed terms on
the right hand side of (3) is positive. Hence, from (3) and (5),

$$\sum_{t=1}^{T''} (w'_t - w''_t)\, a^t > 0 \qquad (6)$$

That is, *the present discounted value of a woman's wages over her work-life
of T" years will be less than that of a man, even though both could have
joined the firm at the same time, have the same education and
experience/seniority in terms of years on the job and have the same marginal
product during the T" periods.* This wage differential depends, from the
preceding analysis, on T', T" and T. The larger is T'/T" - that is, the

relative expected stay of men compared to that of women with the firm - the larger will be the right-hand side of (3) and the larger will be the wage differential. Similarly, this differential will depend positively on the acquisition period for firm-specific skills. This was assumed above to be the period T.

Note that this model, just as other job-attachment models (Becker, 1975; Okun, 1981; Hall, 1980, pp. 100-101), determines the present value of the total compensation to the worker over his employment period. What matters to the firm is this total amount, with the actual pattern of payment - lump sum or one of various possible streams - being indeterminate. Thus, a variety of wage and productivity paths for career workers are consistent with equations (1) and (6).

Equation (6) can be used not merely to show wage *differentiation* between males and females but also to show wage *discrimination* between them. Wage discrimination, in the context of this model where both males and females receive less than the present value of their marginal product over their work-life, may be defined to exist if females receive a smaller proportion of this marginal product than the males. Such discrimination is obvious from equation (6). (See also the Appendix to this chapter). Such discrimination does not occur in the usual human capital models which do not incorporate the replacement of workers in the job position.

4.2 Wage discrimination and hiring and training costs

The preceding analysis established its results under the assumption of the costless acquisition of firm-specific skills. If there is a positive cost of hiring and training, the pattern of this cost has to be specified in order to derive its implications for wage differentiation. These implications are easy to see in the case where such costs are incurred for a new employee in the first period of employment. This was the assumed pattern of cost in chapter 3. In this case, if this cost is \$c, the firm would incur \$c of hiring and training costs for a male worker and \$(T'/T")c for the sequence of female workers over T' periods. Since the firm is concerned only with the present discounted value of rents, net of training costs, that it receives from workers, (1) becomes modified to,

$$\Sigma_{t=1}^{T'} (m'_t - w'_t) \, a^t - ca = \Sigma_{j=0}^{T'/T"-1} \Sigma_{t=1}^{T"} (m"_t - w"_t) \, a^{jT"+t}$$

$$- c \, (a + a^{T"+1} + \ldots + a^{(T'/T"-1)T"+1}) \qquad (7)$$

66

Wage differentiation by sex

so that,

$$\Sigma_{t=1}^{T'} (m'_t - w'_t) \, a^t = \Sigma_{j=0}^{T'/T''-1} \Sigma_{t=1}^{T''} (m''_t - w''_t) \, a^{jT''+t}$$

$$- c \, (a^{T''+1} + \ldots + a^{(T'/T''-1)T''+1}) \qquad (7')$$

This equation is identical with equation (l) except for the addition of the second term on the right hand side of the equation. This term specifies that the firm's share of the rents from the female workers falls by the present discounted value of such costs for (T/T" - 1) female workers. The firm will not hire female workers unless their lower wages compensate the firm for this cost. Hence, the larger *costs* of hiring and training the full sequence of female workers as compared with the cost of training a single male worker over T' years, implies that women will receive an even smaller proportion of their marginal product in wages than equations (1) to (6) had implied and that the wage difference between male and female workers would be even greater than given by (6).

4.3 A female-male sequence versus an all female sequence

The preceding analysis considered the alternative of a male worker versus a *sequence of female workers*. However, the firm may be able to use, without a special cost or penalty, any combination of male and female workers in the sequence. In view of the preceding analysis, the least discriminatory possibility is one where the female worker is followed by male workers. In this case, under the assumptions of section 4.1, the firm will be indifferent between employing a male worker for T' years as against the sequence of a female worker followed by a male one if and only if:

$$\Sigma_{t=1}^{T'} (m'_t - w'_t) \, a^t = \Sigma_{t=1}^{T''} (m''_t - w''_t) \, a^t$$

$$+ \Sigma_{t=1}^{T'-T''} (m'_t - w'_t) \, a^{T''+t} \qquad (8)$$

where $m'_t = m''_t$ for t = 1, ..., T", and the costs of hiring and training are again set to zero for simplification. Hence,

$$\Sigma_{t=1}^{T''} (w'_t - w''_t) \, a^t = \Sigma_{t=1}^{T'-T''} [(m'_{T''+t} - w'_{T''+t})$$

$$- (m'_t - w'_t)] \, a^{T''+t} \qquad (9)$$

67

where our assumptions imply that the right side of equation (9) is positive since a male worker with $(T'' + t)$ years of experience generates a higher rent that one with the tth year, $t < T$, on the job and, therefore, increases the firms' profits by a greater amount. Hence,

$$\Sigma_{t=1}^{T''} [(w'_t - w''_t) \, a^t] > 0$$

and the female worker gets paid less than an *equally competent* - that is, with identical productivity on the same job - male worker, because the *male worker behind her* in the sequence will generate less rents for the firm than if he had been hired from the beginning and the female worker never hired at all.

The wage reduction for female workers is less under (9) where the female worker is followed by a male one than under (3) where there is a sequence of female workers. Hence, *the firms which are restricted to hiring only female workers will discriminate more in terms of wages than ones which are not so restricted.* The so-called *'women's professions'* are an example of the former. Our analysis shows that such professions will pay lower wages than professions in which men and women workers can be interchanged. Therefore, *breaking down the segregation of job positions between male or female ones will also reduce wage discrimination.*

This analysis can be easily extended to the case where male workers consider that they will suffer some psychological or social loss if they were to take on a job formerly occupied by a woman and require a premium to compensate for this loss. In such a case, the premium required will further reduce women's wages.

4.4 Differences in abilities and wage discrimination

The preceding section assumed that all workers are identical in their abilities and knowledge before joining the firm. This is patently unrealistic. This section instead makes the weaker assumption that men and women have the same distribution of abilities. We continue to assume that workers have identical education and general skills before joining the firm and that the acquisition of firm-specific skills is by costless learning on the job, though neither of these assumptions are critical to our results.

Consider the case of any two workers i and j with differing abilities but with identical employment periods T'. The workers can be of either sex. The profit-maximizing firm is indifferent between employing either of the two workers if the present discounted value of its share of the rents from the two are identical. That is, if:

$$\Sigma_{t=1}^{T} (m'_{it} - w'_{it})\, a^t = \Sigma_{t=1}^{T} (m'_{jt} - w'_{jt})\, a^t \tag{10}^8$$

Equation (4) was that $\partial r/\partial m > 0$. Its justification, from the human capital literature, was that any increase in rents due to additional firm-specific skills would be shared between the firm and the worker. In the present context, some of the differences between the marginal products of different workers would be due to differences in abilities. It is quite likely that the more able workers will tend to acquire more firm-specific skills than less able ones over any given period with the firm. In fact, abilities have to be translated into skills to result in productivity and these skills would be both general and specific ones. It seems reasonable, therefore, to continue the assumption that $\partial r/\partial m > 0$. Hence, from (10), the less able worker j, with $m'_{jt} < m'_{it}$, will receive a smaller proportion of his marginal product than the more able worker i.

From equation (10), *a less able worker will receive a lower present discounted value of the wage stream for two reasons. First, his marginal product will be lower. Second, the firm has to retain the same amount of rent from both workers and will, therefore, have to pay the less able worker a smaller proportion of his marginal product.* These conclusions apply to both male and female workers with identical employment periods.

Sections 4.1 to 4.4 have so far provided two reasons for wage differences: different staying periods with the given firm and differing abilities. A firm could then employ both men and women workers, with differing wage distributions for the two groups and with the mean wage for women being significantly below that for men. Since the two wage distributions could partly overlap, some women could earn the same wage as some men, but the former will have to be more able and have to have a higher productivity than the latter.

Greater realism can be introduced into the analysis by assuming that the extent to which superior abilities can increase the marginal product in a given job is limited.[9] This assumption limits the possibility that the more able women could receive the same wage as the less able men in a given job: their marginal product may be higher but not sufficiently so for it to compensate fully for their shorter stay with the firm. It also limits the wage variation within the male and female groups. Therefore, for some jobs, wages could differ somewhat within each group but the best paid woman could be paid less than the worst paid man.

4.5 Turnover, abilities and occupational segregation

The payment of blatantly different wage rates by a given firm for a given job usually imposes some costs on the firm. These costs may arise from the possible infringement of laws and social customs, or may arise from dissatisfaction among the discriminated women employees. Since the output of career workers is not totally a technical datum but depends upon their morale and attitudes, employee dissatisfaction could result in a loss of productivity and cut down on the firm's receipt of the rents from women workers. This would follow from the literature on efficiency wage models (as, for example, in Akerlof and Yellen, 1986), on 'norms' in the workplace (as for example in Elster, 1989 and Rebitzer, 1993) and on 'fairness' (as for example in Rima, 1984; Hicks, 1974; Okun, 1981, and Krueger and Summers 1987). This feedback effect would further reduce the firm's incentive to hire female workers for the same job category as males. Firms may, then, choose to separate the sexes into differing job categories, with those staffed by men paying more than those staffed by women, even though both may require the same abilities. This does not contradict profit maximization. In fact, as the earlier analysis shows, such behaviour is a consequence of long run profit maximization.

Continuing the earlier assumption of identical distributions of abilities among men and women, and further assuming a hierarchy of career jobs catalogued in a descending order by the kind and amount of skills required, we can caricature three cases.

a. The 'topmost' *career* jobs - requiring the highest abilities and with long periods of specific skills acquisition through numerous promotions - will be staffed only by men, if men and women were to be paid the same wage, or there would be substantial differences in wage rates, unless there are countervailing pressures (discussed below). Taking the top managerial jobs as an example of these, and assuming that wage discrimination by sex in these is extremely difficult since the managers know and usually even set the firms' salary structure, our analysis, other things being the same, implies that such jobs will be held almost wholly by men. However, other things may differ and countervailing pressures would reduce and may even wholly offset this tendency. One such pressure would be the need for firms to show to regulators and policy makers that there is no occupational discrimination - even at the top, highly visible echelons in the firm.

b. In the 'intermediate' *career* jobs, and assuming that a firm cannot discriminate extensively between the sexes for similar jobs, there seem to be several possibilities. In the first one of these, firms would employ both men and women in the same category of jobs or in similar jobs, paying both roughly the same wage, but with women possessing superior abilities relative to men. To illustrate, it seems to be part of the folklore among women that a woman has to be twice as smart as a man to hold the same job and get the same wage. Lazear and Rosen (1990) point out that this may not happen in the initial narrowly categorized jobs but that female workers require greater ability to win promotions to higher paying jobs. A second possibility is that firms would employ both men and women of roughly equal abilities in the same category of jobs or in similar jobs, but with women paid less than men. This may involve monetary and/or nonmonetary costs of overt wage discrimination. A third possibility is that there would be parallel sets of jobs requiring roughly the same abilities and experience, but with some largely staffed by men and the others largely staffed by women, but with the latter paying less than the former. A fourth possibility - really a variation on the preceding ones - is for the firm to divide a 'job path' into a set of narrowly defined jobs, without wage discrimination within each of these narrow job categories but with discrimination in promotions, with the result that female workers would require greater ability for promotions (Lazear and Rosen, 1990). In fact, the percentage increase in male workers' wages is significantly higher than in female workers' wages during the early years of employment (Loprest, 1992). Of these four possibilities, if the costs of open discrimination in employee dissatisfaction and legal and social penalties were high, the first, third and fourth possibilities would be more common than the second one. The former represent a form of hidden wage discrimination. The latter represents open wage discrimination.

c. The 'lowest' rung of the ladder of career jobs is *casual* or almost casual jobs. In these jobs, men with a long term commitment to a job do not earn a rent premium for this longevity. Consequently, men would tend to prefer career jobs unless the casual jobs have relatively high wages by virtue of their occupation and industry. Men would be forced into casual jobs if they are barred by lack of ability from rent-paying career jobs or if firms' experience with them had shown that they did not in effect stay for long with any one firm. However, the women excluded from career jobs for reasons given above would have to go into casual jobs. More of them would then come from much abler sections of the distribution. Hence, a larger proportion of the female labour force than of the male one will be in casual jobs and on average will have a higher level of ability.

That is, while men dominate the top career jobs, women, relative to men, will be concentrated more into the casual jobs and those career jobs which are close to being casual ones. The intermediate career jobs will show open wage discrimination only if its costs to the firm are not too high. If they are high (or were low but are increased by 'equal pay' legislation or the pressures of a new social morality in favour of wage equality), open wage discrimination will turn into its hidden forms. In one of these, men and women would receive the same wages for the same job, but the women will have to possess superior abilities. In possibly the more common case, there would evolve parallel sets of jobs, with some staffed by men and paying higher wages while others are staffed by women and pay lower wages.

Note that this shifting of women into more casual jobs, compared with jobs held by equally able men, occurs both by virtue of firm's and of women's choices. This was pointed out in chapter 3 in discussing the rental value of a career job and is worth repeating here. Firms shift women, with a shorter expected stay with the firm, to more casual jobs because the firm, if it paid identical wage rates to men and women, would earn a lower rent/profit from giving a career job to women. But if it paid an appropriately lower wage to women to earn the same rent/profit as from men on the job, it may face a penalty cost or a loss in productivity arising in the context of efficiency wages, thereby again yielding it lower profits from employing women.

In terms of women's choices, for women to get a career job, they would have to assure the firm the rental value of the job by accepting a lower wage than men do. This decrease in wage tends to be greater in career jobs rather than in casual ones, which do not have a positive rental value, so that women may get higher wages in the more casual jobs. Accepting a job with the highest offered wage would, therefore, mean that women end up in relatively more casual jobs in the economy.

Expectations play a role in occupational segregation. The firm, at the time of hiring, does not know how long a job candidate will stay with it. It forms its decisions on the basis of the expected value of this period. If women as a class are expected to have a shorter period, the firm would shift them into more casual jobs or offer them lower wages, so that they seem to choose such jobs. If any female employee, subsequently with the passage of time (several years), shows a long-term attachment to the firm, she would, under the arguments of chapter 3, be beyond the optimal hiring age for the firm and would not be shifted into the higher wage career jobs. *Ex post* indications of attachment to a firm are, therefore, not necessarily enough to assure the absence of occupational segregation.

4.6 Differentiation within male and female categories

The preceding sections have assumed that the length of the workers' stay with the firm was known to the firm. Further, all men had the same length of stay and all women had an identical, but shorter, length of stay. This section considers the question of differing expected lengths of stay with the firm within the male and female categories of workers, under the assumption of identical abilities among the workers.

Legislation outlaws slavery and the courts tend to bar or refuse to enforce against the worker explicit contracts of very long duration, which might constitute indentured labour. To illustrate, while the courts will uphold the universities' system of tenure as a constraint on a university trying to lay off its professors, the courts would not enforce corresponding constraints on the professors not to leave the university for the term specified by the tenure system. Knowing this, the universities have adjusted the tenure system to bind the universities but not the professors to the long employment contract implied by the tenure arrangement.

The firm also does not in general know the actual period for which an applicant will stay with it. It has to form some estimate of this period. One of the low-cost methods of doing so is to categorize workers by easily accessible information such as sex, race, age, etc. To introduce this element into our analysis, assume that the firm classifies all male applicants into m categories, each with a different expected period of stay with it, with a worker in the ith group having a shorter expected stay than a worker in the (i + l)th group, with i = 1,..., m. Similarly, let all female applicants be categorized into n groups, again in a ascending order of expected stay with the firm. The division into groups within males and females could be on the basis of race, age, education, etc. It is quite possible that some male groups may have lower expected lengths of stay than some female groups. Assume that the firm only takes into consideration the average expected stay and ignores the distribution within each group. Since the rent model implies that each firm prefers a longer duration of expected stay with it for career jobs, it will pay a premium for the longer expected duration. Wage and occupational discrimination will, therefore, occur within the male and female categories, as well as between them.

Further, assume that women's groups would have a smaller expected dispersion of the duration of expected stay than men's groups. In particular, for young females, the expected duration of stay with a firm was until recent decades only a few years so that its absolute dispersion due to differences in education and race, etc., was relatively low. Given this lower dispersion, the

page 86 of 256

rent model implies that the wage differences among female groups would have been less than among male groups. The earlier arguments on occupational segregation can also be applied to the case of a lower dispersion of average expected stay among women of different races. These imply that occupational segregation will be less among women of different races than among men of these races. That is, discrimination on the basis of race will be less among women than among men.

In the context of the United States, empirical studies indicate that white males and black males have a wider dispersion of the expected period of employment, especially with the same firm, than white females and black females. Our analysis implies that this would cause the wage differences to be greater among the former than among the latter. Further, the latter are more likely to share the same occupations than the former.

Furthermore, if the differences in the expected period of employment with a given firm are less between white females and black males, than between white females and white males, the former are more likely to share the same occupation and have a smaller difference in wages than the latter.

4.7 Wage discrimination and increased longevity

Assume that there occur increases in the longevity and ability to continue working until later in life due to changes in consumption and living standards, and due to the advances in medical knowledge and practices, such as have occurred through most of this century in most economies. Such changes would reduce the productivity declines occurring in the later stages of life and, therefore, reduce the rent decline at the same time. The analysis of chapter 3 then implies that the optimal retirement age would increase for workers who are expected to keep working with the firm upto this age.

Further, assume that the male workers will stay with the firm upto the higher retirement age which is the new optimal age from the firm's perspective. Also assume that the female workers are expected to leave the firm before the age at which the innovations in health and longevity take effect, and that there are no changes in their expected period of stay with the firm. In terms of the analysis of section 4.1 above, these assumptions translate into an increase in the expected employment period of male workers from T' to say T'^ while that of female workers remains unchanged at T".

For career jobs, this exogenous increase in the expected employment period of male workers from T' to T'^ will increase the period over which these workers yield positive rents to the firm and hence the present discounted value of these rents from their employment. Therefore, the right hand side of equation (8) will increase in magnitude, thereby implying an increase in the wage differential between male and female workers. For given male wage rates, this means that the wages of female workers would fall. These results hold even though there are assumed to be no changes in the abilities and education of the male and female workers.

Conversely, if there are costs to the firm of open wage discrimination, the increased longevity of male workers would imply increased occupational differentiation of a form such that the desired extent of wage differentiation is achieved.

4.8 Wage differentiation and innovations

Now assume that there occur innovations which cause an increase in the period for which female workers are expected to stay with the firm. These could be innovations in fertility rates causing decreases in the number of children, accompanied by increases in child care facilities. There could be decreases in the length of the working day such as to allow women to work fulltime and still manage to care for their families. There could be technical innovations in terms of labour saving devices for work done at home. There could also be technical innovations in the work place which could make such work more attractive to females. Other innovations can be terms of social customs and ideas. These are example of some of the changes that have occurred in recent decades and which seem to have dramatically lengthened the labour market commitment of female workers. There could also be many other changes producing such an effect.

For the formal analysis, assume that while the above changes increase the female employment period with the firm from T'' to $T''^\wedge$, they leave the male employment period unchanged at T'. This exogenous change implies a decrease in the amount of the right hand side of equation (3), so that the male-female wage differential will decrease. In the limiting case, if $T''^\wedge$ becomes equal to T', the wage differential will be zero, so that the former wage and occupational discrimination would tend to disappear.

The preceding section had adduced increases in the longevity of workers as a possible factor making for increases in the male-female wage differential. This section has mentioned various types of innovations which would have the effect of decreasing this differential. The focus in the illustrations of innovations has been on the long run changes. There can clearly be many different exogenous changes with differing long run and short run effects, so that it would not be unreasonable to find this differential decreasing in some years and increasing in others, or with differing trends over different periods.

4.9 The duration of employment, labour supply and education

Sections 4.1 to 4.6 were concerned solely with the effects on demand, wages and occupational structure of women's shorter expected period of employment with a given firm. The latter, however, also affects the human capital investments that will be optimal for women. These effects are both direct and indirect.

As shown above, assuming identical abilities between men and women, the shorter expected duration of stay with the firm by women implies that their lifetime earnings will be smaller. Consequently, the present discounted value of the net return to any investment by women will also be smaller and, *ceteris paribus*, the optimal investment in human capital will be smaller for women than for men. This will be especially true for firm-specific skills, but it could also apply to general skills, since the two types of skills often play complementary roles in many occupations. The human capital models developed in recent years, especially by Mincer and Polachek and cited above, have established the extent and nature of some of these effects.

The smaller female investments in general and specific skills, in turn, further reduce the average female wage and contribute to women's occupational segregation. Thus, the supply side effects arising from workers' decisions accentuate the demand side effects derived above for firms' behaviour. The two would also interact to increase the wage and occupational differences between males and females.

Furthermore, there are also likely to be feedback effects of wage and occupational differentiation upon labour force stay and intermittency. The existence of such simultaneity on the labour supply side is well recognized in the human capital literature (Sandell and Shapiro, 1978; Mincer and Polachek, 1978).

Simultaneity may also exist on the labour demand side. Here, the effects are less clear. On the one hand, a firm responding to a transitory fall in demand may choose to lay off a better paid male worker rather than the lower-paid female worker, thus saving more on labour costs. On the other hand, the firm may want to retain the more experienced and more rent-generating male worker as against the female one who may choose to leave after some time anyway. The net effect of these tendencies may favour either males or females.

Conclusion

As we have mentioned earlier, wage and occupational discrimination is too significant and too pervasive within countries and across countries to be susceptible to any single explanation. There can clearly be a variety of factors making for its existence and extent. Recent decades have seen a proliferation of models identifying several of these factors. Some of them have been discussed in the introduction to this chapter. Among these are models of discrimination based on discrimination in preferences at some level or other. Some models rely upon discrimination and segregation among job categories, rather than wage discrimination within narrow job cells, or in promotions. The reason given for such discrimination may be 'social custom'. Still other models rely upon elements of monopoly or monopsony power. There are also statistical theories of discrimination focusing on the differential reliability of productivity indicators with respect to different groups of workers. Other models focus on the pattern of labour force participation.

This chapter looked at the firms' decisions in the presence of firm-specific skills and how these contribute to wage and occupational differentiation. Such differentiation can be considered as 'justifiable' from a profit maximizing viewpoint or as 'discriminatory' and 'unfair' since it means that workers with identical *current* productivity would be paid different wage rates. In any case, the model presented above shows that economic discrimination is consistent with neoclassical intertemporal profit maximization.

Our labour rents model not only provides an element making for wage discrimination against women, it also explains their segregation into jobs which are closer to being casual ones, with a lesser accumulation of firm-specific knowledge and lower seniority premiums. These are jobs in which labour mobility does not do very much to increase or decrease the wage received. Women thus have more mobile skills on the whole. The converse of this segregation of women into more casual jobs is that women would be scarce in the 'high-paying' jobs in which the acquisition of firm-specific skills is extremely important. This occupational differentiation is derived from the existence of the costs of open wage differentiation, with these costs including legal and social ones, as well as the decreased productivity from worker dissatisfaction, etc. This basis for occupational differentiation is different from that of the varying atrophy rates among occupations used in the human capital literature, with differences among males and females in the time out of the labour force.

Our model above is a general one and can be applied to explain discrimination among workers of different races. Here again, the consequence of different periods of expected stay with the firm is wage discrimination and occupational segregation.[10]

The return to human capital investments is greater the longer the period of employment using those skills. A shorter expected labour force stay for a female entrant to the labour force means that the return to investment in her education, training, etc. will be less than for similar investment in males with a longer labour force stay. Households would then find it economically optimal to invest more in male children's education than in female ones. Educational institutions may also reflect such a general preference on the part of households and firms. The result would be discrimination within the family and society against females.[11]

Both the supply side and demand side effects of a shorter uninterrupted stay with a given firm are thus in the same direction in the rent and the human capital models. They, therefore, reinforce each other.

What differentiates this chapter's analysis from other models in the human capital approach or earlier work on labour turnover models? These have, in general, assumed that workers will be paid a wage equal to their marginal product. As such, their analysis belongs to the category of general skills. Further, there is no discrimination - defining this as 'equal wage for equal work', that is, for identical current marginal product - in these models. By comparison, our model assumes that workers with firm-specific skills are paid less than their marginal product (Becker, 1975, ch. 2; Okun, 1981, ch. 2). This chapter then proves the optimality (from the firm's viewpoint) of discrimination: a woman with the same current marginal product as a man has to be paid less than the man. Further, as pointed out in the chapter 1, while other human capital models focus on the worker, not on the job, our model shifts the focus to jobs. This shift in focus and the emphasis on firm specific skills is also the basis of the model of Lazear and Rosen (1990). However, we also rely on the replacement of workers over time on the given job. This consideration is missing from virtually every other model.

In comparison with other models of discrimination, our analysis does not rely upon discriminatory preferences of workers, firms, parents or spouses, etc., as other models of discrimination tend to do. Nor does it rely upon the existence of less than perfect measuring devices for the ability and future productivity of prospective employees, as the statistical models of discrimination do (See, for example, Aigner and Cain (1977); Lloyd and Niemi, (1979, Chs. 4, 5)). Our model also establishes the possibility of discrimination under the assumption of perfect competition and, therefore, does not rely upon monopoly or monopsony for its arguments (Madden, 1978). However, several or all of these factors can exist in any given context in the real world.

This chapter did not present any empirical tests to support its theoretical findings. Data on rents retained by firms does not exist so that this paper's hypotheses cannot be directly tested. At a more general level, various empirical studies, often appended to the human capital models, have already established that labour force participation patterns are a major determinant of wage and occupational differentiation.

Various excellent summaries of the empirical evidence on discrimination have been published recently (see, for example, Hamermesh and Rees, 1988, ch. 13; Adnett, 1989, ch. 6; Gunderson, 1989; Lazear, 1989; Smith and Ward, 1989; Fuchs, 1989; Bergmann, 1989). In general, the empirical studies tend to show that while women's average wage can be as low as 40% below men's average wage, much - but not all - of this difference[12] can be explained by differences in qualifications, labour market experience, and 'seniority' within the firm and 'completed job duration'. Of these, seniority is a measure of time already spent on the job and thus an indicator of the period over which firm-specific skills may have been acquired. Completed job duration is an *ex post* measure of the total stay of a worker with a given firm. It is a rough approximation to the period that the worker is expected to stay with the firm, with the expectations defined as those held by the firm in the hiring period. So far, only a few studies have tested for the impact of completed job duration on wages. Among these, Abraham and Farber (1986) find that workers on jobs with longer completed duration earn significantly more in every year on the job. That is, if expectations were assumed to be in line with *ex post* realizations, such workers from the beginning of their career - that is, before they have acquired much experience and seniority - are paid more because they were expected to have a longer job duration with the firm. This is in line with the analysis of this chapter. However, note that the analysis deals with expected job duration or conversely with expected interruptions, not with past ones. Blau and Ferber (1991) caution that the data from the latter may not yield results valid for the former. Their study on the anticipated earnings of undergraduate students showed that while male and female students with similar education expected to earn similar wages at the beginning of their careers in the same types of jobs, women expected shorter work lives, lower wages later in their careers and less promotions.

The broad lines of our conclusions are also consistent with the empirical findings of Polachek (1981) on the effects of labour force intermittency on occupational differentiation among men and women. He found that more hometime - that is, time out of the labour force - decreases the odds of being in a managerial or professional occupation and increases the odds of being a clerical or sales person. Polachek interpreted these findings in the context of a human capital approach - a worker's choice format - with higher atrophy rates for higher paid skills. These results are also consistent with the approach of this chapter on firms' decisions in the presence of a variety of costs of open wage discrimination. Polachek's findings should, therefore, be interpreted as estimates of the reduced form coefficients, encompassing both labour supply and demand influences.

We have already mentioned that the observed pattern of wages indicates that there do not exist significant wage differences within narrow job categories while there do exist significant differences between male and female workers in their rates of promotion (Groschen,1991; Lazear and Rosen, 1990). To explain this in the context of our model, we have to first address the notion of jobs in this model. Career jobs were envisaged as having significant firm specific skill requirements which take a significant time to learn. Such jobs should then be thought of as a career path, divided into a ladder of narrowly defined job cells, each representing stages in the extent to which the skills are required. If there are any costs - either monetary or non-monetary one - to explicit discrimination in wages, such costs are likely to be reduced by dividing the career path into narrow job cells with uniformity of wages within any one cell but with different promotion possibilities. This is especially so in recent times with the heightened awareness of discrimination, and with equal pay legislation and more active enforcement of it. Hence, the analysis above implies that wage differentiation would not be observed within narrow job cells, but would appear as differential promotion possibilities. Female workers would have a lower chance of promotion - or show greater abilities for an equal chance - than male workers since firms expect greater job interruptions and separations, based on their past experience, from female workers.

The impact of exogenous changes on the long run male-female wage differential was illustrated in this chapter through the analysis of two types of exogenous change. One of these was the increased longevity of workers raising the optimal retirement age for male workers but not changing the much shorter period for which females are expected to stay with the firm. This lowered female wages and increased the wage differential. Such an exogenous change would seem to have been a major long run development in the first half of this century. The other type of exogenous change was one which caused females to stay much longer with the firm and raised the firm's *expectation* of this period. This caused an increase in female wages and reduced the wage differential. In the limit as the period for which females are expected to remain with the firm becomes as long as the male one, the wage differential disappears. A variety of technical and societal changes occurring over the last couple of decades have tended to bring this about. Among these are the reduction in the time needed for completing the family work in the home, the reduction in the number of children in families, the increases in the number and variety of child care facilities, the improved health of children and women, the lighter equipment in the workplace and the changes in workplace practices accommodative to women workers. There have also been changes in the social ideas and mores about women seeking paid work, the kinds of professions they should seek and those open to them, etc. Laws making discrimination against women and other workers have been another positive development. In general, these have resulted in an overall dramatic increase in the long run expected labour force participation rates of almost all ages of workers and especially of young female workers. They have also resulted in a dramatic increase in the time firms expect the female job applicants, if hired, to stay with the firm. The result has been a very considerable long run narrowing of the male-female wage differential, especially of the younger workers, as well as reductions in occupational segregation. The actual experience of several western economies with changes in wage and occupational differentiation between males and females was briefly presented in the introduction to this chapter.

Appendix

This appendix illustrates diagrammatically the argument of this chapter under additional simplifying assumptions. These are:

$$m_t = m_0 + x\,t \tag{A1}$$

where m_0 is the marginal product of a worker at the time of joining the firm, t is the year on the job and x is the improvement in productivity each year due to the acquisition of firm-specific skills. Further, assume that

$$r'_t = k'\,x\,t \tag{A2}$$

$$r''_t = k''\,x\,t \tag{A3}$$

where r_t are the rents retained by the firm. k' and k" are constants. The superscript ' is again used for females and the superscript " is used for females. Hence,

$$w'_t = m_0 + (1 - k') \times t \tag{A4}$$

$$w''_t = m_0 + (1 - k'') \times t \tag{A5}$$

The firm is indifferent between employing a male worker versus a sequence of female ones if the rents it retains from them are equal. That is,

$$\sum_{t=1}^{T'} (k' \times t) \, a^t = \sum_{j=0}^{T'/T''-1} \sum_{t=1}^{T''} (k'' \times t) \, a^{jT''+t} \tag{A6}$$

Therefore,

$$k'/k'' = [\sum_{j=0}^{T'/T''-1} \sum_{t=1}^{T''} t \, a^{jT''+t}] / [\sum_{t=1}^{T'} t \, a^t] \tag{A7}$$

where the right hand side is less than one, so that $k' < k''$. Hence, the firm retains a smaller share of the male worker's rents than of the female workers' rents. In other words, given a male and a female worker with *identical* productivity, the female worker will be paid less.

Assuming a zero rate of interest so that $a^t = 1$ for all t, (A7) yields

$$k'/k'' = [T'/T'' . \sum_{t=1}^{T''} t] / [\sum_{t=1}^{T'} t]$$

Figure 4.1 shows the exogenously given male worker's marginal productivity path over time as m', his wage path as w' and the rent retained for profits as the triangle Am'w'. The point A gives the inexperienced worker's productivity. Assuming $T' = 4T''$, the four female workers' productivity paths are given by the lines Am''_1, $T''m''_2$, $2T''m''_3$ and $3T''m''_4$. Their wage paths after deduction from their productivity of a rent equal to the area of the triangle Am'w' are shown by the lines Aw''_1, $T''w''_2$, $2T''w''_3$, $3T''w_4''$. Comparing the male and the female workers employed from A to T'', while both workers have the marginal productivity path upto T'' as m''_1, the male worker has the wage path w'_1 and the female worker has the lower wage path w''_1. The reason for this discrimination lies in the lower rents retained by the firm from subsequent workers. Thus, from time 3T'' to 4T'', this rent from the male worker is the area Cm'w'D which is much larger than the rent retained from the fourth female worker, given by the area $3T''m''_4w_4''$. Note that by equation (A5) *all female workers in the sequence of female workers and at the same stage in their careers have the same productivity and are paid the same wage. But the - one and only - male* worker at the same stage in his career has the same productivity but is paid more.

The deviation of k'/k" from unity can be viewed as a measure of discrimination.

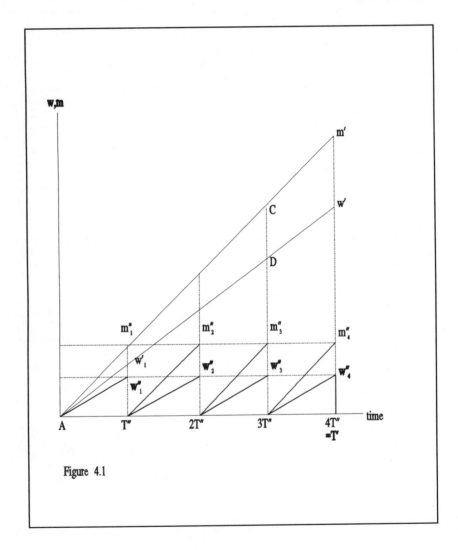

Figure 4.1

Wage differentiation by sex

FOOTNOTES

1. This identification problem is different from the simultaneity problem in estimation. The former in this context refers to the identification of the estimated coefficients as being labour demand or labour supply ones while the latter refers to the two-way causality between labour force patterns and wage patterns. The latter has been studied in several empirical studies (Sandell and Shapiro, 1978; Mincer and Polachek, 1978), while the former is virtually ignored.

2. Note that throughout this book, the words "he", "his", etc. are often used as generic terms to refer to both men and women. The context will clarify the actual meaning.

3. This is meant as a *ceteris paribus* assumption. In general, as the human capital models show quite convincingly, education and pre-labour force training will be affected by the expected intermittency and duration of work-life.

4. The assumed exogeneity of T' and T" is clearly a simplification. It is shared with several other studies (for example, Polachek, 1981). A more general analysis would allow for the endogeneity of T' and T", without, however, affecting our qualitative results. Chapter 3 derives T'. T" is then to be taken as determined by the workers' preferences and their reservation wages.

5. The model, in fact, requires perfect competition only in the labour market for its results. If monopoly or monopolistic competition exists in the product market, marginal revenue product (MRP) would replace marginal product (m) everywhere in the chapter, without changing any of our arguments or implications.

6. In the case of casual workers, as shown in chapter 3, T is any number: the worker can stay as long or as short a period as he or she wants.

7. Medoff and Abraham (1980) presented empirical evidence to show that for white male professional and managerial employees, increases in wages over time cannot be fully explained by increasing performance and hence by productivity increases, so that the wage in any given period need not equal productivity in that period. However, Abraham and Farber (1986) have a contrary finding.

8. In the absence of enforceable work contracts, and a sufficient lack of trust to prevent any backward or forward loading of rents received by the firm, it seems reasonable to reformulate (10) into the stronger statement that

$m'_{it} - w'_{it} = m'_{jt} - w'_{jt}$ for all t.

That is, the rents received by the firm from the two workers are identical for each period.

9. The limiting case of this occurs in the job competition model of Thurlow (1979) in which marginal productivity is identified solely with the job and not the worker filling it. Lazear and Rosen (1990) also use a jobs based model of discrimination.

10. To reiterate, actual discrimination in the real world can be due to many factors. This paper focuses only on one of those, within the *ceteris paribus* clause that workers of all races are otherwise treated as being identical.

11. While the analysis of discrimination by race has been suggested as being similar to that by sex, there obviously would not exist discrimination by race within the family.

12. See Smith and Ward, 1989; Fuchs, 1989; and Bergmann, 1989, for quite different views on the extent of actual wage and occupational differentiation.

5 Discrimination against Hiring Older Workers

The existence of wage and occupational discrimination in hiring older workers, with this term defined such as to exclude workers continuing in their existing employment, is pervasive in the economy and is by now well established[1] (Gordon, 1959; Kleiler, 1978, ch. 9). Several explanations for this discrimination have been offered in the literature. Among these explanations are those flowing from the human capital approach. This approach, in cases of firm-specific skills, implies that hiring and training costs will cause wage differentiation or discrimination by age in the hiring of new workers. It also implies that the costless - or with cost - acquisition of firm-specific skills over time will similarly bring about discrimination by age (for example, see Ehrenberg and Smith, 1985, chs. 5, 14). While these causes of discrimination by age are well known, they have not been integrated in the literature in a formal model of the optimal age of hiring.

As chapter 3 showed, an optimizing firm with a given wage and marginal productivity path over time, will have a unique optimal hiring age or, in some cases, a set of such ages for its career workers. It would, then, prefer hiring the career workers at those ages and will, therefore, discriminate against workers of all other ages for filling its career jobs. This discrimination will occur against both younger and older workers than the optimal age ones. In the case of casual workers, chapter 3 showed that the firm would be indifferent as to the age of its job applicants if it did not have to pay for their hiring and training costs.

The existence of hiring and training costs incurred by the firm clearly leads the firm to hire workers who are likely to stay longer with it (Oi, 1962). Similarly, if the firm incurs other costs which are independent of the

Discrimination, Retirement and Pensions

length of worker tenure with the firm, the firm saves on these costs by hiring workers with longer rather than shorter job tenure. Hutchens (1986, 1987) has recently shown that such costs, even though not hiring and training ones, also exist in Lazear's (1979) incentives model of mandatory retirement. However, such models do not take worker replacement or firm-specific skills into account and are, therefore, quite different from the one presented in chapters 3 and 4, as well as in this chapter. What is more pertinent here is Hutchens' empirical finding that jobs in which there is discrimination in hiring against older workers are characterized by pensions, long job tenures, comparatively high wages and mandatory retirement. Our model, presented in chapter 3, is consistent with these findings.[2]

Section 5.1 elaborates on the model of chapter 3. Section 5.2 examines the relationship between the skill acquisition costs and the hiring age. Section 5.3 derives the reduction in wages that a worker older than the optimal hiring age by one period must accept in order to get the job. We label this reduction as the discrimination premium. Section 5.4 examines the implications of our framework for discrimination against older workers.

5.1 The optimal hiring age model

Our concern in this chapter is, again, mainly with the career workers. However, we will also show that job attachment does not in general exist for casual workers and a firm is not better off hiring such workers at some ages rather than at others.

As in chapter 3, we assume that the firm operates in perfectly competitive output markets and maximizes the present discounted value of its profits. Our focus in this chapter will be on the optimal hiring age. Therefore, given the analysis of chapter 3 for the determination of the optimal number of jobs and the optimal retirement age, we simplify in this chapter by narrowing the analysis to the case in which the firm maximizes the present value of the firm's share of the net rent from each job position, for the given optimal number of jobs and a given optimal retirement age. The marginal productivity function, with its arguments as the education, experience and age, etc., of the worker, is assumed to be given. So is the wage function. For reasons given in chapter 3, the firm's share of the rent from firm-specific skills is designated as the difference between his marginal product and his wage, and is a function of the arguments determining his marginal product and his wage. In the case of career workers, chapter 3 showed that this 'rent' - a short form for the firm's share of the rent from the worker's firm-specific skills - depends upon the number of employees, the hiring age and the period for which the worker has been employed. In the case of casual workers, this rent does not depend upon the hiring age and the period for which the worker has been employed. The firm maximizes the present discounted value of this rent less the present discounted value of the training and hiring costs involved, from its job positions.

The human capital literature generally assumes that the hiring and training costs incurred by the firm are incurred only at the time of hiring and are a constant. These were also the assumptions made in chapters 3 and 4 above. However, they are quite inappropriate in analyzing the hiring age since the cost of training depends upon the capacity to learn and the latter depends upon the hiring age: the very young and the very old may, *ceteris paribus*, take longer to learn than workers in their twenties and thirties. This cost also depends upon prior education and experience. While this cost would vary among workers of different ages, prior education and experience, the assumption of otherwise identical workers - that is, identical in terms of innate abilities - implies that the training cost *function* can be assumed to be identical among the sequence of workers. This cost may be incurred over several periods, rather than only the initial one.

For the reader's convenience, we reproduce in this section some of the main equations and results of the analysis in chapter 3, modified to take account of the dependence of costs of skill acquisition upon age. Since our concern is not with the optimal number of workers but with who will be employed to fill a given job, we start the analysis here with the present value V of the net rents from a given job position for the firm. The modified form of the relevant equation presented in chapter 3 would be:

$$V = \int_{h_1}^{R_1} r\, e^{-i(t-h_1)}\, dt - \int_{h_1}^{R_1} c\, e^{-i(t-h_1)}\, dt$$

$$+ \int_{h_2}^{R_2} r\, e^{-i(t+T_1-h_2)}\, dt - \int_{h_2}^{R_2} c\, e^{-i(t+T_1-h_2)}\, dt + \ldots \qquad (1)$$

where

V	Present value of the net rents accruing to the firm
r	Firm's share of the rents from the job position
c	Hiring and training costs incurred by the firm
r'(=r-c)	Firm's net share of the rents from the job position
i	Interest rate
t	period
T_k	Duration of employment of the kth worker by the firm

R_k Retirement age (= $h_k + T_k$) of the kth worker
h_k Hiring age of the kth worker

Given the identity of the rent and cost functions for each worker in the sequence, (1) becomes, as argued in chapter 3,

$$V = \int_h^R r\ e^{-i(t-h)}\ dt - \int_h^R c\ e^{-i(t-h)}\ dt$$

$$+ \int_h^R r\ e^{-i(t+T-h)}\ dt - \int_h^R c\ e^{-i(t+T-h)}\ dt + \ldots$$

Hence $V = \dfrac{e^{iT}}{e^{iT}-1}\ \{\int_h^R r\ e^{-i(t-h)}\ dt - \int_h^R c\ e^{-i(t-h)}\ dt\}$ (2)

$$= \dfrac{e^{iT}}{e^{iT}-1}\ A \tag{2'}$$

where $A = \{\int_h^R r\ e^{-i(t-h)}\ dt - \int_h^R c\ e^{-i(t-h)}\ dt\}$ (3)

and $T_k = T$, $h_k = h$, $R_k = R$. Note that the definition of A in (4) is slightly different from that in chapter 3 above.

The firm maximizes the presented discounted value of its profits from its n job positions. That is, it maximizes

$$\pi = \int_0^n V\ dx \tag{4}$$

$$= \int_0^n \dfrac{e^{iT}}{e^{iT}-1}\ A\ dx \tag{4'}$$

Our focus in this chapter is on the hiring age so that the optimal number of job positions and the optimal retirement age are assumed to be exogenously specified at n* and R* respectively. This leaves the hiring age as the only endogenous variable in equation (1). Therefore, the firm maximizes π with respect to the hiring age h. The first order condition for a maximum is then:

$$\dfrac{\partial \pi}{\partial h} = \int_0^n \dfrac{\partial V}{\partial h}\ dx = 0 \tag{5}$$

$$\text{Define} \quad B = \{\int_h^R r \, e^{-i(t-h)} \, dt \} \tag{6}$$

$$C = \{\int_h^R c \, e^{-i(t-h)} \, dt \tag{7}$$

$$Y = \frac{e^{iT}}{e^{iT}-1} \{\int_h^R r \, e^{-i(t-h)} \, dt\} \tag{8}$$

$$X = \frac{e^{iT}}{e^{iT}-1} \{\int_h^R c \, e^{-i(t-h)} \, dt\} \tag{9}$$

$$\text{So that} \quad A = B - C \tag{10}$$

$$V = Y - X \tag{11}$$

Therefore, equation (5) becomes,

$$\frac{\partial \pi}{\partial h} = \int_0^n \frac{\partial Y}{\partial h} \, dx - \int_0^n \frac{\partial X}{\partial h} \, dx = 0 \tag{12}$$

5.2 The optimal hiring age for career workers

In the case of *career* workers, $\partial B/\partial h$ is not equal to 0 for all h, so that $\partial B/\partial h$ cannot be taken to be identically zero. Solving the first order condition (5) is difficult and this condition was simplified in chapter 3 to:

$$\frac{\partial V}{\partial h} = 0 \tag{13}$$

This yields,

$$\frac{\partial V}{\partial h} = A \frac{\partial}{\partial h} \frac{e^{iT}}{e^{iT}-1} + \frac{e^{iT}}{e^{iT}-1} \frac{\partial A}{\partial h} = 0$$

$$= \{i(V-A) + \frac{\partial A}{\partial h}\} (\frac{e^{iT}}{e^{iT}-1}) = 0 \tag{14}$$

$$- \frac{\partial A}{\partial h} = i(V - A) \tag{14'}$$

As argued in chapter 3, V is the present value of a given job position to the firm. Correspondingly, (V-A) is the present value of the job position flowing from workers after the first one in the sequence of workers filling the job position and i(V-A) is the rental value of the position per period on the basis of the productivity and wages of workers subsequent to the first one. (14') implies that at the optimal hiring age h*, the firm increases its profits by this rental value by hiring the worker during period h.

In the case of *career* workers, $V > A$, so that the right side of (14') is positive. Hence (14) requires that

$$- \partial A / \partial h > 0 \qquad\qquad (14'')$$

That is, at the optimal hiring age, the firm must lose a positive amount of rents from the first worker's employment because of the delay in the hiring age. Note that this does not necessarily require a positive rent during the first period of employment but a decrease in the present value of the rents over the worker's total period of employment. However, at the very young ages, the physical and mental immaturity relative to the requirements of the job could be such that postponement of the hiring age could yield a net increase in rents. The firm would not find it optimal to hire at such ages.

(14') from the replacement model projects a different picture of the firm's decision processes than the usual one given by analysis confined to the existing worker's employment or to the current sequence of workers for all its jobs. Such an analysis would be applicable when the firm intends to retire the job position or close the firm. In this case, $V = A$, and the optimality condition would be,

$$- \partial A / \partial h = 0 \qquad\qquad (15)$$

Comparing (14') and (15), (14') requires a greater net gain - equal to [i(V-A)] - at the marginal hiring age than (15) and, therefore, a more restrictive policy on hiring ages. Hence, confining the analysis of the optimal hiring age to a single worker, as is usually done, rather than the sequence of workers filling a job position would be erroneous unless the optimal policy for the firm were to retire the job position with the retirement of the current worker. (15) indicates a weaker interest and response than the firm would actually have in being moved away by public policy from its optimal hiring age pattern.

From (14'), an increase in the relevant rate of interest increases the net rental value required at the marginal hiring age.

5.3 The optimal hiring age for casual workers

As shown in chapter 3, the rents r from a given job position are independent of the hiring and retirement ages for casual workers, though they are a function of the hiring age for career workers. Therefore, for casual workers, for a given job position,

$$B = \{r \int_h^R e^{-i(t-h)} \, dt \}$$

$$\frac{\partial B}{\partial h} = r \, \frac{\partial}{\partial h} \{ \int_h^R e^{-i(t-h)} \, dt$$

$$= - r \, e^{-iT} \tag{16}$$

$$However \quad Y = \frac{e^{iT}}{e^{iT}-1} \, \{r \int_h^R e^{-i(t-h)} \, dt\}$$

$$= \frac{r}{i}$$

$$So \; that \quad \frac{\partial Y}{\partial h} = 0 \qquad for \; all \; h \tag{17}$$

Hence, the profit maximization condition when the firm's share of the costs of hiring and training is *constant* is:

$$\frac{\partial V}{\partial h} = - \frac{i e^{iT}}{(e^{iT}-1)^2} \, c = 0 \qquad if \; c > 0 \tag{18}$$

$$= 0 \qquad\qquad if \; c = 0 \; for \; all \; h \tag{18'}$$

(18) implies that the profit maximizing value of T goes to infinity for c > 0. In the context of workers with finite lives, this implication would translate to hiring workers from *birth* to *death* and favouring the worker with the longest expected lifetime. This implication is not realistic. (18') for c = 0 implies that all values of h satisfy the optimality condition so that the firm would be indifferent as to the job applicant's age. This condition is met if the costs of hiring and training were zero. This condition would also be met if there are costs of hiring and training but the worker bears - or pays for - the full amount of these costs. The firm would then not pay any part of these costs, so that c = 0 for all h. Under these conditions, the firm would be indifferent as to the age of the job applicants for its casual jobs.

The next section deals with the case where the hiring and training costs are not constant and the firm has to pay for some or all of them.

5.4 Skill acquisition costs

The analysis of chapter 3 had assumed for both career and casual workers that the firm's share cost of hiring and training is independent of the age at hiring. In reality, this cost would depend upon the age at hiring since the very young workers will lack physical and mental maturity and may also have had less years of schooling than older workers. Similarly, the very old may lack the mental and physical agility of younger trainees. Therefore, the cost of bringing each worker up to a given level of skills would vary with the age at hiring.

The optimal pattern of training or learning firm-specific skills may also be staggered over time: certain skills have to be developed and used on the job for some time before another set can be learnt efficiently. This ties in with the concept of promotion ladders, where a worker has to show ability to learn and use the skills of one level to earn promotion, with another set of skills being learnt after the promotion. Therefore, there may be not only an optimal age of initial hiring but also optimal ages of promotions to new positions.

To investigate the influence of age upon the cost function and through this cost upon the optimal hiring age, rewrite (14) as,

$$- \partial B / \partial h + \partial C / \partial h = i(V - A) \tag{19}$$

where $\partial B / \partial h$ is likely to be negative since, for the given retirement age, postponing the hiring age reduces the periods over which rents are earned. As explained earlier, this term will be approximated under certain assumptions by the present discounted value of the rents generated by the worker in his last period of employment, i.e. at his most experienced level, rather than by the rent generated in the first period of employment when he has not yet acquired firm specific skills. It will be larger the larger are the rents generated and therefore the greater are the firm-specific skills eventually acquired. In rough terms, the impact of this term is: hire the worker as soon as he becomes capable of learning, or starting to learn, the skills required for the job so as to maximize the period over which he will use the skills and yield rents to the firm.

$\partial C / \partial h$ would be approximately zero if the training period is less than the employment period and if the mental and physical abilities of the worker were invariant in the neighbourhood of the hiring age. However, the latter is often not so. The training cost function C(.) is likely to be convex in h, with $\partial C/\partial h < 0$ at quite young ages with relatively inadequate but increasing physical and mental powers. It would have $\partial C/\partial h > 0$ beyond some age h_0. At the relatively young ages, increases in age lead to an improved ability to learn new skills and adjust to a new environment - from an educational institution to a job or from one job to another. This would tend to lower the costs of training. For older workers, with declining mental and physical agility and with decreased powers of learning and adjustment relative to the skill requirements, it is likely that $\partial C/\partial h > 0$. The ages of full or peak powers in this respect can be designated as ones at which $\partial C/\partial h = 0$. This part of the worker's life can stretch over many years. However, for convenience, we will assume it to be a unique age and designate it as h_0. It will be referred to as the 'peak age' or peak period.

In the case of *casual* workers - that is, with $\partial B/\partial h = 0$ - the various possibilities would be:

(i) The cost of hiring and training is positive for all hiring ages and the firm is required to pay a positive amount of this cost. In this case, the firm's profit maximization goal implies that $T \to \infty$ and workers will be hired for the longest period possible since this will minimize the hiring and training costs over the sequence of workers.

(ii) The cost of hiring and training is positive for all ages and the worker pays the whole of this cost, so that, as far as the firm is concerned, $c = 0$ for all h in equations (1) to (4). In this case, $\partial V/\partial h = 0$ for all h and the firm would be indifferent as to the age of its job applicants.

(iii) The cost of hiring and training is zero for all hiring ages, and neither the worker nor the firm has to pay any such cost. The conclusions for the firm's optimal hiring age are as in (ii).

(iv) While the cost of hiring and training paid by the firm is positive for some ages, there exist some ages for which it is zero. An example of this is a convex cost function with minimum cost being zero, at say age h_0 - designated above as the peak age. Then, $\partial C/\partial h = 0$ at h_0. For casual workers with $\partial B/\partial h = 0$ for all h, $\partial V/\partial h = 0$ at h_0, and the optimal hiring age from the firm's perspective will be h_0. Therefore, for casual workers, applicants younger or older than h_0 will not be hired unless they were willing to pay their costs of hiring and training or accept correspondingly lower wages.

For the case of *career* workers, $\partial B/\partial h > 0$. To analyze the different cases relevant to career workers, again assume that C(h) is convex in h, with a minimum at h_0. At the optimal hiring age h^*, $\partial C/\partial h$ can be positive, zero or negative. Therefore, h* may be less than, equal to or more than h_0.

The optimizing condition (18) incorporates two opposing factors. One of these is the firm's desire to extend the employment period and thus increase its rents from the firm-specific skills. Ignoring the impact of the hiring age on the path of productivity and the firm's share of the rents in the neighbourhood of the hiring age - for instance, by incorporating the impact of any immaturity into the training cost function and assuming wages to be inelastic with respect to current productivity - the term $\partial B/\partial h$ is likely to be negative for career workers since increasing h reduces the employment period. The other factor is the firm's desire to delay the hiring age to the one where its share of the hiring and the training cost is at its minimum.

Among the considerations taken into account in the following comments are the following. The cost function is assumed to be convex, with a minimum at h_0. The worker's productivity is concave in the age of the worker, with low but increasing productivity at relatively young ages and with productivity again declining at relatively older ages. The firm's concern is with its share of the rents and these would also depend upon the wage. Minimum wage laws at low productivity levels could imply a negative share of the rent for the firm. However, the rents cannot remain negative through all ages; otherwise, the worker would never be hired. Note also that the retirement age is being taken to be exogenously given for the analysis of this chapter. We comment briefly on some of the possibilities in such a context.

For $h* < h_0$, the worker would have declining hiring and training costs at the age of hiring. In this case, the worker's mental and physical powers for acquiring firm-specific skills would still be increasing at the hiring age. Nevertheless, the firm chooses to hire him if the skill acquisition period is long and the decrease (from the delay in the hiring age) in the firm's share of the rents accruing from such skills is relatively significant.

For $h* = h_0$, the worker is hired at the peak period for acquiring skills. Younger workers will impose additional training costs which are not offset by an increase in the firm's share of the rents from the longer employment period. Older workers will also impose higher hiring and training costs and also decrease the firm's share of the rent through a shorter employment period.

$h* > h_0$ seems to be an unlikely, though possible, occurrence for several reason. The firm can reduce its hiring and training costs by merely hiring workers earlier. Further, since the worker is beyond the peak period of his capacities for learning the firm-specific skills, he is not likely to have a higher marginal product and yield a higher share of the rents to the firm than a younger worker of age h_0. Furthermore, delaying the hiring age reduces B since such a delay reduces the employment period.

However, note that B and $\partial B/\partial h$ also depend upon the path of wages. If minimum wage laws or other rigidities turn the firm's share of the worker's rents to a negative amount at h_0, but leave it positive for older ages, h^* could exceed h_0.

Different occupations would have different rent and training cost functions. Therefore, the optimal hiring age will vary among different occupations. However, as argued above, it is likely that $h^* \leq h_0$.

Casual observation suggests that these implications of our model are empirically valid. While different occupations do have different hiring ages, workers tend to be hired in their late teens and early twenties in most career job ladders. Mental and physical powers seem to be still increasing at these ages. At the same time, there is a reluctance to hire 'old' workers in their forties and fifties.

To draw out more implications of the influence of the cost and rent functions on the hiring age, would seem to require specifying their specific forms. Little is known about these specific forms so that we choose not to proceed along this route.

5.5 The discrimination premium

For a somewhat more limited analysis than the one given above, consider the case of a given wage path w(t) with its implied optimal hiring age h^*. Assume that the firm will maintain this hiring age for all workers beyond the first one in the sequence, but wishes to be able to substitute workers of different hiring ages as the first worker. Further assume that it is considering hiring two workers X and Y, with X as the optimal age worker hired at h^* and with Y hired at age h', where $h' = h^* + 1$. Also assume that the training costs incurred by the firm are only in the first period on the job, both workers are paid the same wage, both will be employed to the same age T^* and both have the same rent function $r^*(.)$. Also designate the first period as period 0, so that each worker starts in period 0, with X working for a total of T^* periods and Y working for a total of T^*-1 periods.

If the optimal age worker X is hired, the present value of the firm's share of the rents from him and the subsequent workers after him on the same job is,

$$V^* = \{ \int_0^{T^*-1} r^*(t)\, e^{-it}\, dt - c + r(T^*)\, e^{-iT^*} \} + (V^* - A^*) \tag{20}$$

where $A^* = \int_0^{T^*} r^*(t) \, e^{-it} \, dt - c$. The expression {.} on the right hand side of (20) equals A^* and separates the present value of the rents from the worker X into that from him during the periods upto T^*-1 and that in the period T^*.

However, if the worker Y - older than the optimal hiring age by one period - were to be hired, the present value of the firm's share of the rents from him and the subsequent workers would be,

$$V' = \int_0^{T^*-1} r^*(t) \, e^{-it} \, dt - c + e^i \, (V^* - A^*) \qquad (21)$$

In (20), the optimal worker X works for T^* periods. In (21), the worker Y works for only (T^*-1) periods and is replaced by other workers who work for the optimal period T^*. In (21), the contribution of the latter to the present value of rents is not (V^*-A^*), as in (20), but is $e^i(V^*-A^*)$ since their contribution will start one period earlier - that is, during the Tth period.

Since V^* is the optimal amount, $V^* > V'$. Hence from (20) and (21),

$$r(T^*) \, e^{-iT^*} + (V^* - A^*) > e^i \, (V^* - A^*)$$

which implies that,

$$r(T^*) \, e^{-iT^*} + (1 - e^i) \, (V^* - A^*) > 0 \qquad (22)$$

The left hand side of equation (22) specifies the present value of the loss to the firm from employing a job applicant older than the optimal hiring age by one period. Since this loss is positive, the firm would not be willing to offer the job to such older applicants and will be considered to be discriminating against them.

If the firm were to be made indifferent between hiring workers X and Y, both workers must yield the same present value of the firm's share of rents to the firm. That is, indifference in hiring and therefore the absence of discrimination in making a job offer requires that $V^* = V^{*'}$, where V^* is as specified by the optimal hiring and retirement ages of the workers (corresponding to the X worker) and $V^{*'}$ is the present value of the rents that the 'older' worker Y will have to yield to the firm. This condition requires that Y's rent function $r'(.)$ differ from X's rent function $r^*(.)$. $r'(.)$ is then endogenous. Formally,

$$V^{*'} = \int_0^{T^*-1} r'(t) \, e^{-it} \, dt - c + e^i \, (V^* - A^*) \qquad (23)$$

From (20) and (23), for V* = V*',

$$\int_0^{T^*-1} r'(t)\, e^{-it}\, dt - \int_0^{T^*-1} r^*(t)\, e^{-it}\, dt =$$

$$r(T^*)\, e^{-iT^*} + (1 - e^i)\, (V^* - A^*) \qquad (24)$$

where, from (22), the right hand side is strictly positive. Hence, the older worker Y will have to yield a larger present value of rents than the younger worker X over the common (T-1) periods of employment, with this amount specified by the right hand side of equation (24). Given identical marginal productivity functions, this requires that over the common (T-1) periods the present value v(w') of *wages* w' received by Y must be less than the present value v(w*) of *wages* paid to X. From (24), given identical marginal productivity functions over the first (T-1) periods, this amount is given by,

$$\int_0^{T^*-1} (w^* - w')\, e^{-it}\, dt = r(T^*)\, e^{-iT^*} + (1 - e^i)\, (V^* - A^*) > 0 \qquad (24')$$

and,

$$v(w^*) - v(w') = r(T^*)\, e^{-iT^*} + (1 - e^i)\, (V^* - A^*) > 0 \qquad (24'')$$

v(w*) - v(w') is now the present discounted value of the cost to the worker of postponing the hiring age by one period. This difference can be designated as the 'wage (discrimination) premium' for being older by *one period* at the time of hiring. By extension, the older the worker relative to the optimal hiring age, the greater would be this wage discrimination premium. There would then exist an age difference between the actual age and the optimal hiring age for which the reduction in v(w) is sufficiently large for it to fall below the reservation wage, so that the worker would no longer accept the job offer. If this age difference becomes sufficiently long, v(w) could even become negative, so that there would not exist a monetary reason for the worker to consider accepting the job offer.

5.6 The optimal hiring age and discrimination

Solving (14') would yield the optimal hiring age for the firm as,

$$h = h(\underline{r}, \underline{c};\ i,\ R,\ n) \qquad (25)$$

where $\underline{r}$ is the vector of variables appearing as arguments of the rents r(.) function and $\underline{c}$ is the vector of variables appearing in the skill acquisition costs c(.) function. Among these variables is the wage path and the path of mental and physical powers relative to the job requirements. R is the exogenously specified retirement age and n is the firm's optimal number of jobs positions. Note these are themselves functions of r(.) and i.

(25) specifies the firm's preferred hiring age for workers in a given job position utilizing firm-specific skills. Given that r(.) and c(.) differ among occupations, the function h(.) is likely to be different for different occupations. If r(.) and c(.) differ for a given occupation among firms - such as when firms differ in size or employ different technologies - h(.) will also differ among firms even for the same occupation category.

Equation (25) determines a variety of hiring ages for different values of the arguments. In particular, different exogenously specified wage paths over the worker's work-life will determine different hiring ages. Workers could then be hired at any point in their life provided that they were willing to accept an appropriate wage pattern.

Equation (25) specifies the demand function by firms for the hiring age. It, along with a supply function for the hiring age given by workers' preferences, will determine the market wage path over time. The endogenous variables of the system would then be this wage path and its resultant rent path. Conversely, given the market wage path to a firm, the rent path for a given job position in the firm can be deduced and the optimal hiring age for the job can be found from (25).

In the long run, the market wage path over the workers' employment periods is likely to be the endogenous variable of the economy. Most workers enter the labour market in their teens and twenties and want a job soon after entry. The standard market wage path must then be one which provides the entry to most jobs at that period of life. This is especially so for career jobs with long-term job attachment. Consequently, the optimal hiring age for this endogenously determined standard wage path would be the one at which most workers enter the labour force.

However, given wage path flexibility such that the labour market clears for the various ages of the available workers, the labour market would specify a variety of wage paths and hiring ages in the economy. Each worker, no matter how old or how young, could be employed in a given occupation at some wage path relevant to him. It is worth noticing that what is relevant here is not the wage in the first period of employment but the present value of the wage path over the worker's period of employment with the given firm and its implied share of rents for the firm.

A longer period of employment increases the net present value of the rents from a worker due to the effect of experience on productivity, along with the hiring and training costs being spread over a longer time span. As against this, physical, emotional and mental immaturity during the early part of the period of employment can lower productivity and the net present value of the rents. Consequently, while the former factors argue for earlier hiring ages, there is a downward limit - imposed by a tradeoff between the effect of these factors on the net present value and that of immaturity at very young ages - to the ages at which V(h) will continue to increase as the hiring age decreases. Further, the educational and training schemes of society and firms etc. are likely to be adjusted to the age or narrow set of ages at which most workers want to enter the labour force. This seems to occur mainly though not totally in the late teens and twenties in prosperous, modern economies, which is roughly the age of attainment of physical and mental maturity for most workers. There is, then, a strong presumption for assuming that V(h) is at a maximum for hiring done at these ages - called the optimal hiring age for most occupations. It is lower at other ages. That is, the workers will have to accept lower lifetime earnings v(w) if they are younger or older at the time of hiring than the optimal hiring age.

Institutional explicit and implicit wage rigidities do clearly exist in the economy and tend to impose a cost on firms which pay 'older workers' - that is, those who are beyond the optimal hiring age, as defined above - lower wages than the workers hired at the optimal ages (the 'optimal-age workers'). Such a cost may be in terms of morale of the older worker in question and his co-workers when they see him being paid less than younger workers on the same type of job. This cost is discussed in greater detail in chapter 6 and is related to the notions of fairness and norms in the workplace. The firm can avoid this cost by paying the same wages to both the older and the optimal age worker. But wage equality would imply that V(.) is lower for the former than the latter, so that the firm would not hire the older worker, all other things - especially wages - being the same.[3]

The nature of the preference by firms for optimal age workers - when all workers are paid identical wages - is shown by our previous arguments. The spreading of the costs of hiring and training over a longer employment is an element in this preference and is much emphasized in the literature (for example, see Ehrenberg and Smith 1985). However, as our analysis shows, this preference would exist even if the hiring and training costs were zero. Further, the hiring and training costs usually incurred by firms do not seem to be large enough relative to annual wage rates to matter over lifetime periods of employment.

A more significant factor than hiring and training costs could be the firm-specific rents attached to a job and the firm's share of them. To illustrate this role, consider a firm hiring a worker X at age 25 and a worker Z at age 45, with both retired at age 65 and with Z being replaced by a worker Y at his retirement. Assume that there are zero training costs and both have the same marginal product for the firm during their first 20 years on the job. Both workers would then generate the same rents for the firm's share if they were paid the same wage during these 20 years. Yet, as our analysis shows, the firm would still get a higher present value of its rents over an infinite horizon by employing X because he would be an experienced worker, with high rents, at his age 45 and would be with the firm for another 20 years. Compared with him, the older worker Z's replacement would be the worker Y with lesser experience on the job than the last 20 years of worker X's employment and will yield a lower rent to the firm than the latter. Z imposes this rent reduction on the firm by virtue of his smaller period of employment. If the firm was to be indifferent between hiring X or (Z and Y) combination, then Z must be paid less than X even over the first 20 years on the job when both have the same marginal product. To the older worker and, in fact, under common definitions of discrimination,[4] this wage differentiation would appear as discrimination.

Our arguments above have generally been in the context of a single occupation with firm-specific skills. There are, in the economy, a variety of occupations with differing degrees of firm-specificity and, consequently, with different degrees of the required wage premium. This premium is zero for casual workers who bear their own hiring and training costs. Further, since there are costs to what is perceived as wage discrimination, as the wage premium often is, firms will not find it optimal to create this wage premium in career jobs in which the firm-specific rents are relatively small.

5.7 Unemployment and underemployment among older job losers

In career jobs with large wage premiums to be paid by older job applicants, the resulting wage justified for older workers seeking a job may be low enough to seem like blatant and socially unacceptable wage discrimination, so that firms would incur too high a cost to practising it. They would, then, take the less costly alternative of not hiring such workers. Further, the low resulting wage may be less than what the same worker can get in casual and semi-casual jobs, or below their reservation wage. We would then see both higher unemployment rates among older workers with firm-specific skills (Osberg, 1988; Gera and Rahman, 1989) and, when they do get jobs, a tendency for such workers to be pushed into less firm-specific categories of jobs and hence with lower wage paths relative to those in the occupations they had pursued in their earlier years in the job market.[5] Our theory also implies that this wage decline will be zero for casual workers and will be lesser for workers trained initially in less firm-specific skill categories.

The wage premium, for a wide variety of forms of the rent function, is likely to increase with the age of the worker being hired. For some occupations, there may exist hiring ages beyond which the firm will not be willing to pay even a positive wage to the worker being hired.

At the other end of the scale, workers younger than the optimal hiring age also have to pay a wage premium to get the job. However, society rarely interprets lower wages in their early years on the job as being discriminatory, as it does for older workers. There are two reasons for this in the context of our analysis. First, the younger workers have visibly lower marginal productivity than both optimal age workers and older ones in the early years on the job because of the former's visible immaturity. A lower wage, then, seems justified. Second, the younger workers' initially lower wage will catch up with that of the optimal hiring age workers, or they can leave and start afresh in another job at that age. By contrast, if the firm is to get adequate rental value of the job position, the older worker's wage may never catch up with that of the optimal hiring age workers.

Conclusion

The existence of the preference by firms for 'younger' job applicants over older ones is well established. So is the recognition in the literature that the costs of hiring and training and the existence of firm-specific skills can bring about this preference. This chapter and chapter 3 set out the formal analysis of this effect in an intertemporal model with replacement of workers over time in the firm's job positions. They derive the optimal hiring age, showing it to be any age in the case of casual jobs with workers bearing their own hiring and training costs and quite specific in the case of jobs requiring firm-specific skills. A wage premium would have to be paid to the firm by younger and older career workers.

Defining, as before, discrimination as the payment or receipt of a wage less than that received by another worker with the same current marginal product, the payment of a wage premium in career jobs will be seen as discriminatory by older job applicants, but need be so perceived by applicants younger than the optimal age ones. In the case of the older applicants, their productivity during their own years of employment could be the same as those of the optimal hiring age workers but, in order to be get the job, they are paid less. The younger workers often seem to be less mature and less productive, so that the lower wages paid to them tend to be viewed as justified and non-discriminatory. Further, the younger workers would have wages equal to those of the optimal age workers when they themselves do reach the optimal age.

While discrimination would generally exist for career jobs, it would generally not exist for casual jobs. One could then, for a given hiring age, rank job categories and occupations by the required wage premium. However, this ranking need not be invariant with respect to the hiring age.

The critical element in our analysis is that the age of the job applicant is important in the wage that the profit-maximizing firm can offer him. And if he is older than the optimal hiring age, he will be offered less than the wage of the optimal hiring age applicant or not be offered the job. Since the latter is a strong possibility because of the costs of open discrimination in wages, as discussed in chapters 1 and 6, there would occur higher rates of unemployment among the older job losers.[6]

The ability of the older job applicant to learn the relevant skills and do the required job properly was assumed in our analysis. However, older applicants with superior abilities than the requirements of the job may try to get the job, thereby trying to take advantage of the substitution possibilities between abilities and age at hiring. This may lead to the actual employment of some of these workers but in 'inferior' jobs relative to their abilities, thus leading to a form of underemployment. However, discrimination against older job applicants either in wages or not being offered the job, could occur even when their capabilities exceed those required by the job - especially if the increase in productivity from the superior abilities is relatively minor.[7]

Hutchens (1986) found that jobs for which there is discrimination against the hiring of older workers tend to have pensions, long term job attachment, comparatively high wages and mandatory retirement. These are common attributes of jobs with firm-specific skills. These findings are fully consistent with our theory. They are also consistent with almost any model of long term job attachment.

A distinctive implication of our replacement model is that improvements in technology which make succeeding generations more productive than earlier ones would increase the wage premium required of older job applicants. Occupations with rapidly changing technology will show more of these effects than traditional occupations, e.g. computers as against textiles. Another implication different from most other models arises from our emphasis on age-related changes in productivity. Occupations with steeper declines in productivity from ageing will show greater discrimination against older job applicants. Thus, physical sports such as baseball, hockey, etc. show such effects more than office based work. Further, given the costs associated with open wage discrimination, such changes in technology will reduce the retirement age for workers and will lead to higher unemployment and underemployment among the older workers.

FOOTNOTES

1. Clark, Kreps and Spengler (1978, pp. 927-29) present a survey of the job performance capabilities and wages of older workers, as well as the contributions of experience and growth to wages.
2. Hutchens argues that the firm-specific skills model is inconsistent with mandatory retirement. While this may be true of Becker's model, it is not true of our replacement model of firm-specific skills (see chapter 6).
3. Other things are not always the same. An older worker may bring a proven track record and experience in getting along with colleagues or dealing with superiors and subordinates.
4. For example, see Ehrenberg and Smith (1985, p. 443) where discrimination is defined as "the valuation in the labour market of personal characteristics of the workers that are unrelated to productivity". See also chapter 4 above.
5. Hutchens (1986) has drawn a similar finding from Lazear's incentives model.
6. Osberg (1988) and Gera and Rahman (1989) present recent evidence on the relatively high rates of unemployment among older workers in Canada, with most of it accounted by job separations due to the unavailability of previous employment.
7. Spengler (1971) contends that capabilities exceed job requirements for the relevant worker over most of his life.

6 Optimal Retirement Policies: The Firm's Choices

This chapter analyzes the firm's preferred age for the retirement of its workers. In the absence of legislation barring mandatory retirement (MR) policies, this preferred age would in some cases be the basis for setting an explicit retirement age in a MR policy. In other cases, the firm may implement a retirement age as an implicit policy. Even in the presence of laws barring MR policies, the firm would have an optimal retirement age for its workers and may seek to implement it in covert ways. Therefore, the presence of such legislation does not make redundant the study of the firm's preferred retirement age for its workers. This chapter examines the retirement age which the firm would like to implement for its workers. The worker's own preferences on this age are analyzed separately and are dealt with in chapter 8.

The firm's preferred or optimal retirement policies have historically been treated under the heading of MR policies. Among the major theoretical contributions on the basic determinants of these policies are Lazear (1979), Blinder (1981), and Lapp (1985). Lazear's incentives theory implies that the firm will pay a worker over his work-life the present value of his marginal product but in a wage pattern such that the real wage will be below the worker's marginal product in the early years, while being above the worker's marginal product in the later years. Blinder's human capital approach adds to this pattern an initial period in which the sum of training costs paid by the firm and wages exceeds the worker's marginal product. In both Lazear and Blinder, the firm's retirement decision is a layoff and not a replacement decision: the firm will have to lay the worker off at the age at which the present value of the expected marginal product and the wage will be equal:

106

employing the worker longer will result in a loss for the firm. Lapp (1985) bases the firm's preferred retirement on the age limit on an insurance contract offered by the firm to insure its workers against potential, age related declines in productivity. These models imply that the wage of the worker will exceed his marginal product later in life, so that continued employment of the worker becomes unprofitable for the firm and the worker is employed upto a point specified in an explicit or implicit contract and determined by a delayed compensation scheme as in Lazear or an insurance one. The essential characteristic of these models for their implication of MR is then that wages exceed productivity later in life. Such a pattern can also occur for other reasons. Thus, Carmichael (1983) used asymmetric information in a two-period model, with only firms being able to observe productivity and workers only able to know their reservation wage in the second period, so that wages could exceed the marginal productivity of certain workers, without either the firm or the worker being able to identify the workers for whom this occurs.

Each of the factors being adduced in the above mentioned models can clearly exist in the real world, so that each of the above models provides a plausible explanation of the optimal retirement policies within firms and industries in which their particular factor is relevant. By implication, no one theory may be universally applicable to the exclusion of the others. There is then scope for the simultaneous relevance of the above theories, as well as of others.

Our analysis implies yet another theory of the firm's optimal retirement policies, merging elements of our version of the human capital rents-based approach with recent work on the concept of the efficiency wage and on workplace norms affecting work effort. The latter are related to the worker's notion of the fairness of the wage and MR decisions. One aspect of this broader theory, flowing from the analysis of the preceding chapters, emphasizes the firm's retirement decision as a replacement decision rather than merely as a layoff one. This broader theory assigns critical roles to health factors, shifts in skills and productivity among generations and resentment at both wage cuts and the imposed retirement element in MR policies.

An important distinction between our theory and the theories of MR mentioned above is that wages would be below marginal productivity in later years on the job in our theory and above marginal productivity in the other theories mentioned above. The latter property has been considered the *sine qua non* for MR (Hutchens, 1989). This is not so, since our theory produces MR even though marginal productivity exceeds wages at the retirement age in this theory. This result is produced in our model by our reliance on the notion that worker replacement or replacement is an essential aspect of firms' optimizing decisions. This notion seems to be intuitively obvious. Gee and McDaniel (1991) summarizing the evidence on the MR policies of firms in Canada point out that in recent decades, the objective of such policies has been to replace older workers with younger ones. Further, "the politics of mandatory retirement are not really about the usefulness of older workers, although the MR 'debate' is often couched in such terms, rather they are about the maximization of profits" (p.465).

Returning briefly to the distinction drawn in the preceding chapters between casual and career workers, a career worker possesses firm-specific skills, with his productivity in his existing firm higher than in other firms. In the long run, this rent is divided between the firm and the worker, with each earning the return to their respective characteristics. Various forces operate in the short run to enforce this division of the rent. Among these is the desire of the firm to reduce quits and the desire of the workers to reduce layoffs. This division of the rent occurs through a wage being paid which is lower than the worker's actual marginal product but higher than the wage the worker will get in other firms (Becker, 1975; Okun, 1981).[1] Such a division results in long-term attachment between the firm and the worker. Casual workers do not have such rents, rent sharing or job attachment.

The sharing of the rents between the firm and the career worker acts to reduce the possibility of cheating by the worker, i.e., slowing down or shirking on his work. Such an action reduces the rent retained by the firm from what it can get from a replacement worker. It could induce his layoff by the firm, resulting in the loss to him of his share of the retirement rent. At the same time, the possibility of default by the firm, in the sense of the firm laying off the worker before the end of his career, is curbed since such an action would reduce the firm's profits through the loss of its share of the already experienced worker's retirement rent. Given these reasons for the self interest of both the worker and the firm in not reneging on the implicit long term job contract - including its provisions of the worker not shirking on the job and the firm not laying him on the basis of fictitious charges of inadequate performance - a special incentives-based wage stream such as that posited by Lazear, Blinder, and Lazear and Moore (1984) is not required to prevent cheating within the context of our theory. From a more general viewpoint, incentives or rent sharing are only two of the factors which can prevent cheating on the job. To illustrate some others, Fama (1990) relies upon labour market discipline and Gibbons and Murphy (1990) resort to the career concerns of workers, in addition to explicit incentives.

The firm's retirement choices

Looking more closely at wage deferral schemes, a wage stream with extensive deferral of wages implies a degree of trust by workers in firms' management over a long career, often of thirty years or so, through a variety of economic vicissitudes. Unvested pensions - unvested over long numbers of years - similarly seem to require a high degree of trust by the worker in the firm, with vested pension funds neither requiring it nor constituting an incentive not to shirk. The existence of such a degree of trust is hard to believe and is, therefore, not posited in this chapter. Conversely, the firm and the worker interact over a very long period so that a high degree of distrust and animosity also cannot be a normal occurrence and is not being posited. Abraham and Farber (1986) report empirical findings against wage deferral and trust. They conjecture that "risk aversion and uncertainty about whether the firm will honour its implicit commitments seem likely to make many workers unwilling to enter into such arrangements" (p.41).

Firm-specific skills tend to be acquired on the job over a period of time. Promotions occur through this period and then new firm-specific skills relevant to the new job are learned. This pattern with its increases in marginal product - and without the need for an assumption of deferral of wages - implies an increasing wage path, especially over the part of the worker's work-life which encompasses promotions. Further, there tend to occur general increases in productivity in the economy. The evidence on earnings indicates that earnings rise with experience over periods as long as thirty years (e.g. see Murphy and Welch, 1990). However, it is not obvious whether the increases result only from the accumulation of skills and the increases in productivity, or are wholly or partly due to wage deferral schemes.

The length of the job attachment period is affected for a given wage stream by the changes over time in the worker's productivity. This in turn depends upon the worker's physical and mental powers relevant to the job. These in general for most jobs and most workers, are greatest in the early years of one's work-life. They decline eventually.[2] As they do so, marginal productivity declines and the rent generated by the worker is cut. So is the firm's share of this rent. At some point in this decline, the firm's present discounted value of profits is increased by replacing the worker by a younger one who can generate a larger share of rents for the firm. The firm would like to lay off the worker at that point, unless it could cut the worker's wage by a sufficient amount below his declining marginal product to get the same share of the rent from his employment as its share of the rent from his younger replacement. But this produces a discrete downward wage adjustment such that the wage offered falls below the worker's reservation wage at some point, and the worker chooses to leave the job. But if he does not do so, the cut in wages might lower his morale and cause his productivity to fall further through shirking and malfeasance. This is an aspect of efficiency wages (Akerlof and Yellen, 1986) as well as of the notion of a fair wage (Keynes, 1936; Hicks, 1974; Okun, 1981; Krueger and Summers, 1987). It is worth noting here that in the judgement of many economists, "the workplace is a hotbed for norm-guided action" (Elster, 1989, p. 101). This is also the approach of many sociological theories (Rebitzer, 1993, p. 1419). The existing wage is often one of the more sacrosanct norms. For the firm to try and cut this wage is to violate this norm, with resentment and adverse reaction by the worker and possibly also by his co-workers. That is, there may also be externalities if the worker's dissatisfaction is communicated to his co-workers and also affects their productivity. The optimizing response of the firm to declining productivity may, therefore, be to lay off the worker rather than to cut his wages or to cut his wages beyond a certain amount.

The above discussion relates to the determination of the paths of the marginal product and the wage of an individual worker in a firm. But an optimal decision on the retirement of a worker by the firm is a decision not merely on the optimal age of his layoff but also of his replacement by another worker (Gordon, 1960), so that an intertemporal choice framework is required. This was presented in chapter 3 and allowed simultaneous determination of the firm's optimal number of jobs, and its desired hiring and retirement ages. This chapter has a narrower focus, confined to the firm's desired retirement age for its workers. It, therefore, abstracts from the more general analysis of chapter 3 by taking the optimal number of jobs and the hiring age as given.

Further, chapter 3 had presented the analysis for an infinite sequence of workers in continuous time analysis. However, given long-term job attachment, even a sequence of two workers can cover several decades, which seems to be a long enough period for firms to plan for. Firms may then view the retirement decision of a worker as that of replacing him by another worker on the same job, without considering the sequence of workers that might follow the second worker, especially since there may exist considerable uncertainty about the nature of the job and the qualifications of workers far into the future. Therefore, although we can continue in this chapter with the infinite horizon analysis of chapter 3, we have chosen to base the analysis in this chapter on a sequence of two workers. This also has the merit of providing a slightly different perspective on the results on retirement derived in chapter 3. The qualitative conclusions derived remain the same between chapter 3 and this chapter. A reader who would prefer the more general analysis with simultaneous determination of the hiring and retirement ages with an infinite sequence of workers can refer to chapter 3 as the relevant analysis behind the arguments of this chapter.

This assumption of a sequence of two workers in a given job maintains the firm's decision on its preferred age for the retirement of the first worker in the sequence a question of the replacement of a worker by another worker. This has been an essential element of our analysis. By comparison, the retirement decision in Lazear and Blinder's theories is merely one of the layoff of the worker, without hiring another worker for the same job. A consequence of this difference is that our theory allows examination of the impact on the firm's desired retirement ages of technological change in learning over succeeding generations. The better education, training and skills of successive generations would tend to lower the firm's preferred retirement age, especially in industries where such changes have significant effects on worker productivity. Our theory also allows examination of the effects of changes in interest rates on the optimal retirement age: a rise in these rates leads to a postponement of the retirement age.

A firm would want a retirement layoff at a certain point in the worker's age. This point would tend to vary among its workers. However, there are also costs to the firm of laying off a worker on an individual basis. These are well recognized in the literature (for example, see Fox and Kerpen, 1964). The firm often finds that a uniform retirement age among workers in similar employment categories and possibly over all its employees is the least costly method out of various possible layoff patterns.

This chapter views MR policies as a constraint imposed by the firm on workers' work-leisure choices and, therefore, as something resented by the workers (see chapter 8 for the reasons for this). Consequently, the fairness of the various aspects of this constraint becomes an important element in its acceptance. As in Blinder (1981), we view pension plans and their particular provisions as attempts to skew the workers' own optimal retirement age - based on their work-leisure choice - to that specified by the firm. But, unlike Blinder, we view the relative fairness of such plans as important elements in reducing the workers' resentment towards the constraint imposed by the firm's MR policies on their choices.

Section 1 of this chapter presents and evaluates the major existing approaches on the firm's optimal retirement age. Section 2 presents a modified version of the model of chapter 3 in so far as it is relevant to the topic of this chapter. This section probes more closely into the determinants of the rent function than was done in chapter 3. Sections 3 and 4 point out the implications of the model for the optimal retirement ages of causal and career workers. Section 5 examines explores the implications of innovations in technology and health etc. for the optimal retirement age. Section 6 investigates the relevance of the fair wage and the efficiency wage arguments in the context of the firm's optimal retirement ages for its workers. Sections 7 and 8 provide some illustrations of the analysis. Sections 9 to 12 pursue other aspects of the subject of MR. Among these is the co-ordination of MR ages among firms, and with the social security system, and the implications of the elimination of MR by legislation.

6.1 The main existing approaches

The central hypothesis of the Lazear (1979) and Lazear and Moore (1984) model is that firms pay a worker over his work-life a present value of his marginal product (m) but in a wage pattern such that the real wage (w) will be below the worker's marginal product in the later years. This wage path acts as a disincentive for workers to shirk - that is, to cheat by reducing their work effort . The higher marginal product and hence the higher present value of wages due to such a wage pattern, is in the interests of both firms and workers and is therefore preferred by both of them. However, this wage path is such that the wage will be above the value of the marginal product in the worker's later work years. The firm will have to lay the worker off at the age at which the present values of the expected marginal product (Pvm) and of the wage (Pvw) will be equal: employing the worker longer will result in a loss for the firm since his wage at that age will exceed his marginal product and continuing to pay this wage will make the Pvm less than the Pvw.

The Lazear analysis implies that the firm will accumulate a substantial fund in present value terms on behalf of the worker in the early years (with $w < m$) while running it down in later years (with $w > m$).[3] To be significant in the retirement decision, this fund must be large at the turning point in the w-m relationship since it would have been accumulated over many years.[4] Firms never acknowledge the existence of such a substantial fund, let alone acknowledging worker's rights to ownership of such a fund. In any case, the workers must have to have an enormous degree of trust in the firm to accept the firm's holding of such an (unacknowledged) fund on their behalf and maintain this trust over several decades. Such trust does not seem to exist in the real world.[5] Even if it did, it would seem to imply an implicit contract between the firm and the worker that if the firm laid off the worker without his fault, the firm would pay the worker this sum. Such a practice does not exist in any significant form in the modern economy: severance payments are usually too small in this respect.

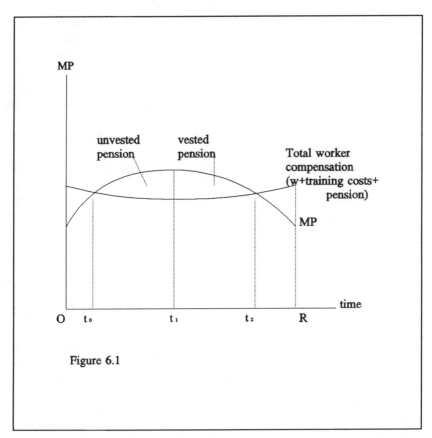

Figure 6.1

Blinder (1981) based his explanation of MR on the existence of training costs and firm-specific skills. These costs, occurring in the early years of employment - period 0 to t_0 in figure 6.1 - are largely borne by the firm and recouped from the worker over a subsequent period. Blinder's 'analysis, therefore, has an initial period in which labour costs (including wages and training costs) exceed marginal productivity. However, Blinder's analysis implies a subsequent wage pattern similar to that of Lazear, with wages above marginal product towards the end of the worker's career and at the retirement age. The focus of both theories is on MR as a layoff decision by the firm rather than as a replacement decision in which the wages and productivity of the new generation of workers affect the retirement age of the initial generation.

More specifically, Blinder assumes that the firm largely or wholly pays the training costs for the acquisition of firm-specific skills (Becker, 1975; Okun, 1981). These occur in the initial stages of the worker's career. Consequently, the total compensation paid to the worker in the form of wages and the firm's share of the training costs exceeds the worker's marginal product in the early years of employment. The firm recoups this overpayment in a subsequent period (see figure 6.1) by paying a wage and accumulating an unvested pension for the worker, with their sum being less than the worker's marginal product. At some point in life (say time t_1), a vested pension is also instituted. But the underpayment continues for many years and is used to build up a fund, as in Lazear's analysis, which is used to pay the worker a wage higher than his marginal product after period t_2 which occurs towards the latter part of his career. Blinder's model is not sufficiently motivated on the reasons for the continuing underpayment, and the subsequent overpayment from t_2 to R. This model does not rely upon Lazear's concept of shirking but uses a w-m path which is similar to Lazear's. Blinder's explanation for this is the firm's desire to reduce quits. But his human capital model with its emphasis on the firm-specificity of skills implies that the worker will lose very significantly if he quits his job with his existing firm for a job with another firm. Blinder's own estimate for this loss, in the case of a worker with a 45 year work-history with 20 years which have been spent with the current employer, is about 24% of his annual wage (Blinder, 1981, p. 23). Jacobson, Lalonde and Sullivan (1993) find this loss for high tenure workers to be very considerable, more so in the early years after job separation but still 25% of pre-separation earnings after five years. The estimated losses are large and occur over a long period in a wide variety of occupations, firms and industries. We suspect that if losses of this kind of magnitude are not sufficiently large to deter quits, imposing a larger loss would also most likely not deter workers from quitting.

The w-m pattern in terms of wage deferral in both Lazear and Blinder is quite similar and requires a considerable degree of trust by the worker in the firm, its firing decisions, its fortunes and his changing bosses over some thirty or more years. This problem of trust is highlighted diagrammatically by figure 6.2 which is a rearrangement of figure 6.1 above, with the modification that t_1 is now the time at which the overpayments of the period upto t_0 are exactly met by the underpayments from t_0 to t_1. The curve ABCD shows the pattern of payments made to the worker by the firm: the convex part AB is wage payments upto the retirement age and CD is pension payments. The worker's productivity is shown by the curve EFGHRT, with the concave part EFGH as the marginal product during the working periods upto the retirement age R and with the zero productivity of the retired years

114

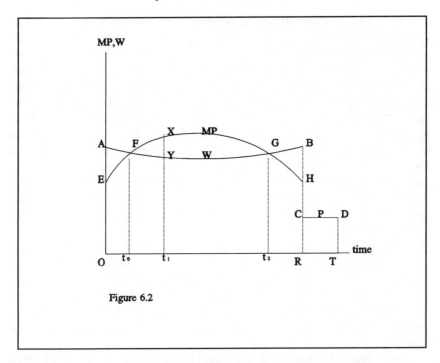

Figure 6.2

shown by the linear segment RT. T is the point of death. In figure 6.2, the overpayment - that is, the total worker compensation less the marginal product - in the period upto t_0 is recouped by the firm through underpayment from t_0 to t_1. Further underpayment occurs from period t_1 to t_2. The accumulation of the fund x given by,

$$x = \int_{t1}^{t2} (m - w) e^{-rt} dt$$

from t_1 to t_2 has an unvested component x_1 and a vested component x_2. Of these, x_2 is the pension component later used to pay the pension P. Its value is specified by,

$$x_2 = \int_{R}^{T} P e^{-rt} dt$$

x_1 is the component used to subsidize the wage from t_2 to R, so that its value is given by,

$$x_1 = \int_{t2}^{R} (w - m) e^{-rt} dt$$

115

Both Lazear's and Blinder's theories fail to explain why x_2 should be vested and x_1 not vested. If the non-vesting of x_1 acts as an incentive for the worker in Lazear's model and as reducing quits in Blinder's model, then not vesting x_2 at least till the retirement age R should increase these effects. The existence of the vested component x_2 - vested from time t_1 in Blinder's theory - can be interpreted as indicating uncertainty, doubt and/or distrust on the part of the workers in their employment being continued by the firm, in its honouring its unvested commitments and in its solvency. But then why trust the firm with the unvested component x_1? And if the possibility of doubt and distrust is strong enough, why has the market not evolved some form of vesting for x_1, with suitable eligibility conditions for collection gradually over the period from t_2 to R? Under such suitable arrangements, the worker would collect his wage equal to his marginal product MP from the firm and an appropriate amount from the vested fund x_1.

While the question of the empirical validity of the wage deferral hypothesis cannot be considered as settled, Abraham and Farber (1986) using a sample of non-union males from the Michigan Panel Study of Income Dynamics, found no evidence of income deferral. They argued that their result might be due to the uncertainty of whether the firm will honour its commitments under such a scheme, a matter of not sufficiently trusting the firm.

We have focused above on the moral hazard element in a wage deferral scheme. A related line of criticism is that there can exist simpler - and presumably less costly - schemes which would prevent shirking. A fee paid by the worker when hired and forfeited if caught shirking, or if fired for shirking, constitutes a penalty which could serve as the inducement not to shirk. In the general case, the worker would post a 'bond' on being hired and would forfeit it if he is caught shirking. Under such a fee or bond posted by the worker, the firm would still be subject to moral hazard in judging whether the worker is shirking or not: the firm itself has an incentive to cheat by falsely declaring workers to be shirking and fire them (Akerlof and Yellen, 1986, ch. 1). Hence, this type of solution to the shirking problem requires bonds being posted simultaneously by the worker and the firm against a job separation, with an extra penalty to the worker who quits voluntarily and an extra penalty to the firm if it fires the worker without adequate cause. This bond should preferably increase as the stake of the firm and the worker in his continued employment with the firm increases, and vice versa. Such a dual 'bond' scheme with the bond increasing in value occurs naturally in the presence of learning-on-the-job of firm-specific skills and is a fundamental part of our model, as argued later in this chapter.

Another substitute for the wage deferral schemes is one based on seniority rights with the firm committed to promoting junior workers on the basis of seniority to a specified number of higher paying jobs. (Carmichael, 1983). In this schema, if workers quit, they lose their accumulated seniority since they would have to start with zero seniority at other firms. If the firm fires them, it has to promote the junior workers into the higher paying jobs and therefore does not save in wages. Neither the worker nor the firm benefits from a job separation; the junior workers then act as a third party benefiting from any job separation. Such junior workers would be the potential replacement workers in our model. A critical element of this schema is the limitation on the number of higher paying jobs. Our theory implies that the optimal number of jobs of each kind and at each level is optimally determined. If the number of higher paying jobs is limited relative to the number of workers who can be given those jobs, the above schema can arise as a natural adjunct of our firm-specific skills framework.

Among other factors which obviate or reduce the need for wage deferral schemes is labour market discipline, as in Fama (1980), and career concerns, as in Gibbons and Murphy (1990). Both are elements of our model.

6.2 The basic model for decisions on retirement

Our basic model for explaining the firm's preferred retirement age for its workers is as specified in chapter 3 and is part of a model in which the number of jobs, the hiring age and the preferred retirement age are simultaneously determined. This chapter uses a simpler version of this model by taking the number of jobs and the hiring age to be the optimal ones, as determined in the model in chapter 3, and focuses only the determinants of the firm's preferred retirement age, including more explicit consideration of the skill learning period and of factors such as health which may affect the productivity path. The latter is incorporated through the variable 'age'.

To start with, chapter 3 had incorporated hiring and training costs into the analysis and shown that the optimal retirement age preferred by the firm would depend upon these costs. Chapter 5 on discrimination in the hiring of older workers had placed even greater emphasis on these costs in the context of the optimal hiring age. While hiring and training costs are an element in the overall model for the determination of the optimal retirement age, we consider them to be of secondary significance in such a decision and drop them from the analysis in this chapter. We also have no objection to Blinder's arguments on the payment of firm-specific training skills by the firm and the possibility of an initial period during which the firm overpays the workers. In Blinder, this overpayment is subsequently recouped by paying the worker less than his marginal product. This recoupment can occur over a short period, as in Blinder, or over the employment period as a whole. In any case, neither the payment of hiring and training costs by the firm nor the pattern of their recoupment plays a critical role in explaining MR in general in any of the three approaches - ours, Lazear's and Blinder's. Further, unless the training costs are still occurring at the retirement age, they are irrelevant to the firm's preferred retirement age since they are in the nature of sunk or fixed costs. Therefore, this chapter largely ignores training costs in its discussion of the determinants of the retirement decision.

As in the earlier chapters, assume that the firm operates in a perfectly competitive market and maximizes the present value of its profits. Also assume that in the job position j the worker's marginal productivity m in a given period is specified by,

$$m_j = m(\tau_j , g_j) \tag{1}$$

where

m marginal productivity
τ the period of acquisition of firm-specific skills
g age at the beginning of the kth period

In (1), $\partial m_j/\partial \tau_j \geq 0$, $\partial m_j/\partial g_j \leq 0$. The presence of τ captures the influence of firm-specific skills. The presence of g, the age of the worker, captures the impact of health and other age related variables upon productivity.[6]

The firm's share of the rent from employing the worker in the jth job position was designated in earlier chapters as r_j. Chapter 3 has a detailed discussion on the nature and measurement of this rent in our model. It was assumed that

$$r_j = r(m_j) \qquad \partial r_j/\partial m_j > 0 \tag{2}$$

As a reminder, the justification for (2) is that firm-specific skills arise jointly from the worker's learning ability and the environment provided by the firm (see chapter 2). The return to these skills will then be split between the firm and the worker, as shown in chapter 2, so that the higher the worker's marginal product due to the increase in his experience, the higher the rent the firm will get to keep from his work. From (1) and (2),

$$r_j = r(\tau_j, g_j) \tag{3}$$

where

$$\partial r_j/\partial \tau_j \geq 0, \; \partial r_j/\partial g_j \leq 0.$$

The firm has been assumed to maximize the present discounted value of its profits and has labour as the only input. Therefore, it maximizes the present discounted value of its share of the rents V_j over all jobs. Dropping the subscript j for simplicity of notation, and with an infinite horizon, the present value V of the firm's share of the rents from the job position j would be:

$$V = \int_{h_1}^{R_1} r\, e^{-i(t-h_1)}\, dt + \int_{h_2}^{R_2} r\, e^{-i(t+T_1-h_2)}\, dt$$

$$+ \int_{h_3}^{R_3} r\, e^{-i(t+T_1+T_2-h_3)}\, dt + \ldots \tag{4}$$

where

V   Present value of the net rents accruing to the firm
r   Firm's share of the rents from the job position
i   Interest rate
t   period
T_k Duration of employment of the kth worker ($= R_k - h_k$)
R_k Retirement age ($= h_k + T_k$) of the kth worker
h_k Hiring age of the kth worker
g   Age ($= h + t$)

As a departure from chapters 3 and 5, (1) assumes that the firm's share of the hiring and training costs is zero.

Assuming all workers in the sequence over time to have identical r(.) functions and with the interest rate i being held constant, the optimal hiring and retirement ages must also be identical for all workers in the sequence of workers. That is, for all k,

$$h_k = h$$

$$R_k = R$$

so that,

$$T_k = T \qquad \text{for all k.}$$

Therefore, from (4),

$$V = \int_h^R r\, e^{-i(t-h)}\, dt + \int_h^R r\, e^{-i(t+T-h)}\, dt$$

$$+ \int_h^R r\, e^{-i(t+2T-h)}\, dt + \dots$$

which simplifies to:

$$V = \int_h^R r\, e^{-i(t-h)}\, dt + \sum_{k=1}^{\infty} e^{-ikT} \{\int_h^R r\, e^{-i(t-h)}\, dt\}$$

$$= \{\int_h^R r\, e^{-i(t-h)}\, dt\} + \frac{1}{e^{iT}-1} \{\int_h^R r\, e^{-i(t-h)}\, dt\}$$

Hence,

$$V = \frac{e^{iT}}{e^{iT}-1} \{\int_h^R r\, e^{-i(t-h)}\, dt\}$$

$$= \frac{e^{iT}}{e^{iT}-1} A \qquad (5)$$

$$\text{where } A = \{\int_h^R r\, e^{-i(t-h)}\, dt\} \qquad (6)$$

The present discounted value of the firm's profits π over n jobs is given by,

$$\pi = \int_0^n V\, dx \qquad (7')$$

$$= \int_0^n \frac{e^{iT}}{e^{iT}-1} A\, dx \qquad (7'')$$

The firm's retirement choices

Under the assumptions mentioned above of treating the number of workers and the hiring age as exogenous for the analysis in this chapter, the firm maximizes (7") with respect to R. The first order condition for a maximum is:

$$\frac{\partial \pi}{\partial R} = \int_0^n \frac{\partial V}{\partial R} \, dx = 0$$

where,

$$\frac{\partial V}{\partial R} = [-i(V-A) + \frac{\partial A}{\partial R}] \, (\frac{e^{iT}}{e^{iT}-1}) \qquad (8)$$

Therefore, the first order condition for profit maximization with respect to the retirement age R becomes,

$$\frac{\partial \pi}{\partial R} = \int_0^n \{-i(V-A) + \frac{\partial A}{\partial R}\} \, (\frac{e^{iT}}{e^{iT}-1}) \, dx = 0 \qquad (9)$$

The corresponding first order conditions with respect to the hiring age h and the number of workers n, had they been maintained as endogenous variables in the firm's decision, were:

$$A = 0$$

$$\frac{\partial \pi}{\partial h} = \int_0^n \{i(V-A) + \frac{\partial A}{\partial h}\} \, (\frac{e^{iT}}{e^{iT}-1}) \, dx = 0$$

The three first order conditions jointly specified the optimal number of job positions - and hence the number of workers employed by the firm - as well as the optimal hiring and retirement ages of these workers. Given the condition that A=0, the marginal worker, with the optimal hiring and retirement ages, would yield a zero present discounted value of the rents. Hiring an additional worker, hiring a worker younger than the optimal hiring age or keeping a worker beyond the optimal retirement age will decrease the present value of the firm's profits and will not be in the firm's interest. However, intra-marginal workers would yield positive rents but it is still not in the firm's interest to hire them at an age younger than the optimal hiring age or employ them beyond the optimal retirement age.

Given that both V and A are unspecified functions of the number of jobs and that it is difficult to solve the integrals in the first order conditions, it

121

was assumed that the solutions to the first order conditions require that the integrand in them be zero. Focusing again only on the first order condition for the retirement age, this requires that (8) is set to zero. Hence, for the interest rate i not equal to zero, profit maximization requires that,

$$\frac{\partial A}{\partial R} = i(V - A) \qquad\qquad (10)$$

We assume without further specification that the second order conditions for a maximum are satisfied by the solutions specified above for the first order conditions.

6.3 The optimal retirement ages for casual workers

We have argued in chapter 3 that in the case of casual workers in casual jobs, our measure of the rent r_j ($=m_j - w_j$) would be a function of the number of workers employed by the firm. It is not a function of the hiring age or the retirement age. The reason given for this was that if a worker was more productive than other workers by virtue of having better general skills (for example, as a result of age or experience), his wage would be correspondingly higher so that the difference between the marginal product and the wage would not be affected.

Since the firm's share of the rent from the casual worker holding the jth casual job position is independent of the hiring and retirement ages and with the firm assumed not to pay any hiring and training costs, the value of V for this job position becomes:

$$V = r/i \qquad\qquad (11)$$

That is, the jth job position is in the nature of a consol yielding the coupon payment r in perpetuity to the firm. Hence, with both r and i being independent of R under our assumptions about casual workers, the first order profit maximizing condition for casual workers in casual jobs becomes,

$$\partial V/\partial R = 0 \qquad \text{for all R} \qquad\qquad (12)$$

(12) holds for all casual job positions in the firm and for all values of R. That is, the firm will be indifferent as to the retirement age of casual workers. Therefore, the firm would not, *ceteris paribus*, have an interest in offering to casual workers implicit or explicit work contracts longer than a

single period.[7] Hence, the question of a firm's preferred retirement age for its workers and a MR policy for them does not arise in the case of casual workers.

To touch briefly on the implications of the case where there are positive hiring and training costs, the analysis similar to that in chapter 5 implies that either (i) the firm would not pay any part of these costs or (ii) the firm pays some part of this cost and would find it profit maximizing to keep the worker until his death! However, since workers can move to other firms without any loss in productivity and wages, and the firm cannot legally compel the worker to stay with it until his death it would not be willing to pay any part of the hiring and training costs as long as they are a variable cost specific to the worker. Case (i) would apply and, as (12) implies, the firm would be indifferent as to the retirement age of such a worker and would not need to impose a mandatory retirement age to terminate his employment with the firm. Conversely, the firm would not have a special interest in inducing any casual worker to stay with the firm by entering into explicit or implicit contracts of long duration.

6.4 The optimal retirement age for career workers

The profit maximizing condition for career workers in career jobs is (10). This yields the firm's optimal retirement age for its workers as:

$$R^* = R(\tau, g, i; h^*, n^*) \tag{13}$$

where τ stands for experience and g for age. As chapter 3 had shown, R^*, h^* (the optimal hiring age) and n^* (the optimal number of workers) are determined simultaneously by the firm's profit maximization.

In (10), V and A are both functions of the firm's share of the rents generated in the job and, therefore, are functions of the experience - representing the worker's acquired firm-specific skills - and age - representing the capacity to work, health etc. - of the worker. Consequently, the optimal retirement age is a function of these variables.

Both V and A are positive for intra-marginal career workers so that, at the optimal retirement age, such workers yield positive rents to the firm. If these workers were kept beyond this retirement age , they would still yield positive rents for some more time, with their marginal product greater than their wage. It would, therefore, seem that the firm could increase its profits by continuing to employing them. This is not so since they are occupying a job position and a younger replacement worker would yield greater rents to

123

the firm. Employing both the initial worker and the replacement worker will also not increase the firm's profits since this would mean an increase in the number of job positions beyond the optimal number. Therefore, the firm would want to replace its workers at the optimal retirement age even if their marginal product exceeds their wage at that age and they yield positive rents to the firm.

6.5 The optimal retirement age and innovations

The optimal retirement age is implied by the intertemporal substitution of workers in the firm's job positions. Suppose there is technological change such that the workers' productivity increases. An identical increase in productivity which increases the firm's share of the rents in each instance of time for all generations of workers including the current one, to α times their former level would imply that $V' = \alpha.V$, $A' = \alpha.A$, and $\partial A'/\partial R = \alpha.\partial A/\partial R$, with $\alpha > 1$, with the prime ' indicating the values of the relevant variable after the technological shift. The first order profit maximization condition after the increase in productivity would be:

$$\partial A'/\partial R = i(V' - A')$$

which yields:

$$\alpha.\partial A/\partial R = i(\alpha.V - \alpha.A)$$

which simplifies to:

$$\partial A/\partial R = i(V - A)$$

which is identical with (10), so that there would be no change in the optimal retirement age resulting from the technological change. This is so even though the firm's share of the rents from the worker would have increased at - and, if the worker had been kept on, beyond - the optimal retirement age.

However, most instances of technological change do not increase the productivity of each generation of workers on a given job in the same proportion. Succeeding generations are often better educated or/and in better tune with the emerging types of equipment - for example, computers and software during the last decade - so that the workers from the future generations possess a better capacity for firm-specific skills and are expected to generate higher rents than the workers, at identical ages and with identical experience, of the current generation. Such technological change will shift the optimal retirement age. To speculate on this, suppose that the rent function for the present generation stays unchanged and that for the future generation shifts upwards. That is, in (10), while A does not change, V increases. Note that V is heavily weighted by the rents generated by the future generations. Consequently, in (10), the right hand side increases, so that $\partial A/\partial R$ must be higher than before the technological change. With $\partial^2 A/\partial R^2 < 0$ in the neighbourhood of the retirement age, this would require a decrease in the optimal retirement age for the current generation of workers.

For casual workers, as discussed earlier, an increase in productivity due to better or more general skills within a technological regime is matched by a corresponding increase in wages so that the firm's share of the rents from a worker's employment in a given casual job position does not change. If we extend this over technological regimes and assume that a shift in technology will not change the firm's share of the rents from its casual jobs, such shifts will not alter the conclusions derived above on the optimal retirement age for casual workers holding casual jobs. That is, the firm will not have an interest in offering long term contracts to casual workers or trying to get rid of them at a preferred retirement age of its choosing. This will be so whether the technological shifts are identical between the future and the current generations or confined only to the future generations.

Comparing the above conclusions for the casual and career workers, technological changes, whether over future generations only or both the future and present generations, may or may not change the firm's share of the rents from the firm's casual jobs. If they do not do so, they will leave the firm indifferent as to the retirement age of its casual workers and will therefore have no impact on the retirement policies applied to such workers. There is, of course, the possibility that some of the workers in the existing generation cannot operate the new technology at all and are not employable under it. For career workers, if the technologically induced increases in the firm's share of the rents are proportionately identical between the future generations and the current one, there would no impact on the optimal retirement ages. However, if such changes increase the rents only of the future generations, the firm would want to retire its current generation of workers earlier than if the technological change had not occurred. Their retirement age would also be earlier than the firm's optimal retirement age for the future generations of workers.

Other changes which can shift the rent function are changes in the general health of the workers. Changes which shift the rent function proportionately at all ages for all generations of workers would not, as seen above, change the optimal retirement age for the firm's workers. However, a considerable part of the improvements in health have resulted in much better health and in the ability to continue working effectively at later ages than used to be the case. Assume that this is such as to shift the rent function upwards much more so at the later ages than at the earlier ones. Without being too specific about it, these 'later ages' may be taken to be the 50s and 60s. In equation (10), such a disproportionate shift would increase $\partial A/\partial R$ - that is, the firm's share of the rent at the retirement age - proportionately more than the increase in V and A, since the latter also include the rents at the earlier ages. Hence, at the previously optimal retirement age, the left hand side of (10) would increase by more than the right hand side. Since $\partial^2 A/\partial R^2 < 0$ in the neighbourhood of the retirement age, optimality would then require an increase in the retirement age. *Ceteris paribus*, improvements in health of the above kind thus lead to increases in the retirement ages of career workers of the current and the future generations.

The development and increasing use of new kinds of machines and tools requiring less strength and agility to perform many jobs, may also allow older workers - whose strength, stamina and mental and physical flexibility have declined from their younger ages - to retain their productivity on the job to later ages, or even merely to slowdown the decrease in productivity with advancing age. Such a technical change would have the effect of increasing $\partial A/\partial R$ more than in proportion to i(V-A) in equation (10) and will, as argued earlier, lead to a rise in the optimal retirement age.

There are clearly many kinds of 'innovations' which can shift the rent functions of career workers. As we have seen above, some of these shifts may be common to the current and future generations, and may be proportionate at all ages. They will not shift the optimal retirement age. Other shifts may be common to the current and future generations but increase the firm's share of the rents more at some ages than others. We have given examples of this from the realm of the improvements in the relative health of older workers and in changes in physical capital which allow the same work to be done at the older ages with less strength, agility and stamina etc. The latter could also benefit the types of workers, such as the relatively weaker men, the relatively weaker women and those with certain kinds of disabilities who may possess relatively less of physical strength and other needed characteristics to do the jobs as well as some stronger men. Such changes were shown to raise the optimal retirement ages for the affected workers of the current and future generations.

There can also be innovations which raise the productivity and the rents generated by future generations more than of the current generation. An example of this would be machines which are more productive when operated by the coming generations than the current one. An example of this from my own personal experience would be computers and their software. Such an innovation would lower the optimal retirement age for the current generation, while possibly, but not necessarily, raising it for future generations. If this innovation was unanticipated and the current generation was already tied into contracts of some sort for the previously optimal retirement age, there would have to be unanticipated 'early retirements'. This topic is dealt with in chapter 9.

6.6 Retirement versus reductions in wages

The theories of MR have as their *raison d'être* the explanation of why firms choose to lay off a worker at the age designated for MR rather than to cut his wages by some appropriate amount. Unfortunately, none of the existing theories of MR really explain in a satisfactory manner why firms resort to MR rather than cutting the worker's real wage w down to or even below the level of his marginal productivity. To see this, consider Lazear's incentives model.

The MR age R_m in the Lazear model is that at which the worker's marginal product, denoted as MP or m, equals his reservation wage $\underline{w}$ (Lazear, 1979, p. 1265, equation 1). That is,

At $R_m - \epsilon$, $\epsilon > 0$, w > m and w > $\underline{w}$

At $R_m + \underline{\epsilon}$, $\underline{\epsilon} > 0$, $\underline{w}$ > m

If at R_m, the real wage w was cut so as to equal m, the worker would retire voluntarily and MR would not have to be imposed on him. Lazear deduces that MR has to be imposed for the firm to get rid of the worker because of his implicit assumption that the firm would maintain the wage path w*(t) it had optimally established (to prevent cheating on the job) *prior* to R_m. Given wage flexibility, the optimal policy for the firm would seem to be to cut his wage to equal his productivity and let him have a choice: accept the reduced wage or leave of his own volition, effectively resulting in retirement. The only reason, then, for the MR decision to be the optimal one for the firm is the implicit rigidity of the w*(t) path - established optimally prior to R_m - being continued beyond R_m.

Now consider Lapp's insurance model. The firm *ex ante* agrees to insure the worker against an uncertain age-related decline in his productivity and finds it optimal to terminate this contract at age R_m, thereby imposing MR at R_m. But the alternative available to the firm in a flexible wages context is to terminate the insurance contract at R_m and reduce the wages to equal m beyond R_m. The worker may choose to retire voluntarily at R_m if w $<$ w or choose to continue working if w $>$ w. In the latter case, R_m is clearly not the optimal age for a layoff, as MR implies, for either the firm or the worker. It is the optimal layoff age for the firm only if the firm is barred from cutting the wage below its pre-R_m level to equal a declining m.

The bottom line to MR being an optimal policy for the firm has to be either some sort of rigidity in the wage pattern or an efficiency wage model. The former could be imposed by custom or law, by union rules or the resentment by the worker against a wage cut. It could also be due to the cost of monitoring changes in marginal productivity. Each of these factors has been cited in the institutional literature on MR. Note that the efficiency wage argument does not argue for wage rigidity but rather for the dependence of the worker's productivity on his wage relative to some reference wage.

The relationships in the workplace between the firm and its workers and among the workers themselves have numerous norms, some maintained with greater commitment and some with lesser one. These informal norms often regulate the work effort put in by the workers (Elster, 1989; Rebitzer, 1993, p.1419). In particular, Keynesian economists have generally emphasized the importance of relativity in labour supply decisions (for example, see Rima (1984)). Further, a number of writers (Hicks, 1974, pp. 64-67; Okun, 1981, ch. 3; Krueger and Summers, 1987; among others) have argued that workers judge their wage in the context of notions of 'fair' or 'just' wages relative to some benchmark. We translate these ideas in the current context to mean that a worker would resent a wage that he considers to be unfair. Such resentment may show itself in quits, more so in early rather than later years of one's work-life, and in forms of shirking and malfeasance on the job, which lower the worker's productivity.

There can be a variety of factors that can make a worker view his wage as 'unfair'. A cut in wages *perceived* by the worker to be unfair seems to be such a factor. The worker cannot measure his own productivity and may view himself late in his work-life as doing the work just as well as he used to do when younger. The assertion of many a worker laid off by reason of age is often that he is still as good as he ever was. Given this attitude, a reduction in his wage would be viewed by the worker as unfair. The firm's response to the declining productivity or the increasing age of the worker by cutting his wage is then self-fulfilling and self-defeating: the cut in wages lowers the worker's morale and causes his productivity to fall further. Since the work-place is rife with both norms and politics, there may also be other repercussions in terms of the co-workers' morale and time spent on politicking rather than on the job, thereby inducing reductions in their productivity. The firm's optimal response to a worker's declining productivity due to his advancing age may, therefore, be to lay off the worker, rather than to cut his wages. Okun (1981, p. 131) argues that such considerations "make layoffs a 'clean hands' solution relative to temporary cuts in pay".

A somewhat related alternative to these ideas on a fair wage and resulting wage rigidity is the concept of an efficiency wage. Such a wage has been defined as one where a worker's productivity depends positively upon his wage (Akerlof and Yellen, 1986). Such an assumption can be based on Hick's or Okun's notions of a fair wage or fair play. It can also be justified on other grounds (see Akerlof and Yellen, 1986, p.2 for some of these). Among these reasons, the most relevant for our model is that a worker's productivity depends on his morale and that a worker would tend to shirk at wages less than some reference wage.

A number of efficiency wage models have been presented in recent years to show that cutting wages in the presence of the positive dependence of the effort and the marginal product on wages may reduce the firm's profits (Solow, 1986; Shapiro and Stiglitz, 1984; Foster and Wan, 1986; Salop, 1986; and Weiss, 1986, among others). To illustrate this, assume that the firm's short-term production function can be written as,

$$x = x(e(w)n) \tag{14}$$

where x is output, e is effort per worker, w is the real wage rate and n is employment. Assuming perfect competition, the firm's profits in real terms are,

$$x(e(w)n) - wn \tag{15}$$

which gives the profit-maximizing conditions as,

$$\partial x/\partial n - w = 0$$

$$\partial x/\partial e \cdot \partial e/\partial w - n = 0 \tag{16}$$

which yield $w^*=f(n)$, where w^* is the profit maximizing wage rate.

Alternatively, substituting for n from (14), $w^* = w^*(x)$. A wage w less than w^* reduces the firm's profits and will not be optimal.

The specification in (14) of the effort function e(w) with $\partial e/\partial w > 0$ is incomplete unless the wage w is specified with respect to the appropriate reference wage. Thus, in the incentives model, "to induce its workers not to shirk, the firm attempts to pay its worker more than the 'going wage'" (Shapiro and Stiglitz, 1984, p. 433). Here, the 'going wage' for the given occupation and industry is the reference wage. That is, the Shapiro and Stiglitz argument suggests rewriting the effort function as,

$$e = e(w/w\#)$$

where w# is the reference or 'going wage'. The reference wage may be real in some contexts and nominal in others. Arguments have been presented in the literature for each of these possibilities. In terms of the past experience of a given worker filling a given job, the reference wage for the job may be the wage recently experienced by him in that job or even his past peak wage. There may be more than one relevant reference wage.

To incorporate the efficiency wage arguments in our framework, assume that the worker's morale and productivity suffer if his nominal wage W falls relative to his reference nominal wage W#, i.e., the wage that he considers to be a fair wage. For simplification, a reasonable approximation to this reference wage will be taken to be the recent past peak nominal wage[8] which the worker had received from his firm. Under this assumption, aside from the peak wage, we are not really concerned with the wage the worker receives over the intra-marginal years of his work-life since the wage path does not enter the marginality condition, equation (16) above. To determine the impact of the marginal period's wage on the retirement decision of the firm, note that for the given worker in the jth job position,

$$r = m - w$$

For a constant price level over time, now define the effort function e such that,

$$e = e(w/w\#)$$

From (14), the worker's marginal product m depends positively upon e. Then, for constant prices and a cut in nominal wages such that $w < w\#$,

$$\frac{\partial r}{\partial w-} = \frac{\partial m}{\partial e} \cdot \frac{\partial e}{\partial(w-/w\#)} \quad \frac{1}{w\#} \quad - 1$$

where w- is a cut in real wages corresponding to the cut in W. The right hand side in the above equation may be positive, negative or zero. That is, a cut in the marginal period's nominal wage of the first worker would reduce both his marginal product and his real wage, so that the firm's rent from him could increase or *decrease*. *Ceteris paribus*, the optimal retirement age will be postponed in the former case; in the latter case, it will become an earlier one. Clearly, in the latter case, it is not to the advantage of the firm to cut nominal wages since this would reduce the worker's rent and the firm's share in it, and hence, reduce the firm's profits. Further, even in the former case, if the nominal wages of both the initial and the replacement workers are cut such that the equality (16) continues to hold, the optimal retirement age will not change. Consequently, the circumstances under which the firm can reduce a worker's wage close to his retirement years and find it profitable to retain him are severely circumscribed. With the retirement ages far in the future - long after the hiring ages - and with the impact of a cut in nominal wages on marginal product involving a moral hazard element and varying from worker to worker, few firms may find it profitable to adopt a policy of nominal wage cuts as a serious alternative to a MR policy.

If, as assumed above, the fair reference wage is the nominal wage W# rather than its real value, W#/P, where P is the price level, the firm can allow the real wage of the worker to decline up to the rate of inflation without triggering a reduction in effort. This possibility allows some reduction in real wages in inflationary periods and allows the worker to be employed even after the decline in his productivity has set in. That is, periods with greater inflation are more likely to show decreases in real wages, with continued employment, than periods with lower rates of inflation. This implication holds only if the reference wage was a pre-specified nominal wage, as the Keynesian literature tends to assume, rather than a real one, as the efficiency wage literature tends to assume.

We used the peak nominal wage as the reference wage for purposes of illustration. The reference wage would depend upon the particular context of the worker. The economy may then have a variety of reference wages. A reference wage appropriate to a worker who recognizes the decline in his productivity might be a ratio of some real wage to marginal product from his past experience, assuming that this marginal product is easily observable.

The argument for wage cuts over MR, with the wage varying with a declining marginal product, also requires that the firm should be able to measure this marginal product at zero or negligible cost and that the worker trusts the firm's assessment of it. There are often significant costs of monitoring performance and productivity (Slavick, 1966; Rebitzer, 1993), especially in large firms. Further, if the worker cannot easily verify the firm's assessment of his productivity, a layoff may be preferred by the firm and the worker to the prospect of *continual* wage cuts as the MP declines over time.

An additional reason for MR in our theory is as follows. In order to employ a worker beyond R*, which is the firm's preferred retirement age for the worker, the firm would have to pay him a wage which is not greater than his MP less the average rent the firm would keep from his (younger) replacement's employment. If his MP falls sufficiently or the employment of the replacement worker is extremely profitable, this difference would become *negative*, implying a negative wage beyond R*. In a less unfavourable context, this optimal wage could be positive but could decline sharply beyond R*, making wage cuts embarrassing for the firm to offer and inducing severe resentment from the workers. The efficiency wage argument would then imply continual declines in productivity due to this resentment, in addition to the age-related decline in productivity. It is this possibility of *continuing* wage cuts beyond R* rather than a single downward adjustment - in addition to our arguments on the rental value of the job position - which are vital to the firm's preference for a policy of MR over wage cuts as the optimal rule.

6.7 A diagrammatic illustration

Hutchens (1985) has recently pointed out that MR is incompatible with the standard theory of human capital, arguing that "specifically trained workers receive a wage less than their VMP (value of the marginal product). In that case MR would be irrational; firms would want to keep workers with a wage less than VMP" (p. 21). This argument applied to the replacement model of this chapter would imply that the firm could increase its profits by hiring the replacement worker while keeping the older one, since both have a wage less than VMP. This conclusion is incorrect, as was shown in chapter 3. We repeat below the gist of that analysis in the context of a simple, one period model used for illustration purposes.

In a one period analysis, the profit maximizing firm has an optimal number of jobs or positions for a given wage rate and a given marginal productivity pattern. Assuming diminishing MP (m) of labour, figure 6.3 shows the MP curves for two types of workers. Assume that the MP of 'older' workers is given by AB and the of 'younger' workers by CD. For a wage rate w, the optimal number of older workers, if younger workers were

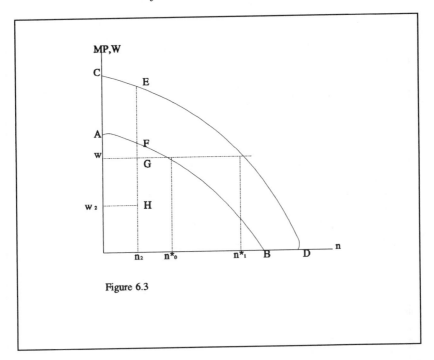

Figure 6.3

not available, would be n^*_0. But if the latter were available, a younger worker, for any intra-marginal position, say n_2, yields a higher 'rent' (= m-w) than an older worker, so that the firm will not hire or keep the latter. Further, in this case, at the marginal position n_1^*, $w = m$ for the younger workers but $w > m$ for the older workers, so that the latter will again not be hired or kept. Consequently, if the more efficient younger workers are available, the firm would not retain the less efficient older workers at identical wage rates even though for intra-marginal positions such as n_2, the older workers have $w > m$.

The older worker can be retained if his wage is reduced sufficiently to make the rent (m-w) from him identical with that from a younger worker: that is, the older worker will have to accept a lower wage to get the job, and, if already employed, accept this lower wage or be laid off (retired). Figure 6.3 also illustrates another of our arguments. For the job position n_2, the older worker will be retained if his wage is reduced to w_2 (with GH = EF). This could be a sufficiently drastic cut in wages to be embarrassing for the firm to offer and for the workers to accept, so that Okun's 'clean hands' notion may make retirement preferable to a wage cut for both the firm and

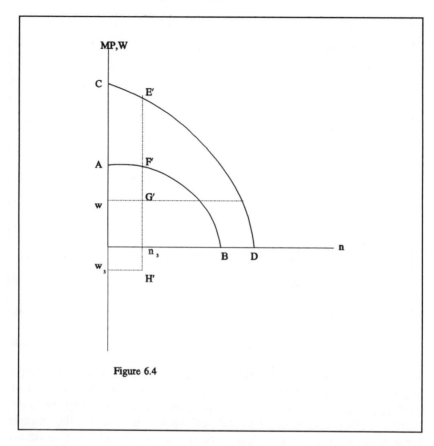

Figure 6.4

the worker.

In an extreme case, shown in figure 6.4, at position n_3, the wage cut required to make the older worker competitive with the younger one gives a wage rate w_3, which is negative since the required net rent for employment is E'G' and G'H' = E'F'. Clearly, retirement rather than keeping on the older worker at a negative wage will be the only feasible outcome in this case.

6.8 Team sports: an illustration

Professional team sports are in a sense reflective of firm-specific skills: a player's productivity depends upon knowledge of other players' strengths and weaknesses, in short on being 'part of the team'. Age-related declines in productivity also tend to be severe in physical sports at relatively early ages, with young replacement workers being more profitable than older existing ones. Our model predicts that the team owners would have a preferred retirement - and replacement - age and that a specified retirement age as in MR plans should be common in such physical team sports. Further, with wages tracking MP, wage increases up to the peak performance period, with wage declines thereafter, should be common in such sports.

In reality, team sports do not seem to have MR. What they do have is employment contracts of a fixed duration or with the termination date at the firm's option (and sometimes the player's). The fixed duration contracts can be viewed as a form of MR. Those with an open termination date at the firm's option serve the same role as MR under conditions of considerable uncertainty about the worker's MP. Such contracts, along with the considerable wage increases followed by wage decreases in the major professional leagues, provide evidence for our theory.

We have argued above that the optimizing firm may find that in order to employ a worker with declining productivity while extracting the due rent from him, the firm may have to offer a negative wage (see figure 6.4) or, in any case, a 'ridiculously low' wage. An illustration of this can be provided from team sports where a weak aging player on a team could have a positive MP, in the sense that he stops some shots, etc., but leads to the team losing a sufficient number of games to cut into the ticket sales and result in losses for the team's owners. His replacement by a younger superior player could lead to sufficient wins to increase sales and lead to profits. The optimal wage offer to the weak aging player would then be a negative one. But if the available replacements were no better than him, then he would be retained and the optimal wage offer to him would be a positive one. Hence, the duration of employment - that is, period up to MR - and the optimal wage offer, for given MP near the termination date, depend critically upon the expected performance of the available replacements.

The number of players or positions on a team is usually fixed and the above arguments may seem to be based on this fixity. However, in the long run, this number need not be arbitrarily fixed but is likely to be optimally determined by the team owner's profit maximization, with the team owners lobbying and politicking to change the number of these fixed in the past to their currently optimal number. In fact, the number of jobs for each position on the field is also likely to be optimally determined in the long run.

Our analysis above also shows that workers are kept into the declining years if there is heavy discounting of the rents from replacement workers. This occurs if the interest or discount rates are high and/or if the period of employment of the initial worker is long. The latter tends to be shorter in physical team sports than in office-bound professions. The latter should then show a much stronger tendency to employ workers well into their declining years than physical sports do.

By comparison, Lazear's incentives model would imply that the aging player would have a rising wage path, contrary to general experience, over his employment period. But there may be an even more fundamental refutation of Lazear's theory involved here. It is reasonable to infer that players would like to continue to play and be paid until late in life, perhaps as late as in other occupations. This usually occurs from age 60 to 70 years. Their reservation wage need be no higher than in other occupations. The MR age in the incentives model is that at which this reservation wage equals the marginal product. There is no reason to expect this equality would occur in the twenties and thirties in professional sports when it occurs at much later times in other occupations. In fact, the popular belief seems to be that players are laid off or retired at a date of the team owners' choosing although the players would like to continue playing even at reduced salaries. Such behaviour is consistent with the predictions of our theory.

6.9 Co-ordination of retirement ages

Firms generally do not have a customized MR age, distinct for each worker, but offer a common one, at least for each class of occupations (Kreps, 1961; Fox and Kerpen, 1964). Several considerations within the context of our hypothesis indicate why this should be so. One of these is that the model implies a firm's preferred retirement *age* for given patterns of acquisition of firm-specific skills and of health. The firm offering a MR age at the time of hiring will be trying to judge these patterns over a long and uncertain future. Given the degree of uncertainty, it might be best for the firm to fix a common retirement age at which the profit maximizing condition (10) is likely to be met by most workers and make *ad hoc* arrangements for odd cases. These can consist of some early layoffs, early retirement, 'golden handshakes' and re-hiring on a special basis after the set retirement age, etc. Some of these policies are related to pensions and are considered in chapter 9.

The second consideration making for a common retirement age within the firm is the cost of designing individual retirement ages. To be optimal, from equation (10), each worker's marginal product towards the end of this career will have to be assessed, as well as that of the worker replacing him. Further, an individual retirement policy is apt to be viewed as a layoff by those retired earlier than others. This could raise problems of morale and dissatisfaction among workers.

A third consideration is that the workers may apply a concept of fairness to their retirement ages, as to their wages (Gordon, 1960; Kreps, 1961). Thus, older workers may feel very upset if their firm's retirement age is earlier than that of other similar firms. The existence and importance of norms in the workplace is again worth emphasizing. As pointed out above, "one often finds informal norms among the workers that regulate their work effort" (Elster, 1989, p. 101). The retirement ages offered by other similar firms is often one of these norms. For a firm to offer a lower retirement age would be a violation of a norm and could cause its workers to reduce their effort and productivity. A retirement age consistent with the general one for similar occupations eliminates this risk.

Similar considerations are likely to induce firms to have a uniform MR age for broad groups of its occupations and sometimes for all its employees. Usage of a societal norm for the retirement age, such as the age at which social security payments start, may make the firm's retirement policy more acceptable to its workers and cut down on the morale problems that could occur. This would imply that a positive relationship is to be expected between the age at which social security benefits start and MR ages in common usage.

6.10 Workers and mandatory retirement

We have not said anything so far on the worker's decision on continuing to work versus retirement. Our analysis has implicitly assumed that the firm confronts the worker being hired with an offer that includes the opportunity to acquire firm-specific skills, thereby generating retirement rents and sharing in them until a retirement age specified by the firm. The retirement age is part of a package offer. It may or may not be in the worker's own individual interests. Given a choice between the specified retirement age and its absence from an otherwise identical package, the worker would prefer the latter since this would keep his options open and let him decide later in his career on the retirement age that is optimal for him. This is not to say that the worker does not willingly choose a package with a MR age over other packages available in the economy, the latter without a MR age. In the context of our hypothesis, the former would have the relative advantage of offering the possibility of acquiring firm-specific skills and hence of earning a higher wage than in occupations without such a possibility. But the acquisition of firm-specific skills leads to long-term (implicit or explicit) job contracts, which the firm finds it optimal to terminate at a certain age of the workers. Therefore, while workers may willingly choose job offers with a MR clause, finding it in their interests to accept the package containing them, it is not necessarily in the interest of any given worker or of workers generally to have such a clause in their contracts.

The sets of considerations that go into utility maximization - tastes and individual's income or wealth - are quite different from those that go into profit or present value maximization. The former are dealt with in chapter 8. The latter were considered in this chapter. The rest of this section briefly touches on some of the reasons for the differences in the firms' and workers' preferred retirement functions.

If the MR age was an individual good, freely traded in the market and not merely part of a package, one could assume that trades in this good would match firms and workers wanting the same retirement age. However, the retirement age is the end point of an implicit work contract which jointly produces acquisition of skills, marginal product and wages and eventually a retirement decision by the firm. We should not, therefore, expect that the firm's preferred retirement ages are necessarily those in the workers' interests.

It is in the interest of firms to employ workers while they are sufficiently healthy. At the same time, ignoring the palliative aspects of having a job, workers can best enjoy retirement - that is, full-time leisure - when they are in good health. This would imply that if workers had acceptable levels of resources to retire earlier than the firm's preferred retirement age, they would do so. But if they had inadequate levels of resources for the retirement years, they might want to retire later than the firm's preferred retirement age.

6.11 Some implications of our framework

6.11.1 At the core of our ideas on retirement is the importance of firm-specific skills, the nature of retirement as a replacement rather than a layoff decision, the decline in productivity at older ages and the decision on the retirement age as a unilateral decision by the firm. Auxiliary elements of our framework are the resentment by the worker of MR as a constraint on his work supply decision, and notions of fairness. This section draws the implications of these ideas and compares them with the implications of other theories on MR as well as with the established empirical knowledge on MR.

Long term job attachment in our model flows from the existence of firm-specific skills and the sharing of rents between the firm and the worker.

The larger these rents are, the stronger is the bonding of the firm and the worker and the more important is MR as the replacement decision. Consequently, career rather than casual (general skills only) jobs would be likely to have MR. To illustrate, construction and farm workers would not be likely to face MR, even though their professions may seem to be very susceptible to the possibility of shirking and malfeasance and should have MR according to Lazear's theory. In reality, these industries do not tend to have MR (Parnes, 1981, p. 156). By comparison, office workers would be more likely to face MR.

Further, neither firms nor workers find it optimal for career jobs to have hirings on an hourly or piece-rate basis so that jobs with these will not tend to have MR policies (Fox and Kerpen, 1964, p. 17). This is also explained by Lazear's theory (1979, p. 1277) in that piece-work constitutes a compensation scheme designed to make workers perform optimally so that his incentives scheme and MR are not needed for such workers. In terms of Lapp's insurance scheme, piece-rate workers are as likely to need insurance against age-related declines in productivity as time-rate workers so that both should show the same likelihood of MR.

The strength of job attachment and its converse, the likelihood of low turnover, are greater for firm-specific jobs than for ones with only general skills. Hence, low worker turnover in firms indicates a higher probability of firm-specific skills and hence of MR policies.

Of any two firm-specific skill occupations, the one with the longer skill-acquisition (training, learning on the job, etc.) period would tend to have a steeper MP and wage path. Since general skills tend to be learnt to a proportionately greater degree prior to job acceptance - for example, in schools, universities, training institutes etc. - and tend to have shorter skill-acquisition periods on the job, jobs with steeper wage profiles will tend to be more firm-specific skill ones and have a higher probability of MR. Lazear found a positive relationship between the steepness of the wage path and MR, interpreting the wage increases along the path as unanticipated ones. His unanticipated variable (AWG - E(AWG)) measured the wage growth not explained by the worker characteristics of sex, colour, education, marital status, urban-rural residence and age of first job. This variable did not exclude learning-on-the-job to which firm-specific skills are related, so that it could capture the influence of anticipated wage increases from firm-specific skill acquisition. Lazear's finding of a positive correlation between (AWG - E(EWG)) and MR can thus be interpreted as evidence consistent with our hypothesis.

6.11.2 Firms do not have a specific optimal retirement age for casual workers and would be willing to retain them as long as the workers themselves want to work. Therefore, if a MR age were to be imposed by the firm as an upper limit dictated largely by the worker's declining health and his inability to perform the job, it would tend to be later than for career jobs. To the extent that company sponsored training programs are indicative of firm-specific skills, such programs will be associated with lower MR ages, as they are (Leigh, 1984). Further, general training is indicative of casual jobs with higher MR ages. Such training is often given in vocational schools, as well as the armed forces. Leigh found that such training and the age of MR were indeed positively correlated. Conversely, career jobs with workers and firms losing from a separation, would have longer job tenure than casual ones but would have earlier MR ages. Consequently, the length of job tenure and the age of MR should be negatively correlated, as Lazear (1981. p. 1282) and Leigh (pp. 527-9) confirm.[9]

In the U.S., since blacks tend to be more concentrated in more casual jobs, they would have later ages of MR than whites, if the effect of education was controlled. Lazear (1981, pp. 1282-3) finds it to be so, though offering an explanation for it in terms of the white variable proxying higher property income. Leigh (1984, p. 527) confirmed this finding.

Since discrimination has tended to force white women into more casual jobs than white males, they are less susceptible to MR policies by virtue of their sex but if they are subjected to MR, they will tend to have higher retirement ages.

Since more educated workers would tend to have a greater ability to acquire firm-specific skills, the level of education and jobs with MR would be positively correlated. Further, since the more educated workers would tend to have greater ability to learn new techniques and thereby update their skills, their knowledge and skills would become outdated less slowly in a changing world and their replacement by new workers would become profitable for the firm at a later age. Hence, while the more educated workers are likely to face MR policies more often than the less educated workers, the MR ages for any given type of occupation would be higher for the more educated workers (Lazear, 1979, pp. 1281-82; Leigh, 1984, pp. 527).

Firms suffer a loss from the separation of a worker with firm-specific skills, whether this separation is full-time - a quit - or a part-time one. In the latter case, the worker continues working on a part-time basis. By comparison, a casual worker can be employed on a full-time or part-time basis without such a loss. Consequently, part-time work is less likely to be associated with MR and, if MR is imposed, would be positively correlated with the age of MR. Leigh (1984) confirms this.

Technical improvements which are 'embodied' in workers usually require changes in their education and training prior to their taking on the job or soon after. They often increase the productivity and the amount the firm gets in rents - e.g., with a constant proportion or even a somewhat lower proportion of rents to marginal productivity - from replacement workers more than from the currently employed - and especially the older - workers. Our model implies that this would increase the likelihood of MR and lower the optimal retirement age. If this technical change was unanticipated, it could not affect the pre-set MR age for the current generation but would induce the firm to institute more generous early retirement plans to the current generation (but not future generations) of workers. More rapid technical change would, therefore, lead to firms 'buying out' jobs from more workers and to an increase in the number of induced early retirements. The number of early retirement plans and the amounts offered in them, and the wage difference between workers of different generations would then be positively correlated.

If the embodied technical change was anticipated but was uncertain as to timing, our model implies that the firm would protect itself by having MR and by reducing the MR age. Occupations with more static skill patterns would thus have a lower probability of MR and later MR ages. Intuitively, rapidly evolving fields of work tend to retire workers earlier than others. Further, since more rapid embodied technical change and wage increases between 'generations' - with each generation representing a different level of embodied technology - are positively correlated and such technical change and MR are also positively correlated in our theory, the increases in wages between generations and MR are also positively correlated in our theory.

6.12 The elimination of mandatory retirement policies

The general trend of ideas in recent years has been to treat MR policies as an aspect of discrimination against older workers and therefore to call for legislation to make MR policies illegal. If such legislation were to be enacted, what would be its effect in our context?

If the jobs are casual ones, the firm would not have a preferred retirement age and would not suffer a loss in profits if it lets the workers retire at their preferred ages. This is, of course, so if the nature of the skills - that is, whether general or firm-specific - is the only factor determining whether the firm has a preferred retirement age or not. In such a case, legislation to eliminate MR policies would not affect the age at which casual workers retire, and would not impose any private or social costs on the firm or the economy.

For career jobs, with the possible conflict (see section 6.10 above and chapters 8 and 9 below) between the workers' preferred retired age (R^h) and the firm's preferred retirement age (R^f), the abolition of MR as illegal would lead to different responses depending upon whether R^f is greater than or less than R^h. (See chapter 9 for a more detailed version of the following analysis).

First consider the case where $ER^h < R^f$. Prior to the abolition of MR, it would be profitable for the firm to induce the workers to stay until R^f. To do so, it would have instituted a 'conventional pension plan', defined as one in which the firm pays workers with $ER^h < R^f$ to increase ER^h to R^f. However, assuming a normal distribution of R^h, this would lead half of the workers to stay with the firm for some periods beyond R^f. Previously, the MR policy would have got rid of such workers. Without the MR policy, the firm would suffer a loss if such workers continue working or if it has to bribe them to leave at R^f. The firm may then find it profitable not to institute the conventional pension plan or to do so to a limited extent so that ER^h remains less than R^f and most of the workers leave by R^f. Hence, the abolition of MR would lead to a reduction in conventional pattern plans. This would be detrimental for workers in monetary terms.

Now consider the case where $ER^h > R^f$. Prior to the abolition of MR policies, this would have caused the firm to institute MR or a 'pattern plan', defined as one in which the firm pays its workers to lower ER^h to R^f. Presumably in these cases, the firm would have suffered a relatively significant loss from keeping workers older than R^f. If the legislation prevents firms from forcibly retiring such workers, it would have to increase its early retirement bonuses and increase its coverage and benefits under the pattern pension plans. Alternatively, it could continue to employ the workers until the age at which they wish to retire. This could be beyond R^f, thus imposing an inefficiency on the firm and the economy. In the short-run, for workers close to R^f, the unanticipated removal of MR provides an opportunity to receive an enhanced amount in the early retirement plan, for which the firm had not already provided for through lower wages, or to continue working beyond R^f. Both impose an unexpected and unplanned cost on the firm, so that some impact on its profits should be expected in the short run.

In terms of private or social costs, *the elimination of MR policies by legislation imposes a constraint on the firms' employment practices of career workers. It imposes an inefficiency on firms in the case where $ER^h > R^f$, and*

142

leads to a decrease in their profits. *It would tend to monetarily benefit such workers. For $ER^h < R^f$, it would lead to a decrease in the conventional pension plans or their benefits. It does not necessarily impose an inefficiency in the employment of casual workers, providing there are no restrictions on the downward adjustment of wages as productivity declines with age.*

In terms of employment, there would be some increase in the continued employment of workers beyond the previous MR ages. The workers who would continue in employment beyond the old MR ages are more likely to be in career occupations of the pattern pension plan type. Further, they are ones who are in the upper half of the R^h distribution. This requires examining the determinants of workers' places in the distribution. Standard microeconomic theory specifies these determinants as worker preferences between income and leisure - with the wage as the opportunity cost of leisure - and the worker's wealth. Among the latter would be private and public pension entitlements. Another determinant would be the worker's health. With retirement as a normal good, workers are more likely to retire earlier if they are sick or have more assets or lower wages. Blinder (1981, p. 44), Fields and Mitchell (1984, ch. 2) and chapter 9 below, present the relevant analysis for these assertions.

However, the desire for a minimum level of wealth or annuity at retirement would make the poorer, low wage workers delay retirement. They are then part of the upper half of the R^h distribution, so that more of them are likely to be forced out by MR policies. This is so for blacks in the United States (Parnes, 1981, p. 166).

Conclusion

It has often been suggested that the necessary condition for a firm to have a retirement policy is that, at its preferred retirement age, the firm must be paying its workers more than the value of their marginal product. This explains the profit maximizing firm's desire to terminate the worker and "is the bottom line to virtually all explanations of MR" (Lazear, 1979, page 1264). It is fundamental to Lazear's, Blinder's, and Lapp's models. The theory offered in this chapter and book differs markedly from this line of thinking.

In our theory, in the presence of firm-specific skills, the intra-marginal worker would have a marginal product - that is, for the *marginal* period of work - higher than his wage at the retirement age but is retired by the firm because the firm finds it profitable to replace him by a young worker. The need to retire the first worker arises partly from the decline in his productivity as his mental and physical capabilities decline with increasing age. These factors, in fact, explain the firm's desire to lay off - retire - the worker but it could, alternatively, reduce his wage by some appropriate amount. Our theory explains the firm's choice of the former over the latter by a fair wage or an efficiency wage hypothesis in the overall context of established workplace norms and the impact of violations of norms on effort. According to these, the worker's morale and productivity suffer if his nominal or real - depending upon the context and the established norm - wage, relative to some reference wage from his past experience, is reduced. Since age-related declines in productivity tend to be continual, the implied continual reductions in nominal wages are not, in general, the optimal response to the continual decline in productivity due to ageing, so that this decline would usually result in the retirement of the worker. Unionization with its standardization of wages further rules out the reduction in wages as a response to declining productivity.

Our model, with its emphasis on the sharing of firm-specific rents between the firm and the worker, has a built-in incentive scheme for the career worker not to shirk on the job and for the firm not to fire him unless he does shirk to an extent such that the firm's share of his rents declines below the rental value of the job. Since both parties - that is, the firm and the career worker - lose by a separation, neither is subject to a moral hazard. Further, the firm-specific sharing of rents is simpler than a scheme in which each or both parties post a bond ensuring their performance and good faith. This sharing of rents has the further advantage that the penalties for both parties from a job separation increase as their stake in continued employment increases through accumulation of firm-specific skills and the growth in rents. In this first stage, seniority and seniority premiums cement job attachment. In the later years of life, as the worker's physical and mental abilities begin to decline, so that the rents generated begin to decline and the firm's share of them falls below the rental value of the job, the penalty to the firm from a job separation disappears and the firm replaces the worker by another. In this secondary stage, increases in seniority, with their concomitant ageing, tend to erode the basis of job attachment.

Our analysis makes a strong distinction between career and casual workers. Long-term job attachment and MR are aspects of the former. Casual workers possessing only general skills would be free to move among firms. The firms would neither have an implicit contract for a long-term job with such workers nor would it need MR policies to terminate such workers.

The firm-specificity of skills is not the only possible explanation of long term job tenure. The latter would also result from implicit job contracts.

Insurance against wage and employment fluctuations has been offered as a possible cause of such contracts. Another cause, in the presence of worker heterogeneity, would be insurance provided by the firm against the worker eventually turning out to have a low productivity. Lapp (1985) has based his theory on insurance against an age related decline in productivity. Another possible reason is the wish of unions, as embodied in their contracts with firms. Lazear's (1979, 1981) theory of agency with job attachment and MR has already been discussed above. A seniority based promotion policy could also produce wages higher than productivity in more senior jobs, as in Carmichael (1983), and make MR policies optimal.It is quite likely that there can be a variety of factors making for long-term job tenure and consequently a variety of related reasons for MR policies.

We ourselves have not done any econometric work to support our hypothesis. However, a recent empirical study by Leigh (1984) confirms the general results of a human capital approach, as in this chapter, towards MR. Similarly, the empirical results reported by Lazear (1979) and Lapp (1985) are also consistent with our human capital approach with worker replacement. Further, the individual assumptions that we have used are well-estimated and well-documented in the literature. Among these, the emphasis on firm-specific skills comes from the work of Becker (1975), Oi (1962), Okun (1981), Blinder (1981) and Akerlof (1984, ch.6) among others, and is part of the human capital literature. The role of the replacement of older workers by younger workers in the context of profit maximization by the firm is supported by Gee and McDaniel (1991). The impact of age on ability and productivity can be found in Welford (1958), Clark, Kreps and Spengler (1978, pp. 927-929), Gordon (1960), Kreps (1961), Gordon and Blinder (1980), and Burkhauser and Quinn (1983). Our efficiency wage hypothesis can be considered as a variant of the relative income hypotheses (Duesenberry, 1949; Keynes, 1936; Rima, 1984), of the fair wage concept of Hicks (1974) and Okun (1981) and of the efficiency wage concept of Akerlof and Yellen (1986), among others. Underlying these is the notion of norms. On the role of norms and their relationship to effort, we have already referred to Elster (1989) and Rebitzer (1993). The assumption that there are significant costs of monitoring performance and productivity is supported by Slavick (1966), among others. That firms find it cost-minimizing to adopt a retirement age common for workers in related job groupings comes from such studies as Fox and Kerpen (1964) and Kleiler (1978, ch. 9). The adoption of a socially acceptable retirement age which approximates the age that the firm would otherwise find optimal for itself, reduces the firm's costs in some measure.

The implications derived from these assumptions seem quite plausible. Career, rather than casual, jobs would tend to be associated with MR policies. These policies would then vary among occupations, being least among casual jobs. Since education increases the ability to acquire a higher level of firm-specific skills, the level of education and jobs with MR should be positively correlated.

Since workers with greater education and high levels of firm-specific skills tend to be less unionized, a negative correlation between MR coverage and unionization should not come as a surprise. However, unionization generally leads to standardization of wages so that retirement, rather than a wage cut in response to age-induced declines in productivity, becomes the firm's optimal policy. This leads to a positive relationship between unionization and MR as against the former negative one. The overall relationship could go either way.

Further, given the existence of sex differentiation among occupations, with males concentrated more in career jobs and females more in casual ones, MR policies should be more prevalent among male employees than female ones. To the extent that discrimination against male blacks in the United States has forced them into relatively casual jobs, as compared with white males, they would be less subject to MR policies. But if they were subjected to these, then since their jobs are more likely to be casual ones, their average retirement age is likely to be greater. Both Leigh and Lazear confirm this finding in their work.

Since small firms cannot be taken to be reliable parties to long-term job contracts, lasting over several decades, small firms would not tend to have MR policies to terminate such contracts. Further, MR is a form of lay-off in response to a productivity decline and small firms may be able to monitor such a decline on an individual basis among workers, so that small firms can lay off workers individually as and when their productivity declines sufficiently. They do not need the rigidity of a MR policy. Such policies should then be much less prominent in small as compared with large firms (Slavick, 1966).

Our model in chapter 8 below does not imply that it is in the individual worker's interest to have a MR policy in the firm in which he works or that the age which the firm finds to be optimal for its workers generally is personally optimal for him. One cannot, *a priori*, expect such harmony of interests between a firm and each of its workers. This is not to deny that both firms and workers have an interest in the acquisition of firm-specific skills and, therefore, in long-term job tenure.[10] However, this interest does not extend to being voluntarily bound by a MR policy. Each worker's interest would be to have a retirement age at his option and as determined by his needs, resources and tastes evolving over an *uncertain future*. This is the subject of chapter 8. *Ceteris paribus*, some workers may *ex ante* find it optimal to retire prior to the firm's specified retirement age while others may find it optimal to retire later than this age.[11] Such decisions by workers are made on an individual basis. The firm, then, would try to reconcile the individual's preferred retirement age by tilting its pension plans and other retirement policies to its chosen age. These act as inducements to workers aimed at reducing the possible conflicts over the retirement age. We should, therefore, expect a positive relationship between the existence of pension plans and MR policies, and between their relevant ages of implementation.

In both Lazear's and Blinder's models, workers are assumed to trust the firm in the management of deferred wage compensation owed to them over long numbers of years. Vesting of such funds is recognized by Lazear (1982) to be inconsistent with his incentives model. Vesting of pensions over part of the worker's lifetime, though not over all of it and not of all funds owed by the firm to the worker is part of Blinder's model but there is no real rationale for it in that model. Its presence is a sign of mistrust of workers towards the firm and runs counter to the trust implicit in Blinder's wage-marginal product paths. Our model, cognisant of the general absence of a high degree of trust - or distrust - by the worker in the firm, implies the vesting of any funds owed by the firm to the worker so that a positive relationship, as observed for example by Leigh (1984) between vesting and MR, argues in favour of our model. Vesting in the context of our analysis is analyzed in chapters 7 and 9.

Finally, Abraham and Farber (1986) have recently examined the relationship between seniority and earnings. Their findings on data derived from the Michigan Panel Survey of Income Dynamics, is that most of the cross-section return to seniority reflects omitted variable bias and that the return to seniority in excess of the general retirement market experience is very small.[12] This finding is also substantiated by Altonji and Shakotko (1985). This evidence clearly undermines the empirical validity of the wage deferral path in Lazear's incentives model of MR. It favours an experience or skill accumulation model, such as ours, with wages roughly tracking - though not equalling - productivity.[13]

Our theory emphasizes that the firm's retirement decision is in the context of the replacement of a worker in a given 'generation' by a worker of the next 'generation'. This has the advantage over other theories of allowing us to examine the impact of improvements in knowledge and skills between generations on the firm's preferred retirement age. These reduce this retirement age while increased longevity and improved health would increase it. A change in the nature of jobs such that a lesser amount of physical and mental stamina is required for their performance would, *ceteris paribus*, raise this retirement age. These implications are quite plausible in terms of the experience with the advancing MR ages in this century.

Some of the provinces in Canada and some of the states in the U.S. have passed laws against MR policies or are in the process of considering such legislation. Such legislation allows the worker to retire at his preferred retirement age, analyzed in chapter 8. While this shift in rights between the firm and the worker changes the relevance of some of our comments in this chapter, it does not affect the relevance of our underlying model and its analysis of the age at which firms find it optimal to retire their workers. Deviations from this optimality, and the implications of these deviations, are examined in chapter 9.

FOOTNOTES

1. We have avoided in this description any reference to training costs. They are not at the core of to our arguments on retirement. If they are incurred by the firm for a worker, then the analysis can be rephrased in terms of the net wages (net of training costs).
2. See Gordon (1960), Spengler (1971) and Clark, Kreps and Spengler (1978). It is quite likely that the typical worker's physical and mental abilities will exceed the extent of these abilities required for his job over a part of his work-life, so that the time at which they become inadequate relative to the requirements of the job is the really relevant one. Spengler (1971), figure 0.1, p.6) points to such a relationship between work capacity and work requirements.
3. Medoff and Abraham (1980) published findings suggesting a significant difference between current wages and current marginal product, with the former exceeding the latter for senior workers. Abraham and Farber (1986), however, attributed this return to seniority as reflecting an omitted variables bias.
4. To guess outrageously, consider a worker with an annual pay rising from $30,000 to $50,000 during the first 15 years of service with the firm. If the firm had put aside 20% of the wage (so that m was 1.20 times the wage) in each of these years, the fund would, with compound interest, be several hundred thousand dollars at the end of those 15 years.
5. Okun (1981, pp. 83-92) discusses some of the problems posed by the need for trust and the inherent reasons for distrust among firms and workers.

6. Only the effect of age upon health is relevant here. The impact on health of disease and accidents, etc., unrelated to age, is not relevant in this analysis.

7. There are several other factors, not taken account of here, which could make long-term contracts desirable. Among these would be the heterogeneity of workers, the need and desire for certain forms of insurance, etc.

8. Whether this fair wage should be the nominal or the real one is a moot point. See Okun (1981, ch. 3) and Phelps (1981).

9. Lazear explains this finding as: workers with relatively short tenure periods are ones 'bought out' of their previous labour contracts, through severance pay or early retirement pensions. The new contracts of these workers would contain a later MR age, either because of a lower reservation wage or higher MP profile.

We find the above explanation to be rather a forced one. In Leigh's sample, the workers had been with their firms for at least five years, thus excluding workers who had recently moved between firms. Leigh found a negative coefficient between job tenure and age of MR for such workers.

10. This common interest means that the agency problem is not a serious one within the context of our theory and the ability of the worker to shirk is curbed by his desire not to be fired by the firm in which he has already acquired extensive firm-specific skills and in which he gets paid more than he will get paid in other firms.

11. Hence, in our theory, contrary to Lazear (1979, p. 1283), the age of MR need neither be a social nor private optimal age of retirement for all economic units. In fact, the evidence indicates that the majority of workers do not retire at the MR age set by their firms. A considerable number retire earlier while some arrange for post-retirement work, even within the same firm.

12. Abraham and Farber (1986) point out that the main evidence for deferred compensation schemes, as in incentives contracts, is the cross sectional observation that wages increase with seniority. While their own prior beliefs were that such deferred compensation is significant, the finding of their empirical study was that "there seems to be only a small return to seniority in excess of the return to general labour market experience for the average worker. For both the nonunion professional, technical and managerial sample and the nonunion blue collar sample, the point estimate of the seniority coefficient in the model including a control for job duration suggests that the true return to seniority is on the order of 0.5 percent per year, rather than the 1.4 to 2.0 percent per year suggested by the standard cross section model." (Abraham and Farber, 1986, p. 38).

13. The other major finding of Abraham and Farber (1986) is that: for nonunion professional, technical and managerial employees, "there is no association between pre-job experience and job duration, and introducing job duration as a control variable into the earnings function does not affect the relatively large estimated return to labour market experience. In contrast, among nonunion blue collar employees, greater pre-job experience is associated with significantly longer job durations and introducing job duration as a control variable into the earnings function lowers the already-low estimated return to labor market experience by 20 to 30 percent" (Abraham and Farber, 1986, p. 39).

7 The Rental Value of a Job and Jobs as Dam Sites

This chapter represents a diversion from our topics of discrimination, retirement and pensions to the analytical concept of the rental value of a job position. This term was first introduced in chapter 3 and has been referred to in subsequent chapters. Although there is some mention of it in the literature, it is not in common usage. We use this chapter to elaborate on it and to relate it to similar ideas in the literature. This chapter also relates this concept to the notions of severance payments, early retirement bonuses or 'golden handshakes' and to 'reverse severance payments' in the form of unvested pension contributions.

Chapter 2 using Lancaster's model of characteristics and activities had argued that firms provide, through their organization of inputs and co-ordination of inter-relationships among workers, the characteristics of general and firm-specific environments. Chapter 2 showed that if the characteristics provided by the firm are scarce, the firm will receive a return to them.

Chapter 3 derived the concept of the rental value of a job position. In this context, a job position embodies the general and specific characteristics provided by the firm and represents the opportunity provided to the worker of practising his general and specific skills. The focus on jobs occurs in many labour market theories, especially in theories dealing with labour market segmentation, as for example in Doeringer and Piore (1971). Among other studies emphasizing the focus on jobs are Akerlof (1984, ch. 6), with which we deal extensively below. In a recent study, Lazear and Rosen (1990) apply the notion of jobs, defined by them as a set of technological opportunities, with possibilities of promotions, to discrimination against female workers.

In the context of chapter 3, the rent due to the firm from the ownership of the job position has a present value. The worker whose occupation of the job position maximizes this present value will get the job position. Other workers will be turned away even though their occupation of the job position may yield a positive rent to the firm and increase the firm's profits compared with a situation in which the job position is left vacant. But they do not get the job because their occupation of the job position when more competent workers are available for it decreases the firm's profits.

The notion that the firm owns a job or job position and maximizes the return to it is similar to Akerlof's (1984) notion of a job position as a dam site. Only one dam can be built on a dam site so that a dam which does not fully utilize the site's potential should not be built: its building rules out a more productive dam which better utilizes the site's potential for electricity and water storage, etc. In other words, the type of dam that is likely to produce the maximum return, net of cost, should occupy the dam site; other types of dams, even with positive net returns, should not do so.

This idea has to be placed in the wider context of a river which can have many dams built on it. In this wider context, the resource is the river as a whole. Optimizing the return from dams on the whole river would specify the number of dams on the river and the type of dam for each site. Building a larger number of dams, or larger or smaller sizes of dams, than the optimal number and types of dams would decrease the net return from the river and be suboptimal. In the overall context of the river, a larger dam than the optimal one for any particular dam site, when the number and types of all other dams are already specified at the optimal level, would decrease the overall net return to all dams on the river. However, with the particular dam site taken on its own, the larger dam could have a larger return than the one that was optimal from the overall context. This could presumably occur since the larger dam would create a larger reservoir and produce more electricity than the smaller, optimal dam. It is in this narrower sense of looking at each dam site in isolation that we can legitimately draw the conclusions of the preceding paragraph: a smaller dam than the optimal one should not be built even though it would, if built to occupy that site, yield positive profits. The wider analysis of the returns from the river as a whole yields another conclusion: considered in isolation from other dams on the river, even a dam (say, larger) which would yield larger profits than the (overall) optimal sized one for that site, should not be built, even though that (larger) size would - taking the site in isolation - yield a higher return. The reason for this is that the larger size would have implications - possibly in terms of water flows and silt accumulations - for the sizes and returns to other dams on the river, so that it would decrease the overall return to damming the river.

For a more adequate analysis, we have also to bring into the picture the notion that the dam deteriorates over time, so that its productivity and the return to it eventually begin to decline. At some point in time, it is no longer optimal to repair the dam; optimality requires replacing it with another one. This point in time depends upon the characteristics of the site and the changes in damming technology that may have occurred over time, so that the decision is not merely to take down or remove the existing dam and leave the site idle but to replace it by another. Both intuitively and from our earlier analysis, it may be optimal to remove the initial dam while it still yields a positive return, either taken on its own or in terms of the overall return to all the dams on the river, because its replacement would increase these profits by a larger amount.

For comparison with our earlier analysis, the optimal number and sizes of all dams are specified simultaneously by the optimization problem. The river corresponds to the firm, the optimal number of dams corresponds to the optimal number of jobs, the size/type of the dam corresponds to the education and the skills of the worker hired to fill the specified job position, and the optimal lifetime of the dam corresponds to the optimal duration of employment. A dam which can last much longer than the optimal lifetime for its type and nature of the particular site it occupies corresponds to a worker wanting a longer than the optimal duration of employment for his characteristics and the nature of the particular job position; and a type of dam which will not last the optimal period for the site corresponds to a worker wanting or available for a shorter duration for that job position.

This chapter reviews the notion of jobs as dam sites and investigates their rental/opportunity cost. The notion of the rental cost of a job position leads to a fresh and unusual perspective on workers and jobs. Standard microeconomic theory proceeds by assuming that the firm hires the services of workers to fill jobs and pays workers for these services. This would be the only useful or natural perspective in the job-occupation process if the firm were to get only a zero return from supplying the job position. But in our analysis, the firm receives a return to its provision of the job position. This yields another perspective on the job-occupation process: the firm owns the job position and the workers, as it were, bid for the job position owned by the firm. In this perspective, the workers are taken to receive their marginal product and pay the firm for the amount contracted for the job position. This perspective on jobs and workers is the dual of the first one.

The idea of firms renting or selling jobs to workers is not new. In a slightly different context, Rosen (1972) argues that,

> "Firms supply learning opportunities ... (as) a by-product of market goods production. But provision of learning options is not costless, since productive resources must be diverted away from current production and towards (largely informal) "teaching" and learning. Hence, firms will not provide such opportunities unless they are reimbursed. This is accomplished by, in effect, selling jobs to workers" (p. 327).

Section 7.1 of this chapter explores Akerlof's concept of jobs as dam sites. Section 7.2 derives the opportunity cost and the rental rate of jobs. Section 7.3 illustrates these in the context of the discussions on discrimination in chapters 4 and 5. Section 7.4 examines the implications of the notion that workers have purchased jobs in an implicit contract and act as the owners of the jobs. It also establishes the value of the worker's stake in the job position. Section 7.5 discusses severance and early retirement payments as compensation to the worker for a layoff and the consequent loss to the worker of this stake. Section 7.6 discusses the loss to the firm from a quit, thus requiring compensation by the worker to the firm in a reverse-severance or quit payment. Such a payment may come from the unvested part of the worker's pension fund.

7.1 Jobs as dam sites

Akerlof (1984) viewed jobs as dam sites in the sense that both jobs and dam sites were scarce resources and that just as only one dam could be constructed on a dam site, only one worker could hold or occupy a job position. Further, just as there could be a variety of dams, with differing outputs for the site, there could also be workers of differing abilities/skills, with differing productivities on the job.

The most productive worker (dam) will occupy the job position (dam site). Less productive dams will not be built on the site even if their cost is zero and they have positive output since they will underutilize the site. Similarly, less productive workers will not get the job even at zero wages because the more skilled, even though higher paid, worker has at least a correspondingly higher productivity on the job. In Akerlof's terminology, the casual workers would underutilize the job position.

Akerlof pointed out the similarity between his analysis of jobs as dam sites with that of Ricardian land theory, with putty-clay models and with cost-benefit analysis of dam building projects. In each of these, the inferior forms of an input using a scarce resource will remain unutilized if the available amounts of the superior resource are adequate enough to fully use up the scarce resource.

To illustrate this from Ricardian land use theory, assume two types of land, a good quality one and a poor quality one, and only one kind of labour. As long as there is enough of the better quality land, the labour spent on such land will be more productive and command a higher wage than its productivity and wage on the poor quality land. The latter cannot, therefore, attract labour to work on it even if its price was zero. The reason for this is that this inferior land does not generate enough output to pay the opportunity cost - i.e., the wage - determined by the productivity of the complementary resource, labour, on better quality land, and therefore will not be employed/used. In this analysis, there are at least two types of land and one kind of labour. In Akerlof's context, there are at least two kinds of labour and a given job position. Adapting the Ricardian analysis to this context implies that the less able or less skilled worker filling the given job position may not generate enough output to pay the opportunity cost of the complementary input - that is, the opportunity cost of the job position as determined by its usage by the more skilled labour.

Inherent in Akerlof's argument is the assumption that a job position can be filled by one person only. He argues that the job descriptions in a firm are part of the firm's specific technology and are costly to change in the short-term in response to changes in relative wages. Any such adjustment in job descriptions and therefore in the number of jobs and persons to perform the total jobs required in the firm must then be a long-run phenomenon. In this connection, Akerlof (1984, p. 111) cites Piore (1968) who showed that engineers in US manufacturing do not adjust job descriptions to take account of differing states of the labour market. What this would seem to suggest, at least for the short and intermediate runs, is that job descriptions - and therefore the types of workers optimal for them - may not be very flexible.

7.2 The price and rental value of jobs: jobs as a scarce resource

While we have adopted Akerlof's analogy of a job position as a dam site, we have sought to place this analogy in the wider context of a river being dammed and of dams deteriorating over time, with damming technology possibly improving at the same time. The owners of the damming rights on the river will examine the existing technology and the expected changes in it to determine the expected nature of future replacements, as well as the cost and return from the dams, to determine the optimal number, sizes and lifetimes of the dams to be built on the river. Given these, they can open the bidding for all the dams as a group or individually for each dam site.

In a competitive system, the owners of the right to dam the river at various points will want from any purchaser of that right an amount related to the return net of the cost of building and operating all the dams on the river. Since a dam is a durable capital good, the amount asked for the dam sites has to be defined as the present value of the net returns from the dams over their lifetime. The numbers, sizes and lifetimes of dams that maximize this present value will set the asking or shadow price for the dams as a whole at this maximum present value - as well as the asking or shadow price, size and lifetime of each dam.

Suppose, now, that a builder of dams turns up and wants to bid for the right to build and own a dam on one site only. It will not be optimal to sell him the right to build a dam of a size and lifetime of his choosing - even if he may offer more than the shadow price for the site - since he might choose a size and lifetime different from the overall optimizing one, with consequent detrimental effects for the returns to the other dams. He will be asked to bid for the specified - optimal - size and lifetime for the dam in question and will get the site if he pays the shadow price for it.

Chapters 3 to 6 derived the present value of firm-specific jobs under the assumptions that only one worker at a time can occupy one job position and that firms maximize the present value of profits from all job positions, taken together, in the firm. The qualities of labour were defined in terms of their hiring and retirement ages, though chapter 4 did also touch on variations in the quality of workers based on their differing abilities. Chapter 3 had assumed that all workers were identical at the time of hiring, and therefore would have the same optimal hiring and retirement ages. It had derived the present value of the profits from any designated job position as,

$$V = \frac{e^{iT}}{e^{iT}-1} \ \{\int_h^R r \ e^{-i(t-h)} \ dt - \int_h^R c \ e^{-i(t-h)} \ dt\} \quad (1)$$

$$= \frac{e^{iT}}{e^{iT}-1} \ A \quad\quad\quad\quad\quad (1')$$

$$where \ A = \{\int_h^R r \ e^{-i(t-h)} \ dt - \int_h^R c \ e^{-i(t-h)} \ dt\} \quad\quad (2)$$

156

The rental value of a job

V   Present value of the net rents accruing to the firm
r   Firm's share of the rents from the position
i   Interest rate
t   period
c   Hiring and training costs
g   Age $(= h + t)$
T_k Duration of employment of the kth worker $(= R_k - h_k)$ $(= T)$
R_k Retirement age $(= h_k + T_k)$ of the kth worker $(= R)$
h_k Hiring age of the kth worker $(= h)$

Since all workers were assumed to be identical at the time of hiring, for the optimal hiring, retirement and employment periods respectively, $h_k = h$, $R_k = R$, and $T_k = T$. The firm maximized the present discounted value of profits from all its job positions, so that it maximized,

$$\pi - \int_0^n V\, dx \qquad (3)$$

$$- \int_0^n \frac{e^{iT}}{e^{iT}-1}\, A\, dx \qquad (3')$$

The optimality conditions for the number n, and the hiring and the retirement ages of the firm's workers were:

$$A - 0 \qquad (4A)$$

$$\frac{\partial A}{\partial h} - -i(V - A) \qquad (4B)$$

$$\frac{\partial A}{\partial R} - i(V - A) \qquad (4C)$$

These conditions are taken from equations (4A) to (4C) in chapter 3. They yield the optimal number and the optimal hiring and retirement ages of the workers - with this 'optimality' being from the firm's viewpoint. These yield the optimal values for a given job position of A and V as A* and V*. iV* was interpreted as the rental value of the job position.

$A(n^*, h^*, R^*) = 0$ and $V(n^*, h^*, r^*) = 0$, as are their partial derivatives evaluated at $n = n^*$, $h = h^*$ and $R = R^*$. However, for intra-marginal positions j, $j < n^*$, $A_j(n^*, h^*, R^*) > 0$ and $V_j(n^*, h^*, R^*) > 0$.

The optimal type of worker for any particular job position in the firm is the one who yields the present value V* of the firm's share of the rents for that position. To the firm, V* is the opportunity cost of the job position in question. It is also the price which a competitive bidding for the job position (with its skill, strength, agility, hiring and retirement age requirements as set by the overall optimization) - viewed as a marketed 'dam site' with a specified (optimal) size and lifetime - would establish. In this competition, workers (dam builders) would be as if buying the job position (dam site) and implicitly (explicitly) guaranteeing to the firm a revenue equal in present value to its V*. This scenario envisions the worker as purchasing the job position, paying its contract price V* as a lump sum or in instalments over his employment period and receiving the marginal product of the job as he performs it. A corresponding contract applies to the dam builder who purchases the rights to build the dam on the dam site.

The average instalment per period on the purchase price of the job position would clearly be iV* which can be defined as the rental value per period of the job position. This notion of rental value corresponds to the notion of user cost or rental value of physical capital goods. The analogy is very close. Both job positions and capital goods are scarce resources in the economy. Both are long lasting. Both use complementary inputs, which can be of superior or inferior qualities.

This concept of the rental value of a job position is based on a dual to the standard picture of jobs and workers posited in economic theory. The standard picture in economic theory has almost always approached factors of production as inputs, providing services to firms and receiving a return. Very often, this return is seen as the rental value of the input, such as the wage (per period) for labour services (per period) or such as the rental value of capital. The dual to this picture lies in the firm having a vacancy sold to or filled in by the input. Thus, the firm has a job position for which the worker is hired. If we were to focus on the ownership of the job position by the firm, one could ask the question as to the rental value of the job position to the firm: that is, what is the maximum amount per period - that is, rent - that workers wanting the job position would be willing to pay to the firm to get it. In this scenario, the worker is seen as renting the job position from the firm, paying this rent to the firm and receiving the entitlement to the marginal product from his performance of the job.

In a perfectly competitive one period framework with wages w equal to marginal product m - and, therefore, without any such encumbrances as implicit contracts, transactions costs, etc., which would cause a divergence between w and m - the maximum rental value the workers would bid for the marginal job position is zero dollars. If, however, the firm had a monopoly on a certain type of job position with a large number of workers bidding for it, with their the productivity in the firm being m but in other types of jobs being lower at m', the workers would be willing to pay (m - m') to the firm for the job position. That is, the workers would retain from m their opportunity cost m' and would pay the remainder to the firm as the rental cost of the job position. Conversely, if the job is of a type common enough in the economy but a worker has a special aptitude enabling him to achieve a marginal product higher than other workers can achieve (= m"), the minimum amount this worker has to bid to get the job position is the amount his best competitor can bid for it. This is m". The worker will then keep (m - m") as a part of his wage and not include it in the rental value paid by him for the job position.

Why would the firm not hire non-optimal age workers who may yield it positive rents from employment but not as much as the optimal age ones? As we argued in earlier chapters and as Akerlof argued for dam sites, while the former do increase the firm's profits, the latter increase these profits by more and so will always be preferred to the former. Of course, at the margin of profit maximization, both types of workers would yield zero rents, so that either type of worker could be employed as the marginal one. But a particular worker cannot in general be designated as the marginal one; any member of a set of identical workers would be the marginal one and the optimal set would be the optimal age workers since these yield higher rents than the non-optimal age ones. This argument applied to the retirement age means that, given (2), workers are being retired even though their net rents to the firm are still positive in the retirement period: they are being retired because replacing them in the given job position increases the firm's profits. In the context of male versus female workers - with, by assumption, the former having the optimal hiring and retirement ages and the latter expected to leave before the optimal retirement age - while the employment of female workers would increase the firm's profits, the employment of male workers with longer employment periods increases it by more. Males will get the job; females demanding equal wages will not.

Our analysis in chapters 3 to 6 allows the possibility that wage flexibility could allow workers of different types to bid the same price or rental value for the job position by accepting appropriately lower wage rates. For this to occur, a lower quality (non-optimal) worker would receive a wage which is lower than of optimal workers for two reasons:

    i. The non-optimal workers have a lower marginal productivity and generate lower firm-specific rents. Assuming that they would receive the same proportion of these rents as the optimal workers, the wage due to them would be lower by virtue of their lower marginal productivity and the lower rents generated.

ii. Keeping the proportional division of rents constant between the optimal and non-optimal workers implies that the worker with the lower marginal product would not be paying the rental value of the job position, and would not get the job. To guarantee to pay the firm this rental value requires that the worker with the lower marginal product pay the firm a higher proportion of the rents than the optimal workers do - and retain a lower proportion than such workers.

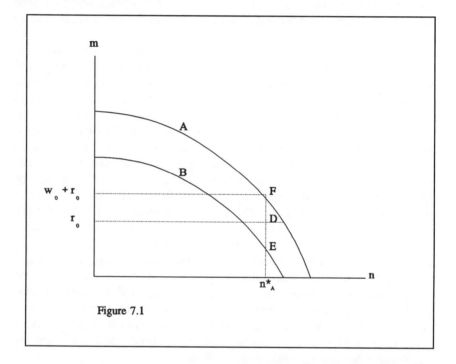

Figure 7.1

The resulting lower wage of non-optimal workers may turn out to be below their reservation wage. This reservation wage may be set by the workers' general skills used in other occupations or by the value of their time while unemployed. In the limiting case, the rental value of a job position to a particular type of worker may even exceed his marginal product in that job position. We illustrate this in figure 7.1.

In figure 7.1, assume a one period analysis, with the optimal type A of workers having the marginal product curve A, with the non-optimal type B of workers having it as B. Let the rental value of the job position n^*_A be r_0

and the wage for both types of workers be w_0. The number of the optimal age workers hired will be n^*_A. At the margin, if $(n^*_A - 1)$ workers have already been hired, the extra worker of type B would have a marginal product given by the point E, so that $(m-w) < r_0$.[1] To bid adequately - that is, to pay r_0 - in order to get the job position, the worker of type B would not get any wages and would have to pay the firm the amount DE out of his own resources. While such cases have been known to occur[2], they are decidedly rare.

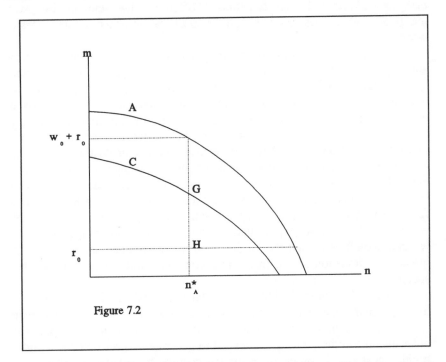

Figure 7.2

In figure 7.2, the non-optimal type of worker C has the marginal product curve C. Again looking at the job position n^*_A and with a required rental value of r_0 of the job position n^*_A, a worker of type C can cover the rent r_0 from his marginal product and get the job *by* paying this rent. But he will have to retain only the wage w_C given by GH which is less than the wage w_0 retained by the optimal class of workers. If w_C is less than the reservation wage of C workers, such workers will not bid enough for the job position and will not get it.

7.3 Non-optimal classes of workers

Chapter 3 established the concept of the optimal hiring and retirement ages for the workers of a profit maximizing firm. In our analysis, this concept applied more to workers with firm-specific skills than with only casual ones. However, classes of optimal workers may also be defined on the basis of abilities, education, handicaps, etc. Note that the optimal classes of workers - that is, those maximizing the firm's profits - are so defined for given marginal product and wage functions. Different wage functions for given marginal product ones could change the specification of the optimal class of workers.

As argued above, the optimal hiring and retirement age workers will be able to bid a higher rental value for the job position than workers of other ages. Other workers who want the same present value of wages as the optimal age workers will bid a lower rental value for the job position in question and not get it. Alternatively, they could bid the same rental value by accepting lower wages and get the job. If we assume that the rent generating function is such that these rents are monotonic decreasing with the absolute deviation of the actual (hiring or retirement) age from the relevant optimal one, discrimination in terms of lower wages offered would increase with this absolute deviation. It is also likely to increase with the degree of firm-specificity of skills. Further, given some rigidity in the acceptable wage, we should also expect that larger proportions of non-optimal age workers would be denied the job in favour of the optimal age workers, the greater the deviation in age from the optimal one and the greater the firm-specificity of skills on the job.

First looking at the hiring age, chapter 5 showed that the dependence of both the rent generated and the cost of training on the hiring age were relevant in determining the rental value of the job position. Job applicants older than the optimal hiring age tended to generate a lower rent and a higher training cost and, in order to get the job position by paying its rental value, would have to settle for a lower wage - set by their marginal product less the given rental value - than the optimal age workers. With the wage declining with the deviation in age from the optimal hiring age, older workers separated from their initial job would face greater wage declines the older they are and the more firm-specific their initial job was. That is, older job applicants would face discrimination in getting jobs or the wage offered because of factors determining the optimal hiring age. They would often and increasingly with age find higher wages - and a greater likelihood of getting a job offer - in more casual types of 'work'.

Looking at the other end of the employment period, workers who are expected by the firm to leave prior to the firm's preferred retirement date will not generate the rents that the optimal retirement age workers will be able to, and will have to offer the firm a lower rental value for the job position and not get it, or settle for an appropriately lower wage. This is the case relevant to workers whose expected employment period with the firm is less than the optimal employment period for the firm. Female workers having the optimal hiring age are often treated by firms as if this were so in their case, so that they are either refused the job or offered lower wages than corresponding male workers. These outcomes also appear as discrimination, though this is now for reasons connected with quitting at ages other than the firm's preferred retirement date.

The legal abolition of the mandatory retirement policies of firms may bring about another reason for wage discrimination. Given an optimal retirement date as far as firms are concerned, classes of workers who are likely to voluntarily quit their jobs later than the firm's preferred retirement date impose a loss on the firm. The firm would like to pay them a lower wage than the workers with quits at its preferred retirement age. That is, it would like to impose wage discrimination for excessive longevity on the job. Employed women may prove more susceptible to this than men since women have a significantly higher life span than men and, *ceteris paribus*, would prefer a later retirement age.[3] Women may then face wage discrimination while young for a shorter expected stay on the job and, if older and expected to stay on the job until retirement, for too long an expected stay on the job.

7.4 Job incumbents as job owners

A worker envisaged in the dual above as bidding for a job position, and buying it, becomes the owner of the job position. As a part of the implicit contract between him and the firm, the worker promises the firm the rental value of the job position. In return, the firm may be envisaged as allowing the worker to consider the job position as his - and thus, recognizes him as the owner of the job position - as long as he continues to generate for the firm the required rental value.

What is the net worth to the worker of his ownership of the job position? In one sense, it is the present value of his expected *wage* path. But the notion of the ownership of the job position arises from the existence of firm-specific skills so that while casual jobs also pay wages, the worker cannot be considered as owning the casual job. Therefore, we might want to specify this loss in another sense: the net worth in period i of employment of a job requiring firm-specific skills might be defined in a more restricted sense as the present value of the *rents* still to be received by the worker from continuing in the job. This amount would equal his wage from the job less the wage he would receive from his general skills in other firms. Designate this present value of the rents as A'_i. However, note that A'_i is a quasi-rent rather than a true rent. Note also that it is the present value of wages rather than A'_i which would have attracted the worker into taking on the job in question and acquiring the firm-specific skills for it. Before taking on the job, the worker would have had the choice of taking up some other job, acquiring the skills for that job and receiving the wage for that job. It is thus the comparison of wages rather than rents received which is *ex ante* relevant for determining which job was taken. Therefore, A'_i is not an appropriate *ex ante* measure of the net worth of the job position to the worker. However, it can be a relevant measure once a worker has taken a job and acquired some firm-specific skills in it.

In general, the firm-specific literature has focused on A'_i as an indicator of the return to the worker's firm-specific skills and as an indicator of the worker's stake in the job position. However, a more appropriate measure of this stake is the loss that the worker would suffer if he shifted jobs in period i. Designate this loss as L'_i. When the worker changes jobs in period i of his employment, he loses the value of the firm-specific skills in his former job but acquires new firm-specific skills in his new job. Assume that the level of general skills is identical in the two jobs, and if we designate the present discounted values of the rents lost in the former as A'_{1i} and those gained in the most attractive alternative job as A'_{2i}, the net loss from changing jobs in period i is,

$$L'_i = A'_{1i} - A'_{2i} \tag{3}[4]$$

where L'_i can be positive, negative or zero. As shown in chapter 5, 'older workers' - that is, older than the optimal hiring age - tend to generate lower rents both for the firm and for themselves, so that older workers changing jobs would often - though not necessarily, since there can turn out be a mismatch between workers and jobs - have A'_{2i} less than A'_{1i}. That is, in the common cases, L'_i would be positive. Such workers would be unwilling to quit their jobs since they would be net losers in a change of jobs. But at the point of entry into the job market, with perfect competition between firms for workers, A'_{1i} equals A'_{2i} so that L'_1 is zero. By extension, young workers in the early years after labour market entry would have low values of L'_i and so would be more willing than older workers to quit. Further, in cases of mismatch and while still in early years on the job, the expected value of A'_{2i} would exceed A'_{1i}, so that L'_i would be negative and a quit would be optimal.

We would henceforth consider L'_i as the worker's stake in the job position in period i of his employment, defining this stake as the amount the worker would expect to lose if he changes jobs in period i of his employment.[5] L'_i varies over the worker's employment period. Early in his career, while the worker has limited firm-specific skills, his alternative wage in other firms is still close to his actual wage and L'_i is low. It increases as he gains firm-specific skills over time and as he gets increasingly older than the optimal hiring age for other firms. The former would increase A'_{1i} while the latter would reduce A'_{2i} in (3). A'_{1i} would eventually tend to decline with age for two reasons. First, as the worker's abilities and stamina decline toward the end of his career, his marginal product would decline and the payment to the firm of the rental value of the job position would leave a smaller rent for the worker.[6] Second, the period over which A'_{1i} is calculated decreases with the number of years (T-i) - where T is the optimal period of employment and i is the period already spent on the job - left on the job and these decrease with age. A'_{2i} is likely to decline as the worker gets older than the optimal hiring age for jobs in other firms, becoming constant at zero when the next most attractive job involves only general skills. L'_i is thus likely to be concave in age.

The concept of the worker viewing himself as the owner of a job position with a positive stake - that is, with $L'_i > 0$ - gives a new perspective on certain aspects of worker behaviour and industrial relations. Among these are severance payments, early retirement payments or sweeteners in pensions, feather-bedding and internal promotions, among others. Of these, severance payments and early retirement payments will be taken up in the next section. We very briefly discuss the others at this point.

Workers in the real world often act as if they own their jobs. Workers on a strike tend to act this way, attempting to deny firms the hiring of replacements for their jobs during the strike and insisting on getting their jobs back at the end of the strike - though firms sometimes try to resist such claims. Workers also try to negotiate or insist on the right to first recall in the event of a layoff due to temporary demand shortfalls. Further, they enter into implicit contracts with firms such that firms will not lay them off even in the event of a demand decline or, if laid off, will keep the job for them when it is again to be filled.

In period i of employment, the worker has the stake L'_i in his job position. To receive this, he needs a predictable wage path and an agreed upon employment pattern. That is, he needs an implicit commitment from the firm about his employment and wage path, or a commitment by the firm to the rules determining these under various contingencies. The job attachment models based on firm-specific skills (e.g., see Okun, 1981) emphasize the existence of such contracts for career workers.

Job separations occur through quits, firings or plant closings. Workers often react to a firing and plant closing as a breach of promise by the firm, involving a loss of net worth for them, and display considerable hostility towards the firm at such times. We should expect such a reaction to firm-induced job separations to be positively related to L'_i. Since L'_i varies over the worker's lifetime, this reaction should show similar variation. Conversely, quits should be negatively related to the time path of L'_i.

A worker who claims ownership of a job position would, from his viewpoint, feel entitled to the expected wage path generated by the job position he had accepted, even if the job position in fact disappears due to the firm's re-organization or adoption of new techniques. Therefore, the workers in such situations in the real world often ask for re-employment in other jobs within the firm, at similar wage rates, and, sometimes, the retention of redundant jobs for them to hold. The latter can be called 'job-security' from one viewpoint and 'feather-bedding' from another.

In owning the job position, the worker owns a risky prospect with a value of A'_i. It is in his interest to increase the expected value of A'_i and decrease the riskiness of A'_i by making the possible outcomes of the prospect as favourable as possible. Policies such as featherbedding are examples of the latter. One way of achieving the former is if the worker can get the firm to commit itself to promote him to more senior positions. However, with a general pyramidical hierarchy of jobs, there are limits to guarantees of such promotions. Failing such a guarantee, workers can improve the outcomes of their risky prospect by insisting that the firm make appointments to more senior positions from within the firm. From the perspective of the firm, it also finds that, in general, the best candidates for senior positions are those who are already familiar with its organization and have a certain amount of firm-specific skills. Consequently, an (implicit) clause more or less limiting promotions to internal candidates would seem to be part of the implicit contract between the firm and the worker.

7.5 Severance payments and early retirement bonuses

The preceding section sketched the time path of the career worker's stake L'_i in his job position. It is zero when he takes up the job and increases as his experience and time on the job increase. It tends to decrease as he approaches the retirement date.

Severance payments are payments made by the firm to a worker if the firm forces an involuntary job separation on him, through firing, plant closing, etc. Early retirement payments are payments made by the firm to induce a worker to retire somewhat prior to the established retirement date or earlier than the worker might want to. They can be viewed as a form of severance payment though perhaps more in the nature of inducements than in the usual case of severance payments.

An involuntary job separation forces the loss of L'_i on the worker, for which the worker would like to be compensated. Severance payments can be viewed as such compensation. Severance payments should then be positively correlated with L'_i, starting from zero in the early years of one's career, increasing with the number of years on the job before declining as the firm's preferred retirement date for its worker is approached. That is, severance payments should generally peak in the middle, and most productive years, of one's career.

While this would be the general hypothesized pattern for severance payments, considerable variation can be expected in practice. For example, universities embody the concept of tenure after a few years on the job and tenure rules out involuntary job separations (except for 'cause'). Consequently, it is early retirement provisions that constitute the main form of severance payments and they often peak at the age at which the eligibility for early retirement starts.

While job separations impose a loss of L'_i on the worker, they also impose a loss equal to L_i on the firm, where L_i is given by,

$$L_i = V_{1i} - V_{2i} \tag{4}$$

where V_{1i} is the present discounted value of the rent still to accrue to the firm if the given (first) worker continues with the job to his retirement age while V_{2i} is the 'resale value' of the job position for the duration the first worker should have kept the job position but did not do so. This resale value is the payment the firm would receive in auctioning off the job position in period i of the incumbent's employment period. This is the increase in its present discounted value of the rents from hiring a new optimal age worker earlier than it would have done so. The net loss L_i by the firm was used in chapter 4 to explain discrimination against female workers, assuming that they were expected to leave the firm before its optimal age of retirement. Note that L_i depends upon the arguments that determine V_{1i} and V_{2i}. L_i is likely to be low in the early years of a worker on the job and increase as his experience and skills mount, declining beyond some point towards the end of the worker's career.

Since both the worker and the firm suffer a loss from job separation and any compensation paid to the worker increases the loss to the firm, the magnitude of severance payments would depend upon the party - that is, the firm or the worker - as well as the factors - such as extraneous market conditions, shirking on the job, deterioration in health and the ability to perform the job, etc. - which are the cause of the severance. The implicit contract between the worker and the firm would allow for justified involuntary job separations - that is, layoff or firing due to the worker's physical or mental incapacitation, shirking, etc. - without compensating severance payments. This may - or may not - also apply to relative and general economy-wide shortfalls in demand. Severance payments may then be payable only in cases of arbitrary firing, managerial changes and the adoption of new techniques.

While the worker would like to be compensated for the full amount of L'_i for any involuntary job separation, severance payments constitute a penalty on the firm in addition to its loss of L_i. Therefore, the firm would be quite reluctant to pay L'_i, so that the actual amount paid could depend upon the bargaining power of the worker vis-a-vis the firm. The bargaining power of workers may be enhanced by unions and even by legislation. On the latter, the elimination of discrimination by virtue of 'age' in some parts of Canada and the United States has increased the rights of older workers to retain their jobs at essentially unchanged wages beyond the firm's preferred retirement dates. Such legislation has increased the expected value of L'_i and the worker's bargaining power since the possibiliy of a court case (against a firing) going in the worker's favour has increased. The dependence of the size of severance (and early retirement) payments on L'_i and on bargaining power suggests that these payments had increased in the 1980s as a result of such legislation. A counteracting factor acting on the actual size of payments in the early 1990s would be the adverse market conditions of the time.

In our approach, severance payments can also be viewed as the amount insured with the firm and payable on the loss of L'_i from a job separation. In this approach, a worker receives a higher wage from his existing firm than the wage he can get from other firms. He would want to insure the (extra) income loss he would suffer from a separation from his existing firm. The firm would be willing to sell such insurance at very favourable rates since it receives a rent from the worker and would suffer a reduction in its profits if it replaced him with another worker. Therefore, it would not undertake this replacement under normal circumstances. However, unexpected changes in demand or in technology, etc., may make it optimal to fire the worker. Severance payments then become amounts payable to the worker, either by explicit contract or by established custom, upon the materialization of such a contingency.

Further, the existence of a fund accumulated by the firm out of the worker's marginal product and owed to the worker suggests the payment of this sum as severance pay if the firm fires the worker. Such a notion easily belongs in Lazear's incentives model and Blinder's version of the human capital model, though, as we argued earlier in Chapter 6, such severance payments seem much too small compared with the likely magnitude of the fund implied by these two theories. Further, such severance payments are often 'vested' in the worker in the sense that the firm is often known in advance to be committed to paying them. But such vesting is inconsistent with Lazear's theory (Lazear, 1979, 1982; Leigh, 1984, p. 516). Furthermore, severance payments tend to increase with seniority until a late age, not decrease beyond some early mid-point, as the Lazear and Blinder theories would imply.

7.6 Reverse severance payments and vesting

The firm has the stake L_i in a worker continuing his job till the firm's preferred retirement age. From (4), the firm's stake equals V_{1i} less the 'resale value' of the job position for the duration the worker could have kept the job position but did not do so. As argued above, this resale value equals V_{2i}.

The firm wants to protect its stake in having the worker continue in the job for the firm's optimal employment period by arranging for an adequate penalty on the worker for leaving the job earlier or by receiving compensation from the worker, or some combination of the two. A worker quitting a job in period i of his employment loses L'_i. For most occupations, L'_i is likely to be low in the early years on the job and is likely to increases with years on the job, before declining as one approaches the retirement date.

Assuming the time patterns of L_i and L'_i suggested above, a worker quitting within the optimal employment period suffers a penalty L'_i - and imposes a loss L_i on the firm. If L'_i is not sufficient to deter a quit or if the firm feels strongly about its loss of L_i, it may require a payment from the worker to the firm, contingent upon such a quit. This can be called a 'quit payment' and would be a 'reverse severance payment'.

In general, it seems difficult and costly for the firm to compel the worker to make a payment to the firm upon a quit, though the firm can in certain circumstances keep the worker's last pay cheque. A less costly mode of collecting such a compensation is by accumulating part of the worker's effective wage in a pension fund, not vesting it and appropriating it in the event of a quit. This procedure decreases the loss from the quit to the firm and increases the penalty to the worker.

While pensions are the subject of chapter 9, a few remarks about it can be useful at this point. Pensions may accumulate with the firm through the firm's contribution and/or the worker's contribution financed through a deduction from his take-home wage. Both of these contributions are really elements of the worker's total compensation or effective wage. In some cases, all or a part of the pension fund accumulating with the firm for a worker is not vested in him until after a specified period of employment with the firm.[7] Further, the firm may insist on retaining all or a part of the unvested pension fund in the event of a quit. What is thus retained by the firm is a form of a reverse severance payment by the worker to the firm. Because the firm retains the possession and ownership of an unvested fund, it is less costly and less cumbersome to collect than if the worker were asked to make a payment to the firm from funds in his control or ownership.

Let the loss to the worker from an unvested pension and any other payment from him to the firm be L'^P_i. Then, the total penalty on the worker from a quit is $(L'_i + L'^P_i)$. The loss to the firm from the quit is $(L_i - L'^P_i)$. The firm may start the worker with a positive L'^P_i - that is, through an unvested pension - but as the worker's experience increases with years on the job and L'_i increases, it may alone constitute an adequate penalty on the worker for preventing unjustified quits. L'^P_i may then be allowed to go to zero. That is, the worker's pension fund may be wholly vested in him. Further, since the firm's stake L_i tends to decrease towards the end of the worker's career, the loss to the firm from the quit decreases so that there is no reason for the firm to insist on a reinstatement of an explicit payment of the type L^P_i later on in the worker's career.

The preceding analysis has shown that an unvested pension fund can be a reverse-severance or quit payment by the worker to the firm. It may also serve other functions. A function which is essentially a part of our arguments but which has not been mentioned so far is that the unvested pension fund can compensate the firm for hiring and training costs incurred by the firm and not collected from the worker or taken directly out of his wages. Such costs are part of the firm's loss from a quit, so that, on a quit, the firm may insist on compensation for this loss out of the unvested pension fund. Blinder (1981) also explains the unvested pension fund as a compensation to the firm for the worker's training and hiring costs.

Note that in our theory the severance payment need not be an adequate compensation to the worker for his loss L'_i nor are quit payments necessarily an adequate compensation to the firm for its loss L_i.

Conclusion

The existence of firm-specific skills focuses attention on the firm's possession of characteristics which lead to the acquisition and exercise of such skills by the workers. The returns to such skills will depend upon their relative scarcity, as in discussed in chapter 2. These returns occur in the form of rents generated by the worker's skills and the firm's environment, and are shared between the worker and the firm. The firm maximizes the present value of its share of these rents by employing the workers with the optimal ages of hiring and expected retirement, as specified in chapters 3 to 5. As the owner of its share of the rents, the firm may be envisaged as auctioning the job position - with parameters established by the firm in the light of its maximization of the present value of its profits - to the highest bidder. The bidder who can bid the highest, while retaining the highest present value of the remainder (i.e., the wages), will be the workers with the optimal hiring and retirement ages. Other workers can meet this bid only by retaining a lower present value of wages. In the limit, this might be negative. These other workers may, therefore, find it unattractive to put in a competitive bid for the job position.

The concept of a job position owned by the firm, seeking the best applicant for it, is similar to Akerlof's notion of a job as a dam site on which the most productive dam should be built. Less productive types of dams will constitute inefficient use of the dam site, a scarce resource. Similarly, the firm, through use of scarce resources, creates scarce firm-specific jobs, for which the optimal-age workers would be the most efficient ones to employ. To properly extend the analogy of jobs as dam sites to our analysis, we suggested extending the analysis of dam sites to apply to a river with several damming sites. Optimizing the return to the whole river determines the optimal number, size and lifetime of each dam built on it.

Workers taking on a firm-specific job can be envisaged as buying the job position until their retirement date or until some set contingency occurs. This is a dual to the usual way of looking at jobs, i.e. with hiring/renting labour services and paying a rent for these services. In its dual, the worker rents the job position from the firm, with a commitment to pay/generate a certain rental value for the job position. Workers who cannot generate this rental value will not be hired or if already hired, will be fired or asked to quit.

Workers as the owners of job positions up to the retirement date would try to improve their return from the jobs by insisting upon internal promotions, internal job ladders, etc. They would also lay claim to the job position even though on strike and try to fight job redundancies through featherbedding or the first right of appointment to other positions within the firm.

A worker owning a job position would be entitled to compensation if the firm separates him from the job position through arbitrary or other action on its part, rather through than because of the worker's fault - such as shirking - or changes in the state of 'nature' such as general demand declines. Such compensation would take the form of severance payments and be related to the worker's stake in the job position. This stake is the present discounted value of the worker's share of the future rents generated by the job less those generated in his new job. Severance payments are a mode of compensating for the loss of this stake without necessarily being full compensation. They would be positively correlated with this stake. In the early and middle stages of the worker's career, this stake and wages tend to increase as his firm-specific skills increase. Consequently, severance payments are likely to be positively correlated with wages during these stages.

Note that there are two opposing sets of factors involved in the determination of L'_i. To illustrate these, a worker laid off after one year of employment loses his share of the rents from then until retirement but may not have learned much in the form of firm-specific skills so that this rent is relatively small. As time passes, the years over which the present value is calculated decrease but the experience accumulates and the magnitude of annual rents increase. The latter are positively related to wages. We should, therefore, expect severance payments to increase with wages. They would also increase with the employment period up to some point in the worker's career, with a subsequent decline.

Severance payments may also be payments under an insurance scheme in which the firm implicitly agrees to pay the worker specified sums upon the occurrence of certain contingencies resulting in a job loss.

Since the firm also suffers a loss from a worker quitting before the firm's optimal retirement period, the firm would try to collect compensation from the worker in the event of an unjustified quit. Such a compensation is often by the worker forfeiting - and the firm retaining - the unvested part of the worker's pension fund.

172

FOOTNOTES

1. We have here made the simplifying assumption that the marginal product of a worker depends only upon the number of jobs already filled, not upon the types of workers in those jobs.

2. For example, where a parent or other beneficiary pays a capital or endowment contribution to 'buy' the job position for a person who is not as able as others competing for the job.

3. Assuming identical utility functions over lifetime consumption and the number of years of leisure (retirement), and with consumption and leisure as normal goods, an increase in the expected lifetime would imply a greater demand for consumption, the number of years of leisure after retirement and the number of years of work prior to retirement.

4. A'_{1i} and A'_{2i} are defined net of any training costs paid by the worker in the period from period i to the retirement age. Further, it avoids complications if the retirement age is assumed to be identical in the two jobs.

5. Note that L'_i is likely to be much smaller than A'_{1i}: presumably, a worker capable of acquiring firm-specific skills in one firm would be able to acquire such skills in his new job.

6. This is somewhat simplistic. The declining (m - r) leaves a smaller wage and not necessarily a smaller share of the rent received by the worker. The time path of the latter also depends upon how wages in alternative occupations decline with age. They may decline faster than (m - r). In practice, then, the second reason given in the text may be the more assured, and important, cause of the decline in A' with age.

7. Usually the unvested part is specified to be the 'firm's contribution'.

8 Retirement —
The Worker's Choice

This chapter sets out our preferred analysis for the worker's choice of his optimal retirement age. Our preferred analysis is that for the uncertainty case. However, we start with the analysis under certainty, as in Burbidge and Robb (1980), Fields and Mitchell (1984, ch.2) and Baily (1987). These studies use an intertemporal utility maximization model with choices over lifetime consumption and leisure during the retirement years. The worker's optimal retirement age implied by this model is not necessarily consistent with his firm's preferred one, so that pension plan provisions and early retirement bonuses etc. are used by the firm to tilt the former to the latter (Fields and Mitchell, 1984; Wise, 1984).

Chapters 3 and 6 had set out the analysis for the firm's preferred retirement age function, specifying the firm's preferred age for retiring its workers as a function of various variables. These chapters had assumed perfect competition and profit maximization in the context of firm-specific skills and derived the firm's preferred retirement age functions for various types of job positions. For a given type of job, this function was independent of the worker's preferences, though dependent upon his abilities, health and wages. Consequently, the retirement age preferred by the firm may not necessarily coincide with that implied by worker's preferences. The firm attempts to coordinate the two through pension plan provisions. These will be the subject of the next chapter.

While the earlier chapters of this book are confined to the analysis of the firm's choices, the worker's choice had to be analyzed in this chapter in order to properly deal with the implications of firm-specific skills for pensions which are the topic of chapter 9. Section 8.1 presents the basic model of choices under certainty. It assumes that the worker maximizes an intertemporal utility function with lifetime consumption and leisure during the retirement years, in a context in which he will learn firm-specific skills and achieve promotions. But he cannot *ex ante* predict the rung that he will achieve along the promotion ladder and, therefore, the wage and working conditions that he will have as he approaches the retirement age. Given this uncertainty, the worker will not decide on his preferred retirement age until late into his career and will show little concern for it early in his career. His general preference will be that the firm not have a mandatory retirement policy. If it does so, he would want it to specify a retirement age which lies at the upper limits of his preferred set of retirement ages for the likely wage and promotion paths. This analysis of the worker's choice under uncertainty is presented in sections 8.2 and 8.3.

8.1 Retirement: the worker's choice under certainty

In the case of certainty, the household's standard behavioral model of choice over consumption and leisure can be adapted to the worker's choice between consumption and leisure in the form of the retirement years. The model adapted in this manner by Fields and Mitchell (1984) is as follows.

Assume that only full time work is available and that the number of hours worked per year for full time work is exogenously specified by the firm. The worker's work-leisure decision takes the form of choosing his lifetime consumption and the number of years which he will take as leisure, out of the years up to his horizon/expected date of death.[1] The worker maximizes an intertemporal utility function U with respect to c_t, $t=g,...,D$, and R in:

Maximize $U(c_g...,c_D, R)$ (1)

subject to:

$$C = Z + b_g - b_{D+1} \, \Omega_t^{-D+g-1} \qquad (2)$$

$$Z = \Sigma_{t=g}^{R} \, w_t' \, \Omega_t^{-t+g} - \Sigma_{t=g}^{R} \, (A_t+a_t) \, \Omega_t^{-t+g} + \Sigma_{t=R}^{D} \, (S_t+s_t) \, \Omega_t^{-t+g} \qquad (3)$$

$$C = \Sigma_{t=g}^{D} \, c_t \, \Omega_t^{-t+g} \qquad (4)$$

where
    c_t consumption in period t

C   present value of lifetime consumption

Z   present discounted value of current and future income

b_g wealth at the beginning of the current period/age

b_{D+1} bequest (exogenously set) at the end of age D

w'   disposable earnings (including public and private pension contributions), net of tax payments

w_t $(\partial Z/\partial t)\ \Omega_t^{t+g}$ = 'Effective wage' in tth period

s   private pension benefits

S   social security/public pension benefits

a   private pension contributions

A   social security/public pension contributions

Ω_t 'discount factor' $[= (1/1+i_t)]$

i   interest rate

R   retirement age (= g + n; R $\geq$ g)

D   (Expected) date of death (D $\geq$ R)

g   current age

n   expected number of years of continued employment with the firm (= R - g)

t   time, in years.

All of the above variables are in real terms. U(.) has the usual neoclassical properties. It is ordinal with $\partial U/\partial c_t > 0$, $\partial^2 U/\partial c_t^2 < 0$, $\partial U/\partial R < 0$, $\partial^2 U/\partial R^2 < 0$. w, a, A, s and S are assumed to occur at the beginning of the period. The bequests at death occur at the end of period D, which is the same as the beginning of period (D+1).

In (1), the post-retirement years equal (D-g-n) and are the period which the worker would like to have in the form of full-time leisure. C is the present discounted value of consumption over the remaining (D-g+1) years of life. (2) specifies that C must equal the present discounted value of wage and pension income over the remaining lifetime plus any current wealth less the present discounted value of any planned bequests at the end of period D. These bequests are not relevant to our analysis and are, therefore, specified to be exogenous. The discount factor Ω_t^{-t} in competitive markets equals (1 + i_t)$^{-t}$ where i_t is the long market rate of interest to period t.

From (3), the present value of the net gain in income from working in period R is given by,

$$\partial Z/\partial R = w'_R\ \Omega_t^{-R+g} - (A_R + a_R)\ \Omega_R^{-R+g}$$

$$+ \partial[\Sigma_{t=R}^{D}\ (S_t + s_t)\ \Omega_t^{-t+g}] / \partial R \qquad (5)$$

176

In (5), the first term on the right hand side is the after-tax wage, the second term is the public and private pension contributions and the last term is the increase in the public and private pension benefits, all in present discounted value terms.

The Lagrangian function for equations (1) to (4) is,

$$L = U(c_g, \ldots c_D, R) - \mu[\, \Sigma_{t=g}^{D}\, c_t\, \Omega_t^{-t+g}$$

$$-\, \Sigma_{t=g}^{R}\, w_t'\, \Omega_t^{-t+g}$$

$$+\, \Sigma_{t=g}^{R}\, (A_t + a_t)\, \Omega_t^{-t+g} - \Sigma_{t=R}^{D}\, (S_t + s_t)\, \Omega_t^{-t+g}$$

$$-\, b_g + b_{D+1}\, \Omega_t^{-D+g-1}\,] \tag{6}$$

The first order conditions for an interior maximum with respect to c_t, $t = g, \ldots, D$, μ and R are,

$$\partial U / \partial c_t = \Omega_t^{-t+g} \cdot \mu \qquad\qquad t = g, \ldots, D \tag{7}$$

$$\partial U / \partial R = -\mu \cdot \partial Z / \partial R$$

$$\Sigma_{t=g}^{T}\, c_t\, \Omega_t^{-t+g} = \Sigma_{t=g}^{R}\, w_t'\, \Omega_t^{-t+g}$$

$$-\, \Sigma_{t=g}^{R}\, (A_t + a_t)\, \Omega_t^{-t+g} + \Sigma_{t=R}^{D}\, (S_t + s_t)\, \Omega_t^{-t+g}$$

$$+\, b_g - b_{D+1}\, \Omega_t^{-D+g-1}$$

where $\partial Z / \partial R$ is the present discounted value of the gain in income or 'effective wage' from working an extra year. Correspondingly, define, $w_R = [\Omega_t^{R-g}\, \partial(Z)/\partial R]$. w_R is thus the effective current wage - not its present discounted value - for working during period R.

Assuming the first and second order conditions for a maximum in the interior of the interval [g,D] to be satisfied, (1) to (4) imply that,

$$R = R(\underline{w}', \underline{a}, \underline{A}, \underline{s}, \underline{S}; g, D, b_g, b_{D+1}, \underline{\Omega}) \tag{8}$$

where the line under a variable indicates that it is a vector of the values of the variable from g to D. Assuming the private and public pension contributions and the change in the future pension benefits to be functions only of wages from g to R, (8) can be rewritten as,

$$R = R(\underline{w}, S_g + s_g; g, D, b_g, b_{D+1}, \underline{\Omega}) \tag{8'}$$

where S_g and s_g are respectively the public and private pension entitlements already existing in period g. An increase in the current effective wage w_R at the retirement age makes work more attractive and causes a substitution effect in favour of work as against leisure, thus tending to increase R. However, an increase in wages also raises incomes and induces an income effect. Assuming leisure to be a normal good, the income effect increases the demand for retirement years and lowers R. The net effect on R of an increase in w_R is thus uncertain.

But if the present discounted value of income is held constant with wages in the neighbourhood of the retirement age reduced and those in earlier years correspondingly increased, the income effect will be zero and the substitution effect will lower the retirement age. A decline in real wage rates in the neighbourhood of the retirement age does not seem to be an uncommon occurrence in the real world.

The substitution effect of an increase in wages only comes into play if wages increase at the retirement age. Suppose that the wages in the neighbourhood of the retirement age remain constant while wages at earlier ages rise. Then, the substitution effect will be zero and only the income effect will be operative. Assuming leisure to be a normal good, such an increase in wages will lower the retirement age.

An increase in the present pension entitlements S_g or s_g causes a pure income effect. With leisure as a normal good, the income effect in this case will lower R. Hence, exogenous and gratuitous increases in private or public pension entitlements unambiguously lower the retirement age.

Under the assumption of leisure as a normal good, increases in current wealth b_g and decreases in the final level of bequests b_{D+1} will similarly lower the retirement age.

The above utility maximizing framework - equations (1) to (4) - assumes perfect certainty. In particular, it assumes certainty as to the age of death, the state of health and wages at each age. The last assumes that the time pattern of promotions and job changes is known at the planning date, long in advance of actual promotions. Since promotions tend to be uncertain and dominate the actual wage path for most workers, we focus in the following section on their implications for the optimal retirement age.

8.2 Uncertainty and the stochastic dynamic analysis of workers' choices

The utility maximization problem in the preceding section involves planning several years, if not decades, ahead. Therefore, uncertainty is likely to affect many aspects of the problem. This, and the following sections, focus only on uncertainty in the wage path, treating it as uncertainty about the number of promotions during the worker's career. The rate of inflation and the worker's state of health are other areas involving a great deal of uncertainty but are not considered explicitly in our analysis.

The standard analysis of the worker's choices under uncertainty employs stochastic dynamic analysis. This analysis usually assumes that the (typical) worker satisfies the von Neumann-Morgenstern axioms of cardinal utility and that he maximizes his expected utility. His decision point is at the beginning of his career. At this point in time, he forms his subjective probabilities - or estimates his chances - of promotion along each rung of the promotion ladder and the wages each rung will bring.

Assume that the worker's lifetime can be separated into 4 stages, each occupying one period. In the first stage - that is, while 'young' - the worker has a job with a known wage. With the future as uncertain, the worker does not know his job status in stages 2 and 3. Stage 2 is that of the middle-age worker. In stage 2, the worker may have the same job/wage as in stage 1, or be promoted one level to a higher job/wage, or may not have a job because he quit or was fired at the end of the first period. In the last case, the worker spends the period searching for another job. Stage 3 is that of the older worker. There are again three alternatives: promotion one level, no job or the same job. If the worker did not have a job in period 2, this translates in period 3 to the worker not having a job, a job at the first level or at the second promoted level. At this stage, the worker may not have a job because he was fired, quit because of job dissatisfaction or took early retirement. Given uncertainty, each of the alternatives in periods 2 and 3 have a subjective probability attached to it. The fourth, and the last, stage is the (mandatory) retirement period with a zero wage. The worker is assumed to choose retirement at some point during period 3. The retirement period thus extends over part of period 3 and over period 4.

Figure 8.1 shows the various outcomes and their related subjective probabilities. An x is an outcome, with p as the probability. The superscript will indicate the period and the subscript will indicate the outcome. The first period has the known outcome/wage x^1_1. The expected outcomes during the second period are x^i_j ,having the probability p^i_j, $i=2$, $j=0,1,2$. The expected outcomes during the third period are x^i_{hj} where h indicates the previous period's outcome and j indicates the current period's outcome. $j=1$ indicates employment at the first job level or rung on the promotion ladder, with the wage as w_1. $j=0$ indicates being without a job, with a zero wage. $j=2$

179

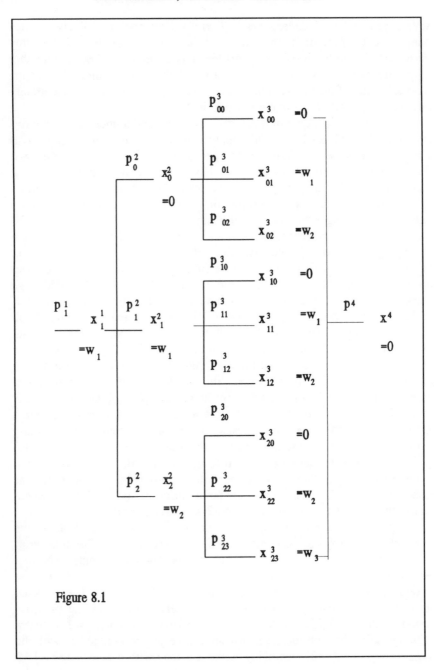

Figure 8.1

means being promoted to the second job level/rung, with the wage as w_2. $j=3$ is the third and last job level/rung, with the wage as w_3. *All outcomes and their subjective probabilities are as envisaged by the worker at the beginning of period 1.*

The von Neumann-Morgenstern axioms assert that the worker is indifferent between the compound prospect in figure 8.1 and its actuarially identical - that is, probabilistically equivalent - simple one in figure 8.2. In figure 8.2, the outcomes are the wages w_j, $j=0,1,...,3$, with probabilities $_1q^i_j$, *where the subscript to the left of q indicates the period in which the subjective probabilities were formulated.* The prospect for period i is written as $_1(w^i, q^i)$. $(w^i,1)$ is written simply as w^i. $w^i_0 = 0$ for all i.

Stochastic dynamic programming requires maximization in several steps. First maximize utility subject to its constraint in period 4, for given levels of wages and consumption in earlier periods. Second, for period 3, maximize expected utility subject to its constraint in period 3, for given levels of wages and consumption in periods 1 and 2, and the optimal consumption level derived in step one for period 4. Third, for period 2, maximize expected utility subject to its constraint in period 2, for the given level of consumption in period 1 and the optimal retirement age and consumption levels derived earlier for periods 3 and 4. Fourth, maximize expected utility in period 1 given its budget constraint and the optimal retirement and consumption levels in periods 2, 3 and 4. The actual computation is quite cumbersome, is not done here and is not needed for the qualitative results we intend to use.

The information given in the paragraphs above and displayed in figures 8.1 and 8.2 yields the optimal consumption and retirement age functions *from the perspective of the worker at the beginning of period 1*, as follows.

$$_1c^i = {}_1c^i(w^1; {}_1(w^2, p^2) ; {}_1(w^3, q^3); b_1, b_5, \Omega) \quad i = 1,...,4 \tag{9}$$

$$_1R = {}_1R(w^1; {}_1(w^2, p^2); {}_1(w^3, q^3); b_1, b_5, \Omega) \tag{10}$$

where

$_j(w^i, q^i)$	the wage-probability combinations expected for period i when the worker is at the beginning of period j
$_jc^i$	ith period's consumption, on the basis of planning at the beginning of period j
$_jR$	retirement age, on the basis of planning at the beginning of period j
Ω	discount factor
b_1	inheritance at the beginning of age 1

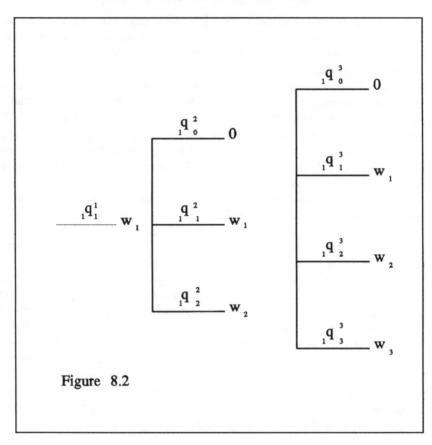

Figure 8.2

b_1 inheritance at the beginning of age 1
b_5 bequest at the end of age 4

In (9) and (10), q^i are the probabilistically equivalent single-stage combinations of the second and the third period's subjective probabilities. b_g and b_{D+1} are, as in the preceding section, respectively the exogenously given inheritance in period g and the bequest at the end of period D. w^i is, as before, the effective wage in i. It includes the change in pension benefits and excludes the change in pension contributions due to employment in period i.

At the beginning of the second period, the second period's wage becomes known. The worker also has a bequest b_2 from the first period. Assuming that there is no other change in the worker's outlook - that is, *the outcomes and the probabilities of the future prospects remain consistent with*

182

those specified at the beginning of period 1 - his consumption and retirement age functions *from the perspective of the worker at the beginning of period 2* with the wage as w^2, would be,

$$_2c^i = {_2}c^i(w^2, {_2}(w^3, p^3), b_2, b_5, \Omega) \qquad\qquad i = 2,3,4 \qquad\qquad (11)$$

$$_2R = {_2}R(w^2, {_2}(w^3, p^3), b_2, b_5, \Omega) \qquad\qquad\qquad\qquad (12)$$

where w^2 is now known with certainty. Note that $_2(w^3, p^3)$ is identical with $_1(w^3, p^3)$ so that the passage of time from period 1 to period 2 did not change the outcomes and their probabilities for the periods still in the future. $_2c^i$ and $_2R$ are consistent with $_1c^i$ and $_1R$.

Similarly, *from the perspective of the worker at the beginning of period 3, with the outcomes in period 3 - that is, the wage w^3 - remaining consistent with those specified at the beginning of period 1,*

$$_3c^i = {_3}c^i (w^3, b_3, b_5, \Omega) \qquad\qquad i = 3,4 \qquad\qquad (13)$$

$$_3R = {_3}R (w_3, b_3, b_5, \Omega) \qquad\qquad\qquad\qquad (14)$$

Finally, *from the perspective of the worker at the beginning of period 4,*

$$_4c^4 = {_4}c^4 (b_4, b_5, \Omega) \qquad\qquad\qquad\qquad (15)$$

Comparing equations (10), (12) and (14), the worker's optimal retirement age can only be determined with certainty in period 3 when that period's wage becomes known and all uncertainty disappears. In periods 1 and 2, equations (10) and (12) show that wages for future periods are uncertain and so is the optimal retirement age: $_1R$ and $_2R$ are *functions* of anticipated future outcomes and their subjective probabilities. Therefore, the rational worker, while still in periods 1 and 2, will not want to make a commitment with the firm on a *specific* retirement age, especially if it was specified to be independent of his actual wage late - that is, period 3 above - in his working life.

At the beginning of period 1, when he first joins the firm, the rational worker has a number of state dependent optimal retirement ages and would be willing to enter into a set of contingent contracts for those. The actual labour market does not have such contracts and cannot have them in the presence of moral hazard, since such contracts would also have to have clauses guaranteeing the payment of certain wages in the same prespecified states in the future and also have to make provision for the uncertain future interest rates. Given moral hazard and the uncertainties as to which workers will be promoted in the future, the firm would not be willing to enter into futures contracts guaranteeing future wage paths under certain contingencies to the worker, with each path having its associated optimal retirement age for the worker.

In (14) - that is, at the beginning of period 3 - the worker's choice of the optimal retirement age is affected by the current wage, and through b_3, by the past actual path of wages, as well as *the degree of uncertainty of wages that had existed over his past periods*. The last is represented by the vectors $_1(w^i, p^i)$, $_1(w^i, q^i)$ and $_2(w^i, p^i)$ which enter into the determination of b_3. Similarly, in a model including pensions, it would also be affected by the private and public pension plan entitlements and any uncertainty that had existed or still exists over their amounts and provisions.

Two basic results follow from this analysis. First, the function and determinants derived in chapter 6 of the firm's preferred retirement age for the worker are clearly different from the functions and contingent preferred retirement ages of the worker. The latter include purely subjective elements - and therefore introduce asymmetries in information between the firm and the worker - such as the worker's utility function and *his perception* of the uncertainty regarding his job, promotions, wages and health. Given the differences in these determinants and the existence of purely subjective elements, as well as differences even in the nature of the functions specifying the worker's and the firm's preferred retirement ages, it is unlikely that - given any set of anticipated (*ex ante*) or actual (*ex post*) values of these determinants - the retirement age preferred by the worker will be identical with the one preferred by the firm. Clearly, the two are likely to be different for most sets of such values. That is not say that they may not, for a fortuitous set of values of the determinants, turn out to be identical, though this will be more of a coincidence than a result of common interests. If an equality is desired between them by the firm, it may have to either bribe or coerce the worker to its desired outcome. Conversely, if such equality is desired by the worker, the worker might have to bribe/pay the firm or coerce it to his desired outcome. In the former case, a usual form of 'bribes' is 'golden handshakes' and manipulation of pensions. This forms the subject of chapter 9. Coercion by the firm seems to exist extensively in practice through explicit or implicit pressures for retirement, which if ignored are sometimes handled through 'establishing' a record of incompetence or even abolition of the specific job held by the worker. An explicit form of coercion is the implementation of mandatory retirement.

enter into a mandatory retirement contract to retire at a specific age far in the uncertain future. Simply put, rationality dictates that the worker only enter into contingent contracts specifying various retirement ages and consumption paths. If the contingent markets are not complete and the needed contingent markets are not available at low cost - as they are not in the real world - the worker's optimal policy is to keep his options open, if he can. In the context of the incentives models, he may be willing to forego this preference because - given the presence of his own tendency to shirk and the absence of any other factors to prevent this shirking - the incentive of the higher wage path in a contract with a mandatory retirement commitment may be enough to compensate him for giving up this preference. However, our model does not allow a tendency to shirk to be effective: the losses incumbent upon losing a job and having to find another in an uncertain and job-scarce environment are by themselves a sufficient prod for the worker not to shirk, so that a payment-deferral scheme is not necessary for this. In this view of the world, the worker does not shirk anyway and his marginal productivity (and wage) would not become higher were he to enter into a payment-deferral incentives contract. Consequently, he would not be paid more to persuade him to forgo his option not to specify an explicit retirement age. Therefore, he would not forego this option. In this view of the world, the worker will specify his preferred retirement age when he is close to retirement and knows the actual values of the determinants of this age. In our analysis above, this occurs only in period 3 - that is, in the period just prior to retirement. If the firm tries to pin him down to a pre-specified age of eventual retirement, he would want a contingent contract. In the absence of such a contract and faced by the firm with a specific retirement age, the worker would resent the firm's action, and would want to be compensated for such an action. Our theory therefore, does not view such resentment as a case of *ex post* sour grapes, as the incentives models tend to do, but as a result of a legitimate divergence of workers' and firm's interests in the presence of uncertainty about future promotions and wage paths - and about future interest rates.

8.3 The impact of the passage of time

The stochastic dynamic analysis above yields the actual path of bequests b_t, consumption c^i and the retirement age R as being determined by past realized wages and by the degree of uncertainty about the future.[2] If this uncertainty were not present and the worker had *ex ante* known his actual wage stream, his consumption pattern and the optimal retirement age are likely to have been different from those in the presence of uncertainty. To illustrate, been different from those in the presence of uncertainty. To illustrate, suppose that the worker never does get fired and gets all the promotions he had expected. Knowing this *ex ante*, would yield in the general case higher consumption in the earlier periods and lower in the later periods than in the uncertainty case. In the latter case, during the earlier years, the worker has to budget for the possibility of lean years ahead and so would have lower consumption. But as time passes and he realizes his good fortune in achieving the highest expected wage levels, his consumption would rise in the later periods and be above the certainty case.

Conversely, the worker who experiences the lowest expected wages as time passes, would have had higher consumption in the early periods and lower in the later ones than if had known his wage path with certainty.

The deviations in actual consumption levels and retirement ages from their mean planned or anticipated levels occur in the above analysis with the passage of time. However, they are not truly unanticipated since the worker *ex ante* knows that the actual values of these variables depend upon which of his expected states actually materializes. Truly unanticipated changes would occur if the probability distribution of the expected wage rates shifts. Thus, in our framework, the worker had anticipated in period 1 the prospect $_1(w^3, p^3)$ for wages in period 3. Suppose that his expectations change during period 2 such that this prospect shifts to $_2(w^3, p^3)$, with $_2(w^3, p^3)$ now different from $_1(w^3, p^3)$. This is a frequent occurrence in the real world since the passage of time often involves new information or the firming or weakening of what was believed earlier. This likelihood of change in the specification of future prospects was the reason for putting in italics and thereby emphasizing the clauses "*the outcomes and the probabilities of the future prospects remain consistent with those specified at the beginning of period 1 ... from the perspective of the worker at the beginning of period 2*" and "*from the perspective of the worker at the beginning of period 3, with the outcomes in period 3 - that is, the wage w^3 - remaining consistent with those specified at the beginning of period 1*" for the derived planned consumption and retirement age functions from the stochastic dynamic analysis above. They were meant to indicate the strong possibility of change in the planned functions as the emerging wage and future prospects shift in a manner inconsistent with the expectations held at the initial point of the analysis, which is the beginning of period 1 in the preceding analysis. For example, in period 2, the worker could develop poor health and now expect to dies in period 3 rather than at the end of period 4. Such a shift would be inconsistent with the expectations held in period 1 and would lead to new planned consumption and retirement age functions which would be inconsistent with worker received an unanticipated two promotions in period such that his wage jumps from w_1 to w_3. This would be inconsistent with his prospect sets $_1(w^2, p^2)$ and $_1(w^3, p^3)$ formulated at the beginning of period 1. It would cause $_2c^2$, $_2c^3$ and $_2c^4$ to differ respectively from $_1c^2$, $_1c^3$ and $_1c^4$. Similarly, $_2R$ would differ from $_1R$.

Is the revision of planned values of the variables emphasized in the preceding paragraphs carping on inessentials or is it a fundamental and large part of the reality that workers face and respond to in the real world? It would clearly be analytically neat to ignore it altogether. But we are dealing with lifetimes, with careers spanning several decades. None of us in middle age can be sure that we anticipated with any degree of accuracy of probabilities the successes and failures that we have already encountered and might encounter. Many of these depend only partially on our own attributes. They also depend on the environment we happened into, the abilities and temperaments of colleagues, and the 'politics' of the situation. Further, they are affected by unpredictable chance encounters and occurrences. Similar unpredictabilities or inaccuracy of past anticipated probabilities apply to health and family matters, etc. These imply that the careers and the health of most workers over the three or four decades relevant to the analysis do take unanticipated and surprising turns, sometimes for the better and sometimes for the worse. Consequently, our emphasis on the role of uncertainty and the possibility of unanticipated shifts seems to be fully justified in an analysis of retirement.

Further, note that the underlying basis of the stochastic dynamic analysis, if it is to be applicable to the individual worker, has to be subjective rather than objective probabilities, which may not even exist or even if they exist, may not be known to the worker, the firm or any other person.

The unanticipated shifts with the passage of time in the prospects would lead the *rational* worker to derive new sets of optimal consumption and retirement age functions than to maintain earlier ones and eventually lead to different actual values than if the shifts had not occurred. If these shifts are fairly frequent, with the subjective expectations tending to change several times over the several decades of the worker's life, the optimal policy implies fairly frequent shifts in consumption and retirement plans, so that the long-term dynamic stochastic analysis would be continuously revised and any particular set of solutions would be of limited value. The *rational* worker would learn this over time and would not use the above analysis. More myopic rules of thumb may then become more useful and common.

Furthermore, dynamic stochastic analysis is based on the expected utility hypothesis. That hypothesis has been called into question in recent years, hypothesis. That hypothesis has been called into question in recent years, especially in the in the dynamic context (Schoemaker, 1982; Machina, 1989). Its applicability would be especially doubtful in a context where the objective probabilities are uncertain and the anticipated subjective probabilities, as estimates of the unknown objective probabilities, for future periods keep shifting with the passage of time and the accumulation of information. Non-expected utility hypotheses in a dynamic context do not usually maintain the consistency of contingent choices as time evolves.

The conclusion of the preceding section using the expected utility hypothesis and its associated stochastic dynamic analysis was that under uncertainty the rational worker would want to keep his options on the retirement age open until the uncertainty disappears. This conclusion is reinforced by the arguments of this section on the subjective nature of the anticipated probabilities and the virtual certainty that they would shift several times during a career spanning several decades. In such a context, the rational worker would be aware of the possibility of significant shifts in his optimal retirement age as shifts in his information and expectations occur. Hence, early in his career, the rational worker will be unwilling to enter into an implicit arrangement with the firm as to a fixed retirement age. In the absence of the required contingent markets - and even in their presence when the probabilities of outcomes are volatile and unpredictable - he will prefer an open-ended employment period, with retirement eventually set at an age of his (eventual) choosing. He can, alternatively, have the firm adopt a mandatory retirement age at the outer limits of his contingent/possible retirement ages, and then retire earlier at his preferred retirement age, the latter known only as he approaches retirement and knows the relevant state. In general, then, the worker would resent the firm's mandatory retirement policies imposing earlier retirement ages. This resentment is likely to be even greater if his firm's mandatory retirement age was set earlier than in other firms, since the latter might be regarded by the worker as a 'norm'.

As against the preference of the worker not to be subject to a mandatory retirement age, we know from the analysis of earlier chapters that firms would want a mandatory retirement age for firm-specific workers. If all firms offering such jobs unilaterally specify such a clause in their contracts, workers who prefer jobs without such a clause would be faced with a *fait accompli*. Workers would then be observed to be accepting jobs with a mandatory retirement clause. Such evidence could be interpreted as evidence of workers willingly entering into contracts with mandatory retirement, with a further presumption that they do so because such contracts are part of an incentive scheme which will yield higher lifetime wages. Such interpretations would be wrong in our view of the world: the incentives schemes may in general be peripheral to the issue of preventing shirking in a world in which the stigma of the loss of a job and the difficulty and cost of finding a new job are high; and there is no compensation for agreeing at the beginning of a career to a mandatory retirement clause operational several decades later. In an environment in which firms collectively pursue mandatory retirement policies, without a preference for them by the workers, the latter cannot individually fight these but would have to do so through collective and political action.

8.4 Policy-induced changes in retirement ages

In (8), the optimal retirement age depends upon the effective wage w_t where the effective wage w_t is the sum of the current disposable wage w'_t less the increase in public and private pension plan contributions plus the resulting increase in public and private pension benefits. This equation was,

$$R = R(\underline{w}', \underline{a}, \underline{A}, \underline{s}, \underline{S}; g, , b_g, b_{D+1}, \underline{\Omega}) \tag{8}$$

Since $\underline{a}$, $\underline{A}$, $\underline{s}$ and $\underline{S}$ depend upon $\underline{w}$, rewrite (8) as,

$$R = R(\underline{w}, \underline{s}', \underline{S}'; g, D, b_g, b_{D+1}, \underline{\Omega}) \tag{8'}$$

where

$\underline{w}$	vector of 'effective wages' ($= w_g,...,w_R$)
$\underline{s}'$	vector of net private pension benefits received on a non-contributing basis ($= s'_g,...,s'_D$)
$\underline{S}'$	vector of net public pension benefits received on a non-contributing basis ($= S'_g,...,S'_D$)

The firm can manipulate the payment of the effective wage w_t through the actual wage w'_t paid during the working periods and the net private pension benefits s'_t paid during the retirement years. The public pension authorities can similarly manipulate w_t through income taxes and the net public pension payments S'_t. They can thus change Z in the worker's budget constraint.[4]

Since $\underline{w}$, $\underline{s}'$ and $\underline{S}'$ can be altered by public policy and $\underline{w}$ and $\underline{s}'$ can be negotiated between the firm and the worker, in the uncertainty case the worker's wage path and his contributions to and benefits from the public and pension plans, will all be uncertain. A worker may then end up with higher

189

or lower pensions than he would have anticipated based on his mean expected wages. This issue is followed up in the next chapter.

Conclusion

This chapter has set out some of the basic analysis of the worker's choice of a retirement age. Given the stochastic intertemporal nature of the maximization problem, a stochastic dynamic programming analysis is the appropriate one in certain contexts and is the standard one used in the literature. However, given the unspecified form of the utility function and the extent of the uncertainty as to the state of nature that would obtain over several decades in the future, this analysis can be seriously inappropriate for a rational worker if objective probabilities are not known or, even if known, are known to be volatile, with unpredictable shifts.

For some heuristic evidence on this issue, consider the 1990-93 recessionary period in most European and North American countries. The duration of the recession and its severity were not consistent with the expectations and predictions - held say in the mid-1980s and even in 1990 - of most economists and market analysts, let alone ordinary workers. According to a *Statistics Canada* survey published in the winter 1993 issue of *Perspectives on Labour and Income*, the result in the Canadian context was that about half of the workers who retired during 1990-92, retired earlier than they had themselves anticipated or planned. Of this group of 211,000 workers, unplanned early retirement occurred because of illness or disability (63,000 workers), closure of plants or layoffs (45,000), incentives received from the firm through a cash-out or an early retirement package (43,000), and other reasons (60,000). Even during the pre-recessions years of 1987-89, the number of workers who retired earlier than planned was 190,000. Of these, illness and disability accounted for 69,000; closure and layoffs accounted for 20,000; and incentives received accounted for 34,000. That is, even in 'normal' times, a very significant proportion of workers retire earlier than planned because of unanticipated occurrences. Further, the economy is known to sometimes produce unanticipated changes which lead to unanticipated revisions in expectations about future jobs and wages.

Comparing the analysis of chapter 6 on the firm's preferred retirement age and of this chapter on the worker's preferred retirement age, with uncertainty and the occurrence of unanticipated events a distinct possibility, there can be no doubt that any harmony of interests on the retirement age between the firm and any given worker must be no more than a coincidence.

In our analysis, with the worker's optimal retirement age as state dependent, what kind of contract would the rational worker want to negotiate with the firm if the contract was to be entered into at the beginning of the worker's employment period? At this point in time, the retirement age is likely to be several decades in the future. Further, the states of nature obtaining so far in the future and those along the way are likely to be highly uncertain. Therefore, the worker's optimal choice would dictate leaving the retirement age open for determination until the states of nature are well enough known or to negotiate the latest retirement age implied by the possible states of nature, with the worker keeping the option to retire earlier. In keeping with this implication of our analysis, workers, in reality, tend to display little interest in the retirement provisions of their employment at early stages of their career: there is too much uncertainty to worry about a possible conflict between the worker's and the firm's preferred retirement ages (Burkhauser and Quinn, 1983, p. 352). Workers at this stage are more interested in improving their employment and promotion prospects - thus attempting to change the possible outcomes that might occur and their probabilities. They tend to get more interested in the retirement provisions of their jobs towards the end of their careers, as the states likely to obtain for them become somewhat better known. Even then, the dominant fact of worker's retirement choices remains their desire to retire at an age of their choosing, rather than at the firm's pre-specified retirement age.

Looking at the other determinants of the worker's preferred retirement age, these include the wage path, pension contributions and the pension benefits. These are susceptible to manipulation by the firm and the government. The former could do so to realign the workers' and the firm's preferred retirement ages so as to make them more consistent with each other. The latter might do so in the interests of public policy. These issues are taken up in the next chapter.

We have not in this chapter focused on the worker's health as a determinant of his preferred retirement age. It is clearly one of the determinants.[5] While the worker's health is partly exogenous in terms of the income variables considered above, it must also be endogenous to a certain extent: the worker's health depends upon income and the conditions of work and, therefore, depends upon the promotions achieved. In general, the possible improvements in health due to higher incomes and to cleaner and safer work conditions often associated with promotions, would encourage later retirement ages.

Better income, with the state of health held constant, in theory has an ambiguous affect on the worker's preferred retirement age. Assuming leisure to be a normal good, sustained high wage levels through the worker's career are likely to lower this age while low wage levels through most of this career with a high one in the final years of work are likely to increase this age.[6]

FOOTNOTES

1. Assuming that skills depreciate more rapidly away from the job than on the job, it can be shown that the optimal pattern of work and leisure will imply bunching of working years, followed by bunched leisure years. The latter will be the retirement period.

2. In the case of normal distributions, this uncertainty can be captured by the expected value and standard deviation of the relevant distributions.

3. Note that he also has larger bequests at the end of period 2 than if he had *ex ante* known that $w^3 > Ew^3$.

4. The firm and the public pension authorities can also alter the time pattern of the pension benefits during the retirement years, possibly shifting/changing the function for R.

5. Burtless (1987) has two excellent studies on this issue by Poterba and Summers, and Baily.

6. Blank (1988) looks at the determinants of retirement and finds that leisure in the form of earlier retirement was in fact a normal good. Since retirement income in his study had increased significantly, there was an associated decrease in the retirement age. Another study confirming leisure to be a normal good is Hogarth (1988).

9 Retirement and Private Pension Plans

This chapter looks briefly at the interrelationship between our analytical framework in the preceding chapters and the nature and provisions of private pension plans. Basically, it views the deviation of pensions from their role of savings or deferred wages as a vehicle for aligning the firm's and its workers' preferred retirement ages.

Chapter 8 presented the analysis of the workers' preferred retirement age. Chapter 6 had done this for the firm's preferred retirement age for its workers. The two analyses are quite distinct and yield different retirement age functions, so that for a given income stream, the worker could prefer an earlier or later retirement age than the firm's preferred one. In particular, for any given class of workers in a given firm, both the expected value and the dispersion of the workers' preferred retirement ages could be different from those of the firm's preferred retirement ages.

Since the firm's preferred retirement age maximizes the firm's profits, workers choosing to retire earlier or later than this impose losses on the firm. The firm can reduce these losses - and maximize profits, given the workers' preferences - by using the pension plan provisions to reduce the conflict between the workers' and the firm's preferred retirement ages. This usage of the pension benefits may mean changing their present discounted value or/and imposing conditions on the age of retirement.

Further, as chapter 8 showed, given the uncertainty about the wage and promotions path, as well as the uncertainty about the extent of asset accumulation and the state of the worker's health etc., the worker would not be able to specify his optimal retirement age until he reaches the neighbourhood of retirement and the uncertainty is resolved. In particular, his job rung and wages operative in the last years of his career need to be known for the determination of the actual retirement age. A high degree of uncertainty may also affect the firm in its determination of the optimal retirement age for any specific worker. While this uncertainty can be somewhat resolved by the firm varying the retirement age with the job rung achieved or with the occupation, such variation is likely to impose certain costs on the firm. Moreover, even with such variation, the firm and the worker may still have differing preferred retirement ages. Since this difference is likely to become known only late in the worker's career, the firm will need to institute special measures, such as pension enhancement for early retirement, only *late* in the worker's career. The delayed vesting and portability provisions of pensions may be used by firms to reduce worker mobility and strengthen worker attachment to the firm (Pesando and Rea, 1977, ch.2) but tend to occur too early in the worker's career to contribute significantly to the alignment of the worker's and the firm's preferred retirement ages.

However, pensions are not just a means of aligning the firm's and the worker's preferred retirement ages. They can also serve - and generally do so - as a vehicle for savings, especially under circumstances where holding them with the firm is preferable - for reasons of efficiency, return and security - than with other institutions (Munnell, 1982). This component of pensions may be treated as one which is 'actuarially fair' and is based on contributions, whether made by the worker or by the firm. Such actuarially fair savings can be viewed as a form of deferred wages, to which the worker is implicitly 'entitled' at the time the contributions are made but whose payment is delayed.

Further, pensions may have an element of insurance under which workers 'buy' insurance from the firm for a certain amount of income/pensions after retirement and pay appropriate premiums to the firm out of their wages.

Out of these and any other roles of pensions, our concern will be mainly with the role of pensions to strengthen worker attachment to the firm and to align the firm's and workers' preferences on the retirement ages.[1]

Section 1 looks at the worker's and the firm's preferred retirement ages and the ways and costs of aligning them. Section 2 examines the issue of vesting of pension funds. Section 3 comments on pensions as savings. Section 4 compares pattern and conventional pension plans and their relationship to retirement.

9.1 Pensions and the divergence in the retirement ages preferred by workers and firms

9.1.1 Chapter 8 had derived the retirement age, R^h, function for workers for the cases of certainty and uncertainty. For the case of certainty, equation (8) in chapter 8 was:

$$R^h = R^h(\underline{w}', \underline{a}, \underline{A}, \underline{s}, \underline{S}; b_g, b_{T+1}, g, T, \underline{\Omega}, \phi) \tag{1}$$

where the symbols - and other related ones - were defined as:

c_t	consumption in period t
Z	present discounted value of current and future income
b_g	wealth at the beginning of the current period/age g
b_{D+1}	bequest (exogenously set) at the end of age T
w'_t	'Effective wage' in nth period $= (\partial Z/\partial n)\,\Omega^t$
s	private pension benefits
S	social security/public pension benefits
a	private pension contributions
A	social security/public pension contributions
Ω	discount factor $(= 1 + i)$
R^h	optimal retirement age $(= g + n)$ from the worker's decision
D	(Expected) date of death/planning horizon
g	current/hiring age
n	years of work left until retirement $(= R - g)$
ϕ	uncertainty

The line under a variable indicates that it is the vector of the values of the variable from age g to age T. Note that (the subscript) h is used in this chapter for 'households/workers' and not for the hiring age. ϕ has been inserted as an argument in the function on the right hand side of (1) to emphasize the role of uncertainty where it does exist.

In chapter 8, the stochastic dynamic analysis for the case of uncertainty had implied equations (9) to (15) for optimal consumption and retirement. The optimal functions *from the perspective of the worker at the beginning of period 1*, were:

$$_1c^i = {}_1c^i(w^1; {}_1(w^2, p^2); {}_1(w^3, q^3); b_1, b_5, \Omega) \quad i = 1,...,4$$

$$_1R = {}_1R(w^1; {}_1(w^2, p^2); {}_1(w^3, q^3); b_1, b_5, \Omega) \tag{2}$$

where

w^1	wage in period 1
$_{i-1}(w^i, p^i)$	the wage-probability combinations expected for period i when the worker is in period i-1.
$_j(w^i, q^i)$	the wage-probability combinations expected for period i when the worker is in period j
$_jc^i$	ith period's consumption, on the basis of planning in period j.
$_jR$	retirement age, on the basis of planning in period j.
b_1	inheritance at age 1
b_5	bequest at the end of age 4

In (2)), q^i are the probabilistically equivalent single-stage combinations of the second and the third period's subjective probabilities. b_g and b_{D+1} are, again respectively the exogenously given inheritance in period g and the bequest at the end of period D. w^i is the effective wage in i. It includes the change in pension benefits and excludes the change in pension contributions due to employment in period i.

The consumption and retirement age functions *from the perspective of the worker at the beginning of period 2 and with the outcomes and their probabilities remaining consistent with those specified at the beginning of period 1*, were,

$$_2c^i = {}_2c^i(w^2, {}_2(w^3, p^3), b_2, b_5, \Omega) \qquad i = 2,3,4$$

$$_2R = {}_2R(w^2, {}_2(w^3, p^3), b_2, b_5, \Omega) \qquad\qquad (3)$$

$_2(w^3, p^3)$ is here assumed to be identical with $_1(w^3, p^3)$ so that the passage of time from period 1 to period 2 did not change the outcomes and their probabilities for the periods still in the future.

The consumption and retirement age functions *from the perspective of the worker at the beginning of period 3 and with the outcome in period 3 consistent with the prospects specified at the beginning of period 1*, were:

$$_3c^i = {}_3c^i(w^3, b_3, b_5, \Omega) \qquad i = 3,4$$

$$_3R = {}_3R(w_3, b_3, b_5, \Omega) \qquad\qquad (4)$$

The reason for repeating equations (2) to (4) here is to stress again that the worker's optimal retirement age can only be determined in a specific manner once uncertainty disappears. In our four period model, uncertainty disappears in period 3 when that period's wage finally became known. Note also that the worker's planned contingent consumption and retirement ages are interdependent.

The broad conclusions from equations (1) to (4) for this chapter are then as follows. First, as far as the worker is concerned, the optimal retirement age R^h is uncertain as long as there exists uncertainty about the wages and pension benefits, health and other relevant variables. This uncertainty may not be resolved except in the neighbourhood of the retirement age. The worker would not, therefore, wish to commit himself to a fixed retirement age until this uncertainty disappears or becomes minor. Second, the income effect on R^h of wage increases at the retirement age are *a priori* unknown. For the *average* worker, it is quite likely that leisure is a normal good so that the income effect of increases in income will lower R^h. However, there would be individual variations both in the size of the effect and even possibly its sign: increases in wages in the neighbourhood of the retirement age would set up conflicting substitution and income effects on R^h, with the overall impact on individual workers *a priori* unknown and probably varying among workers. Hence, if the firm wanted to persuade its workers to alter R^h voluntarily, it could not use reductions or increases in wages to influence R^h with *determinate* and *predictable* effects on all or most of its workers.

In contrast to the substitution effect of *wage* increases producing a delay in the retirement age, increases in *pensions* - other things (including wages) being the same - produce a substitution affect in favour of leisure and hence cause earlier retirement. If the increases in pensions also increase the present discounted value of income, their effect - again assuming a normal income effect - will further lower R^h.

Therefore, at a given present discounted level of income, decreases in wages in years approaching R^h, with compensatory increases in pensions after retirement, will unambiguously lower R^h. An increase in this present discounted level of income, either through an increase in pensions or a lump sum payment - such as a 'golden handshake' on accepting retirement - will further lower R^h. The firm could then rely upon an 'upward tilt' of the wage-pension profile - that is, lower wages in periods prior to retirement and higher pensions afterwards - accompanied by an increase in the present discounted value of income to decrease R^h unambiguously. Conversely, it could use a 'downward tilt' of the wage-pension path and decreases in the present discounted value of income to raise R^h. Tilting the wage-pension path and golden handshakes thus provide the firm with two different - and compatible - instruments for manipulating R^h.

Increases in the present discounted value of income may be brought about not only through golden handshakes on the worker's retirement but also through increases in wages during years earlier than in the neighbourhood of the retirement age. This would be true of periods/stages 1 and 2 in the four period uncertainty model of the preceding chapter. An increase in wages during the middle working years is then another instrument available to the firm for inducing a reduction in R^h.

Different workers are likely to have differing preferences and differing personal factors such as health. For any given firm and given rank or type of workers, R^h will have a distribution rather than a single value. Assume that R^h has a normal distribution with mean ER^h and standard deviation σ^h.

The firm may want to shift ER^h or σ^h or both. We will take the desired change in σ^h to be a reduction in it, though it need not always be so. The firm will need different types of inducements to influence both ER^h and σ^h. Mandatory retirement policies can be a way to achieve an actual retirement age R whose mean ER and standard deviation σ may differ respectively from ER^h and σ^h.

9.1.2 Chapters 3 and 6 presented the model for deriving the firm's preferred retirement age R^f for its workers, with the subscript f standing for the 'firm'. The firm was taken to maximize the present discounted value of its profits. R^f maximized this value. Its determinants were the relevant interest rates and the time path of the firm's share of the rents from firm-specific skills, with this rent being the marginal product less the rental - that is, the wage plus other labour related charges - cost of labour hired for its job positions. The rents generated by both the preceding and the succeeding generations of workers were relevant to the determination of R^f for the current generation of workers. Hence, write the determinants of R^f as,

$$R^f = R^f((\underline{w}^f_0, \underline{m}_0); (\underline{w}^f_{-1}, \underline{m}_{-1}), (\underline{w}^f_1, \underline{m}_1), \Omega) \qquad (2)^2$$

where,

w^f	labour cost per worker (wage plus the firm's pension contributions etc.)
m	marginal product
$(\underline{w}^f, \underline{m})$	wage $(\underline{w})$, marginal product $(\underline{m})$ vectors
0	subscript for the current generation of workers on the job
-1	subscript for the preceding generation
1	subscript for the succeeding generation

Focusing only on the variables pertaining to the current generation, with the others taken as exogenously given, (1) simplifies to:

$$R^f = R^f(\underline{w}^f_0, \underline{m}_0, \Omega) \tag{2'}$$

Further, taking the rate of discount as exogenously given and focusing only on the last period R before retirement, (2) can be further approximated by,

$$R^f = R^f(w^f_R - m_R) \tag{2''}$$

where w^f_R and m_R are the labour cost per worker and the marginal product respectively in period R; $(w^f_R - m_R) > 0$ for intra-marginal job positions, with $\partial(w^f_R - m_R)/\partial R < 0$ for career job positions and $\partial(w^f_R - m_R)/\partial R = 0$ for casual job positions.

9.1.3   Divergence between R^f and R^h will reduce the firm's present discounted value of profits unless the firm can retire the worker at age R^f without incurring any cost arising from that divergence. The nature of some of these costs was discussed in chapter 6 above. Since profits are maximized at R^f, the decrease in the firm's share of its profits for a given worker holding a given job can be represented by the decrease in V, where V is the present discounted value of the firm's share of the rents from the job position held by the given worker.

There are two main and four subcases relevant to the analysis of the divergence between R^f and R^h. These are:

(a) $R^f < R^h$, with subcases:

(i) $R = R^f < R^h$

where R is the actual retirement age. In this subcase, the firm could achieve the equality of the actual retirement age R with its preferred R^f by imposing a mandatory retirement age at R^f or firing the worker at that age. However, since $R^h > R^f$, workers want to stay longer on the job and as discussed in chapter 6, there are likely to be costs to the firm of retiring the worker prior to his preferred retirement age. One of these costs arises from the impact of such an action on the morale of the worker himself while he is still on the job, as well as on the morale of his colleagues, and consequently on the workers' productivity and the firm's share of the rents from his firm-specific skills. Assuming this productivity to be a function of $(R^h - R^f)$ for $R^h > R^f$, the present value of the firm's share of the rents for a given job position will depend negatively upon $(R^h - R^f)$. That is, $\partial V/\partial(R^h - R^f) < 0$.

(ii) $R = R^h > R^f$

Here, the worker retires at an age of his choosing, even when it exceeds the firm's preferred one. In this subcase, the firm also suffers a decrease in V, since V is maximized at R^f and V is assumed to be concave in R.

(b) $R^h < R^f$ with subcases:

(i) $R = R^h < R^f$

This subcase occurs since indentured labour is illegal and the worker can leave employment at any time. Hence, in this subcase, workers will leave at R^h. Since $V(R^h) < V(R^f)$, it is in the interest of the firm to reduce the loss due to too early retirement.

For $R = R^h$, the magnitude of the loss suffered by the firm is $[V(R^f) - V(R^h)]$. The loss per period can be approximated by $[iV - (m_R - w^f_R)]$ where iV is the rental value of the job and $(m_R - w^f_R)$ is the rent received by the firm by keeping the worker on the job in period R.

(ii) $R = R^f > R^h$

Laws against indentured labour rule out this subcase.

The firm may be taken to choose a loss minimizing strategy. One of its possible strategies is to retire the career worker at R^f and pay the worker an amount X such that R^f would also be his preferred retirement age. For $R^h > R^f$, this would be an optimal strategy if the loss through worker resentment at early retirement was high, the compensation needed to change R^h was low and $(m - w^f)$ was much lower than the rental value of the job iV. For $R^h < R^f$, with $R = R^f$, the firm cannot compel the worker to remain on the job beyond R^h. It must compensate him sufficiently to raise R^h to R^f. This would be optimal if the compensation was less than the alternative loss $[V(R^f) - V(R^h)]$ from retirement at R^h.

In the extreme case of casual workers, as argued earlier, $\partial V(R)/\partial R$ is zero for all values of R, so that $\partial[V(R^f) - V(R^h)]/\partial R = 0$. Hence, the optimal strategy for the firm in the case of casual workers is not to pay any compensation for early or late retirement. For $R^f < R^h$, if the resentment at forced early retirement would impose a productivity loss on the firm, the optimal strategy would be to employ the worker until R^h. For $R^h < R^f$, since the casual worker's replacement will generate the same amount of rents as he does, the firm does not lose by letting him retire at R^h and replacing him by another worker. In fact, as argued in chapters 3 and 6, the firm does not really have a preferred retirement age R^f for casual workers. Hence the optimal strategy for casual workers is not to pay them any compensation for early or late retirement. This strategy would also seem to be optimal for workers who fill 'almost-casual' job positions, i.e., career job positions with $\partial V(R)/\partial R$ being close to zero.

Define R^{f*} as the optimal retirement age from the firm's perspective for the *average* worker on the job, where the star refers to the average worker. We first consider the cases where $R^{f*} < R^h$. For career jobs having a high rental value and a high *average* loss $[V(R^{f*}) - V(R^h)]$, 'good workers' - that is, those with higher than the average productivity - will impose a smaller loss on the firm by staying longer on the job than 'bad workers' - that is those with lower than the average productivity. The loss minimizing firm will then be willing to pay the good workers less to retire early, at R^{f*}, than the bad workers. For sufficiently superior workers, the optimal strategy could in fact be to retain them until R^h since, even at R^h, they might generate at least the rental value of the job or sufficiently close to it. That is, *for R^{f*} < R^h, the worse is the worker in terms of productivity, the higher is the optimal 'bribe' to retire earlier than he would otherwise want to.*

Conversely, *for $R^{f*} > R^h$, the firm would find it profit maximizing to let 'bad' workers go at R^h and 'bribe' only 'good' workers to stay until R^f.* This is even more so for truly superior workers.

Therefore, the payment of compensation for changing R^{h*} differs between the two cases of $R^{f*} < R^h$ and $R^{f*} > R^h$ for bad and good workers. Bad workers are bribed to lower R^h in the former case while good ones are bribed to raise R^h in the latter case. Good workers stay on the job until a later age in both cases.

9.2 Pensions and vesting: unvested pension funds

The worker's choice model of chapter 8 viewed pension contributions and benefits as elements of the present discounted value of the worker's real wealth Z. The excess in present discounted terms of pension benefits over employment-related contributions was identical in its implications with the real disposable wage w'. But this excess amount was not a consequence of employment in any given period, it was identical in implications with the exogenously given initial bequest b_g. These remarks implicitly assume that the worker has the same rights of ownership, possession and control over his future rights to pensions as he has over his current wealth and wages, and that the market also treats them identically. These implicit assumptions do not hold up in the real world. There are many differences between pensions and current wages, not the least of them being that the actual value of pension rights is often dependent upon the firm's own interests and solvency, upon the uncertainty about the worker's continued employment with the firm and upon his longevity. These differences explain some of the practices with regard to the vesting of pensions. This section focuses on the issue of vested versus unvested pensions.

Most common types of private pension plans requires the worker and the firm each to make specified contributions to the worker's pension plan. The worker's contributions are usually vested in him from the date he starts contributing while the firm's contributions are often not vested in him - that is, he cannot claim ownership of them - for a designated period after his joining the firm.[3] During this period, the worker's pension fund has a vested portion and an unvested portion, with the latter appropriated by the firm if the worker quits or is fired before the end of the designated period.

The unvested part of the pension fund can be viewed in a number of ways. There seems to be fairly general agreement in the literature that it serves as an inducement to workers to reduce quits and thereby promotes job attachment (for example, see Becker, 1964, pp. 26-27; Blinder, 1981; Leigh 1984). Vesting is inconsistent with the incentives model since it would reduce the incentive for workers not to shirk and also reduces the incentive for them not to quit (Lazear, 1982).

As chapter 3 argued, quits impose a loss on the firm in the case of career jobs, though not in the case of casual ones. The unvested component of pension plans is, therefore, likely to occur more for career rather than casual jobs.

The unvested pension fund acts on the worker as an inducement to reduce quits. But it also acts as inducement for the firm to fire the worker or force him to resign prior to the vesting date, with the firm appropriating this unvested amount. The firm will not do so if this amount is less than the loss to the firm from the job separation. The nature of this loss, due to the decrease in the present discounted value of the rents from the job position from a job separation earlier than at the optimal retirement ages, was analyzed in chapter 6. Since this loss is zero for casual jobs, the moral hazard element becomes dominant for such jobs so that casual workers would not trust the firm with such an unvested fund, if one was instituted for them. In fact, having such a fund jeopardizes their occupancy of the job since it gives the firm an inducement to get rid of them before the vesting date, thus imposing on them the loss of the unvested fund *and* of the job. Casual workers should, then, resist an unvested pension fund, unless there are other provisions for ensuring their continued occupancy of the job.

For career jobs with significant rent accruals to the firm, unvested funds are again not in the interest of the worker if the optimal retirement age R^f is within or soon after an unvested period: in these cases, the future loss to the firm from getting rid of the worker is likely to be less than the unvested fund. Examples of such cases are professional players of physical sports and fashion models.[4] Unvested pension funds are, therefore, unlikely to exist for such workers.

Therefore, unvested pension funds are only likely to be in the interests of both the firm and the worker in the case of career jobs with significant future rent accruals to the firm from continued employment and with long optimal employment periods.

Are the unvested funds out of the worker's past *or* future marginal productivity? As discussed in chapter 6, one approach in the literature considers them to be funds accumulated from the worker's productivity at the time of the firm's contribution into them and as such compensation properly due to the worker even prior to the vesting period (for example, see Blinder, 1981). In this approach, unvested funds are a 'bond' posted by the worker against an unjustified quit. However, there can exist simpler versions of such bonds. In particular, there can exist versions of bonds which are not subject to the exercise of moral hazard by the firm (Akerlof and Yellen, 1986, pp. 4-6).

Our approach in chapter 6 was to emphasize, for significantly large unvested funds, the lack of adequate trust by the worker in the firm in the presence of moral hazard. In our approach, then, the unvested funds must be an expected payment out of the worker's 'future' - that is, after the vesting date - expected productivity. Prior specification of them by the firm is the firm's recognition of the dependence of the worker's future productivity upon the current acquisition by him of firm-specific skills on the job. In short, the firm's contributions to an unvested fund are an indicator, though not a full measure, of the expected increase in future productivity because of continuing current learning of firm-specific skills *and* of the expected duration of the worker remaining with the firm. They cannot be vested in the present because they have not actually accrued yet but are a by-product of current employment and the expected period of employment with the firm. The firm uses unvested pension funds as a signal to indicate its current interest in the worker's future continuation on the job. They are also an inducement to the worker to acquire the relevant skills in the present, with non-acquisition resulting in a job separation before the vesting date. As a corollary, unvested pension funds would not be used in cases where firm-specific skills are not important and/or the optimal duration of employment from the firm's perspective is relatively short.

The existence of unvested funds, therefore, is evidence of the expectation of significant firm-specific rents to be generated by the worker over a long period in the future. These rents are shared between the firm and the worker. The unvested pension funds are then a part of the future rents accruing to the worker as his share. After the vesting date, there must also be another part - out of the worker's share of the rents from firm-specific skills - which will be paid to the worker in current wages and which he would lose if he left the firm for another firm. This limits the possibility of his quitting and allows the firm to recoup from his productivity the amounts specified by it in the formerly unvested pension.

9.3 Pensions as savings

Pension plans represent the accrual of purchasing power in the future, just like the private savings done by the worker on his own and over which he retains control. However, the worker cannot draw upon his pensions until the designated age or date late in life.[5] He is also generally not able to borrow against future pension receipts. These may not prove to be a constraint on his behaviour if his income and optimal consumption patterns would have anyway allowed him to set aside savings equal to or greater than his pension contribution and the firm's contribution on his behalf. We will assume this to be so. Pensions can then be treated as a form of voluntary saving or of deferred wages (Pesando and Rea, 1977, ch. 2). In taking this approach, we do not accept that the usual case of pensions arises from 'employer benevolence and/or familial ties', an approach also discounted by Pesando and Rea (1977, p.11).

The worker may want part of his savings invested in the form of private and public pensions for a variety of reasons. These forms permit portfolio diversification of his overall savings, with 'professional management' by the firm or a designated institution of the pension funds at a low transaction cost to the worker. Besides the benefits from diversification, such management may yield the worker a higher rate of return than he might manage to get on the rest of his savings. A higher rate of return may also come about if pension schemes permit tax deferral either on the original contributions or on their yield. Further, pension plans with a formula as a minimum base would also limit the worker's downside risk, making them an even more attractive investment vehicle. The element of compulsion in pension contributions may also contribute to the appeal of pensions as a savings medium.

While pensions can be considered as a form of savings, they also play other roles. We have already discussed their role in encouraging job attachment. We now turn to their role in aligning the worker's and the firm's preferred retirement ages. As argued earlier in the introduction to this chapter, the existence of uncertainty implies that this role of pensions is likely to occur close to the retirement age and not early in the worker's career.

9.4 Pensions and the retirement age

As discussed earlier, a gratuitous increase in the pension fund contingent upon 'early' retirement would cause a substitution effect in favour of early retirement. Further, assuming leisure in the form of retirement to be a normal good, the income effect would also induce early retirement. The firm can, therefore, use such payments - independent of wages and work -to induce its workers to decrease R^h. Conversely, the firm can use appropriations of the pension funds to induce delays in R^h. Where such a recourse is not available to the firm for legal or other reasons, it may be able to induce increases in R^h by making increases in the pension fund contingent on working for a longer period.

The firm can, therefore, use the present discounted value of pensions and the terms of the pension plans as instruments to induce increases or decreases in R^h.

Given the possibility that R^f may equal, exceed or be less than ER^h, there would exist three types of pension plans.[6] If $R^f = ER^h$, the worker's compensation would be based on his productivity and the rental value of the job, with the firm being indifferent between the division of this compensation into wages and pensions. A pure savings-based - that is - 'actuarially fair' - pension plan would occur and the pension plan would be designed to be neutral in terms of its impact on R^h.[7] If $R^f > ER^h$, the firm would use the provisions of the pension plan to induce increases in ER^h. Such plans are often called 'conventional plans'.[8] If $R^f < ER^h$, the firm would use the pension plan to encourage decreases in ER^h. Such plans are often called 'pattern plans' (Fields and Mitchell, 1984, pp. 57-59).

In the case of $R^f_0 < ER^h_0$, suppose that the firm institutes a pattern plan such that, in figure 9.1, h(R) shifts from $h(R_0)$ to $h(R_1)$, with $ER^h_1 = R^f$.[9] This has two distinct consequences. One is that workers who are in the upper half of the $h(R_1)$ distribution would have an enriched pension plan, greater than in a pure savings-based plan, even though they still wish to retire later than R^f. The firm may then have to institute selective measures tailored to individual workers to induce retirement at R^f, or to institute mandatory retirement (MR) at R^f. The other distinctive aspect is that workers in the lower half of the $h(R_1)$ distribution would also receive an enriched pension, retire voluntarily without further inducement and retire earlier than R^f. In fact, some of these workers would have retired voluntarily before R^f without the special inducements. These are the workers to the left of R^f in the $h(R_0)$ distribution in figure 9.1.

Given that R^f was the firm's profit maximizing retirement age, workers

205

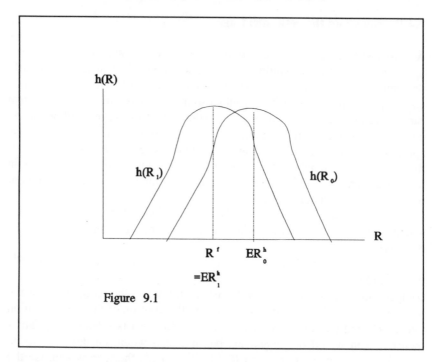

Figure 9.1

retiring later than R^f impose a loss on the firm. Therefore, the general policy of shifting $h(R)$ to reduce ER^h to R^f may reduce this loss but the dispersion of R^h still imposes a loss on the firm. The optimal policy for the firm would be to induce all workers to retire at R^f or to compel them to do so, as in a MR policy, thus eliminating this dispersion also. A MR policy is thus likely to be the least cost policy for the firm, with some selective enrichment of pension plans to reduce worker resentment at compulsory retirement. The fact that MR policies were often in the past accompanied by general pattern pension plans is some indication that firms tried to shift the R^h distribution, including ER^h, even while using the compulsion element in MR.[10]

Therefore, in the absence of MR and given $R^f < ER^h$, the firm would need general pattern plan provisions to reduce ER^h and selective ones to reduce the dispersion of R^h. These may cost the firm more than if MR was possible as a policy.

In the case of $R^f > ER^h$, the firm would use a conventional pension plan to induce later retirement. Such an inducement can be an increase in wages at and after ER^h or an increase in the present discounted value of pensions if retirement is delayed. By comparison, as mentioned earlier, in the case of $R^f < ER^h$, there would be a decrease in wages for work after R^f and/or a pattern pension plan with a decrease in the present discounted value of pensions for a worker choosing to continue on the job beyond R^f.

For some empirical evidence, Fields and Mitchell[11] report that "pattern plans discourage work beyond age 60. An employee in a pattern pension plan who defers retiring until age 65 will receive lifetime benefits about 18% lower than at age 60. On the other hand, conventional plans' present value streams are structured so that the worker who defers retirement until age 65 will receive about 17% higher benefits than if he retired at 60". (Fields and Mitchell, 1984, p. 57).[12] The change in the present discounted value of pensions (PDVPP) for each additional year of work has been computed by Fields and Mitchell (p. 57), as given in their following table.

Change in Retirement Age

Age:	60-61	61-62	62-63	63-64	64-65
Plan type:					
Pattern	-2%	-2%	-5%	-5%	-5%
Conventional	+2%	+14%	0	0	0

9.5 Some rough calculations

For *career* workers, it has been argued above that their preferred retirement age will often differ from the firm's MR one, with MR at R^f, and that firms are likely to use pension plan provisions to move the former to the latter, if only for the purpose of reducing workers' resentment over this difference. Suppose these provisions manage to equate ER^h to the MR date, so that $ER^h = R^f = MR$ age. Further, assume that for workers in good health at ER^h, R^h has a normal distribution around ER^h. Then 50% of those still able to work and in good enough health at ER^h would have taken early retirement voluntarily before ER^h. If b% of the workers retired early because of poor health, then $(b + 1/2 (100 - b))\%$ would have retired voluntarily before the MR age.

Empirical evidence indicates strongly that the majority of workers covered by MR policies do tend to retire earlier than the MR date. Fields and Mitchell (1984, p. 8) report from the Longitudinal Retirement History Survey (LRHS) sample of 1103 white married men, that 48.9% of the men retired earlier than age 65 while 12% of the total sample gave poor health as the reason for such early retirement (see also Clark, Kreps and Spengler, 1978, pp. 935-37; Parnes, 1981, ch. 6 and Burtless *et al* (1987) for the relationship between health and retirement). Our earlier rough guess/prediction with b equal to 12% would have given 56% of the sample as the sum of the early retirees and those voluntarily retiring at the MR date. The LRHS information and our rough approximation are fairly close.[13]

For *casual* workers, the firm has no incentive to impose a MR policy. If one is imposed, it would be as late as the oldest age at which any of its casual workers want to retire. Such a policy would not infringe on the desire of any of its workers to continue working, while allowing others who want to retire earlier to do so. Most retirements would then seem to occur voluntarily or due to poor health. However, other reasons for imposing MR on casual workers must be taken into account here. MR may be at the request or insistence of unions. These reasons will dictate how late the MR age is and how many workers will want to retire before it. However, to the extent that such an age accommodates must workers' preferences, most workers would retire before it.

There are, consequently, strong reasons to expect that a high percentage of career and casual workers in good health would wish to retire earlier than the MR age. If we add to these the workers who retire voluntarily for reasons of poor health, the majority of workers would tend to retire for health and economic reasons and would do so prior to the MR age, rather than being forced out of the job at the MR age.

Further, consider the following at the level of a rough heuristic argument. Assume that we are again dealing with a group of workers with 65 as ER^h (= MR age) and with a normal distribution centred at age 65. Although the expected life expectancy of most males in US and Canada is somewhat over 70 years, it seems that virtually every male worker wants to retire by age 70. Assume, therefore, that the $h(R)$ distribution is such that $ER^h + 2\sigma = 70$, where σ is the standard deviation of R^h. Then 50% of the workers would have preferred retiring at or before age 65, 65.5% would prefer retiring by age 66, 78.8% by age 67, 88.5% by age 68 and so on. If workers retired by MR a year or two earlier than their preferred retirement ages do not feel sufficiently resentful, they may not cite the reason for retiring as being forced out of work by MR. A survey of such workers would show that only a very small percentage of workers would indicate a willingness to continue working beyond the MR age. This is what the empirical survey data does tend to show.

Conclusion

Pension plans were viewed in this chapter partly as savings out of wages left to grow with the employer and partly as a vehicle to adjust the workers' optimal (utility maximizing) retirement age R^h to the firm's profit maximizing one, R^f. A possible conflict between these ages arises in our theory since the two ages are determined by different forces and different economic agents, with uncertainty playing a critical role. Pension plans, or some component of them, are attempts by firms to induce workers to harmonize R^h with the firm's R^f. There would, therefore, be three types of pension plans: pure savings (actuarially fair) plans, conventional plans and pattern plans.

The use of pension plans to orient R^h towards R^f will occur in job positions with firm-specific skills. For casual jobs, since the optimal employment period can be any period, there is no implication for or against long-term job attachment and there is no need for a R^h-modifying policy. The firm would be indifferent between having or not having a mandatory retirement (MR) policy. Therefore, for casual jobs, the firm would not use a pension plan, if one is instituted for such workers, to persuade workers to accept early retirement or postpone it. Further, since casual workers receive wages equal to their marginal product, the firm does not find it profitable to pay them an additional amount in pensions. Hence, any pension plans for casual workers would be pure savings schemes under which workers take less than their marginal product in wages during their working years, with the remainder received later in pensions. Vesting of the accumulating pension sums from the beginning would be normal under the circumstances. So would be the complete portability of such funds.

Further, for casual jobs, since workers do not receive any quasi-rents from their job positions, they also do not have a strong attachment to the firm. Therefore, they would not have a strong preference for maintaining a pension plan with the firm rather than with financial institutions, unless there were other benefits such as lower transactions costs for savings plans with the firm. Hence, in general, casual workers are less likely to have pension plans with their firms, as well as being less likely to be subject to MR policies.

For career jobs with significant rents accruing to the firm, pensions are almost a necessary concomitant of a retirement age R^f preferred by the firm (for empirical evidence on this, see Gordon and Blinder, 1980; Gordon, 1960; Clark, Kreps and Spengler, 1978). While there is likely to be a large savings element in them (Munnell, 1982), they are also meant to reduce quits so that they may not be fully vested or portable in the *early* years on the job (Pesando and Rea, 1977). However, since our model does not assume that workers trust the firm completely, the vesting of the pension funds will occur soon after the worker's savings with the firm start accumulating. Pesando and Rea (1977) report that the trend in recent years in both legislation and the practice of firms has been towards earlier vesting.

With vesting of pension funds and with severance payments having their own determinants in our theory, severance payments are not necessarily a reflection of accumulating unvested pension funds. Further, given uncertainty over R^h through the early parts of workers' careers, the R^h-modifying provisions of pensions will tend to occur late in workers' careers.

We envisaged pattern pension plans as incorporating payments by the firm to encourage earlier retirement in an attempt to decrease ER^h to R^f. Conventional plans incorporate pension benefits which are only available if the worker delays retirements, in an attempt by the firm to increase ER^h to R^f. Given that variations in workers' preferences leave a dispersion of preferred retirement ages, mandatory retirement policies, if legal, could often be the least cost method of adjusting R^h to R^f. The resentment against the compulsory element in such policies could be handled through special payments by the firm in the form of the pattern and conventional pension plans.

Hutchens (1989), among others, pointed out that persons retiring early often receive a larger expected value of pensions than if they continued working to the normal retirement age. The evidence cited by him showed a very significant difference: about \$158,000 at age 55 versus about \$79,000 at age 65 with 40 years of tenure, implying about \$8,000 per year of early retirement. He argued that such an early retirement bonus was a 'puzzle' for human capital theory and in general was incompatible with theories in which wages were equal to or are *less* than productivity, since in such a case the firm would not profit from inducing earlier retirement. In fact, if wages were less than the productivity of the worker, the firm would increase its profits by keeping the worker as long as this condition held. This condition holds in our theory for career workers: part of their productivity is a quasi-rent, which is split between the firm and the worker, so that wages are less than productivity. Hutchen's argument would then imply that the above empirical observation would be evidence against our theory. Our arguments in this and earlier chapters show that this is not so. Our theory in fact predicts such bonuses in certain conditions.

The analysis of chapter 3 showed that the firm has an optimal number of job positions and in the context of the replacement of workers in these job positions, it has optimal hiring and retirement ages for its career workers. Even with wages less than the productivity of a given worker, it may pay the firm to replace him by giving him a retirement bonus so that it can hire a more profitable worker for his job. This can occur if he wants to continue working beyond the firm's optimal retirement age for its workers. It can also occur in the particular context of the worsening of the worker's health and other personal characteristics, or increases in the technical requirements of the job , such that his actual productivity became less than the expected one. Further, early retirement bonuses may also be offered where the job position is being phased out for technical or inadequate demand reasons, and the career worker will lose the anticipated - and implicity agreed upon - share of his quasi-rents, which would have occurred if the job had continued. Consequently, our framework puts forward various reasons for early retirement to include a bonus not offered to those retiring at the normal retirement age, even though the wage may be below the worker's productivity.

FOOTNOTES

1. Burbidge and Robb (1980) is a compact statement of some aspects of this.
2. We have the optimizing condition (4C) from chapter 3 as:
$$\partial V/\partial R^f = i(V - A)$$
where V is the present discounted value of the firm's share of the rents from the jth job position, A is the present value of these rents from the first worker, R^f is the retirement age preferred by the firm and i is the interest rate. The firm's share of the rents from the jth job position in any period equals the worker's marginal product from holding that job position less the compensation paid to him.
3. Some firms seem to require as many as ten years of employment with the firm before vesting their share of the contributions.
4. See chapter 6 for the discussion of such cases.
5. For a thorough treatment of pensions as organized savings, see Munnell (1982) and Pesando and Rea (1977). Burbidge and Robb (1980) analyze the differences between age-conditioned plans - that is, those with pensions starting at a designated age - and retirement-conditioned plans - that is, those with pensions payable only on retirement from the given job.
6. This section assumes that in the case of a difference between ER^h and R^f, the firm would try to use its pension plan, rather than any other instrument such as coercion or mandatory retirement, to induce changes in R^h. Further, it assumes that the firm would try to align ER^h to R^f, rather than to some other value of R^f, though this need not always be so in the real world.
7. The division of the savings channelled into the pension plan between contributions by the worker and the firm is immaterial to this point and our discussion in this chapter.
8. Fields and Mitchell (1984, p. 59) point out that the existence of conventional plans is inconsistent with Lazear's incentives model in which

early retirement is to the firm's advantage and is encouraged by the firm. However, Lazear's model strictly allows only pure savings-based pension plans since in that model R^f are R^h are determined in such a way as to be equal on an *ex ante* basis.

9. We have assumed R^f to be constant in this illustration. However, pattern plans impose a cost on the firm such that R^f could increase.

10. Note that the firms may still have had selective provisions for early retirement to deal with those whose competence was particularly inadequate.

11. Fields and Mitchell based their findings on fourteen pension plans from the U.S. Labour Department's Benefit Amounts Survey done in 1978.

12. Fields and Mitchell also found that pattern plans were most prevalent where workers receive equal pay for standardized work, as in large manufacturing firms while conventional plans are more common where pay is less standardized (p. 54). Further, unionized firms have somewhat later retirement ages and blue-collar workers tend to retire earlier (p. 71).

13. Our predictions are for career workers facing MR policies. The evidence cited from LRHS is for all workers. Further, 65 years need not be the MR age for all these workers.

10   Summary and Conclusions

Discrimination of various types, retirement and pensions are all facets of the labour market so that one would expect some common factors to permeate their determinants. Of course, one would also reasonably expect the converse: there are also likely to exist some independent and isolated determinants of each of these phenomena. This book is a study in the former. It uses the human capital approach and the nature of skills in a profit maximizing context to specify a common model for explaining aspects of these phenomena. Other contributions in the literature have not have sought out such a common or unifying theme, so that these phenomena seem to be largely unrelated from the perspective of the dominant theories explaining discrimination and retirement. This book establishes such a common element and shows its relevance to such diverse labour market phenomena as wage and occupational discrimination against women and minority workers, in hiring older workers, and in firms' desire to impose mandatory retirement, with young workers' indifference to it but with older workers' resentment to such imposition.

The extent and nature of discrimination, and the imposition and the degree of insistence/implementation of forced retirement, etc., clearly differ among various types of jobs. We explain such differences by drawing upon the extent to which the various types of jobs mix general and firm-specific skills.

While the existence and pervasiveness of firm-specific skills has been widely recognized in the literature, their role as a unifying element in explaining discrimination against female workers and against hiring older workers, as well as in explaining retirement practices, has not generally been

213

recognized: the main theories explaining these would work equally well in the absence of firm-specific skills. To illustrate, the dominant theory of discrimination against female workers and minorities explains such discrimination on the basis of discriminatory preferences either by firms or workers (Becker, 1957). Discrimination against hiring older workers is usually based on the firm's desire to recoup the workers' training costs over a longer period. The dominant theory on mandatory retirement seems to be the incentives theory of retirement, which bases its explanation for mandatory retirement on the firm's desire to reduce shirking on the job (Lazear, 1981). None of these explanations has the particular nature of firm-specific skills as an essential feature, especially in a replacement model, even though mention is often made of them in such explanations. However, these explanations would be equally cogent if the workers were purely casual rather than career ones with firm-specific skills. Emphasizing the nature of these skills gives a somewhat different perspective on each of these issues, as well as a unifying framework for them. This unified framework was presented in chapter 3.

Virtually all other theories on the issues dealt with in this book use models restricted to the employment of the worker in question or to the current generation of workers, and it is tempting to opt for such a simplified framework. However, such a restrictive framework for the firm's profit maximizing decisions seems to be particularly inappropriate in a study of hiring - of which discrimination is a facet - and retirement, since the very notions of retirement of one worker and the hiring of another imply the replacement of workers and the turnover from one 'generation' of workers to another. That is, the replacement of one worker by another of a different age - or the rotation of workers of different generations in the job positions in the firm - must be central to explanations of discrimination and retirement. This focuses attention on changes occurring between different generations of workers and their impact on the labour markets. A major such change would be the 'technological' change in skills, through changes in education, training and the advances in knowledge between generations. Another such change would be that in the longevity and health of workers. Such changes alter the productivity of succeeding generations of workers, and, as we showed, alter the nature and extent of the various types of discrimination, as well as the firms' - and workers' preferences - for retirement ages and pensions for the current generation of workers. We relied upon such 'technical' factors for explaining the actual changes that have been occurring in these, though without totally ignoring changes in the ideas and legislation regarding them.

We now turn to a very brief review of the analysis and findings presented in the preceding chapters.

10.1 General and firm-specific skills

Using the possession or lack of firm-specific skills as a distinguishing feature, workers in the economy were divided into casual and career workers. The former do not possess firm-specific skills, the latter do. A similar distinction belongs to jobs. Jobs whose performance leads to the learning of significant firm-specific skills and the utilization of those skills can be classified as career jobs; those without such characteristics would be casual jobs. Applying the same distinction to workers and jobs brings out a point that seems to have generally gone unnoticed in the literature. This is that firm-specificity in the exercise of skills is a joint product of worker's expertise and of job characteristics so that the resulting increase in productivity from such skills is shared between the worker - in whom the skills are embedded - and the firm - which is the owner of the job position. This sharing of the rent/quasi-rent generated by the worker on the job, through higher productivity in the firm over working in other firms, is a long run outcome of competitive labour markets. The payment of part of this rent by the firm to the worker is not merely a gift by the firm to the worker nor is it merely an inducement by the firm to the worker to reduce quits. Nor is the firm's retention of some of this rent necessarily a form of high-handed appropriation of the rents generated through the exercise of the worker's firm-specific skills.

The extra productivity resulting from firm-specific skills is not a rent in the long run from an *ab initio* perspective - that is, before the worker has learnt these skills - though he possesses the potentiality of doing so. He can join one firm and learn the skills specific to it or join another firm and learn the skills relevant to that firm. From this *ex ante* long run perspective, the emphasis is on learning abilities, which are not firm-specific. The worker is entitled to a competitive long run return to them, which in the short run after the skills are acquired takes the form of sharing in the rents generated by such skills.[1]

In the short run, this sharing of the rents is at the discretion of the firm which can deny the worker his long run share or a good part of it, incurring his resentment but without his necessarily leaving the firm. Given the applicability of the notions of fairness or/and norms common in the work-place, or/and of the efficiency wage hypothesis in this context, the firm will experience a decline of the worker's productivity due to his feelings of resentment, so that it may give him a share of the rents to avoid this resentment. But the optimal amount of the rent thus paid to the worker on the basis of short-run considerations can be - and is likely to be - somewhat different from that resulting from long run competitive factors. A variety of actual rent-sharing ratios might then exist simultaneously in the economy so that the wages of workers with identical firm-specific skills would differ among firms. As a corollary, in the short run, different firms would have different actual profits depending upon their actual rent-sharing practices.

10.2 The basic model

This was presented in chapter 3 for the analysis of the firm's decisions on the optimal number of job positions and the optimal hiring and (expected) retirement ages for the firm's workers. The firm was assumed to maximize the present discounted value of its profits, with profits equalling the sum of the 'rents' received by the firm from all job positions in the firm. For a given job position, this rent was defined as equalling the marginal product less the wage for that position. It would equal zero for the marginal job with the optimal hiring and retirement ages but would be positive for the intra-marginal job positions in the neighbourhood of the optimal hiring and retirement ages.

Note that this definition of rents (or quasi-rents) is different from the usual one in the literature on firm-specific skills. With marginal productivity diminishing with an increase in the number of job positions in the firm, intra-marginal workers would have marginal product in excess of the wage rate. This would be so whether the workers have some firm-specific skills or not. For workers with only general skills, wages would rise with an increase in such skills or other superior characteristics, so that the difference between marginal product and wages would not depend upon the possession of such skills or of a favoured age or experience. Hence, in the case of casual workers, the rent would be independent of the level of skills, of experience and of age. In the case of career workers with firm-specific skills, the rent would depend upon the level of such skills and, therefore, upon any superior characteristics which contribute to such skills. Hence, for career workers, the rent would be a function of the hiring age and the duration of employment, as well as of age.

Our model is 'intergenerational', with the replacement of 'older' workers by younger ones at the optimal retirement age for the former. The first order conditions for the optimal number of job positions and the optimal hiring and retirement ages were derived. As usual, the first order conditions implied that the marginal worker employed from the optimal hiring age to the

216

optimal retirement age yields zero rents to the firm. However, for the intra-marginal workers, any given employed worker would yield positive rents to the firm. For such workers, the worker's productivity would exceed his wage even at the retirement age, but it would still be optimal for the firm to replace him by another - younger and higher rent-yielding - worker. The possibility and desirability of the replacement of workers in the job positions in the firm plays a key role in this analysis.

The number of job positions offered by the firm was derived from the optimality conditions and was not arbitrarily fixed.

It was shown that specific optimal hiring and retirement ages are given by the analysis for career workers. The firm would be indifferent as to the hiring and job-separation ages of its casual workers.

A given firm-specific or career job position is like a dam site, in an overall context of the optimal number of dams on a river. The type of worker who best utilizes the job position in the sense of yielding the highest return to the firm would be offered the job. Workers of other, sub-optimal, types will be refused the job.

10.3 Discrimination

In firm-specific jobs, workers with the optimal ages at hiring and leaving the firm would be the ones to get the job position. Assume these to be male ones for the occupation in question. If female workers are *expected* to leave the firm before the optimal leaving age, they will not get the job position unless they are willing to accept lower wages than the optimal male workers, with these lower wages appearing as discrimination against female workers. The costs of open discrimination and the practical limits to the minimum wages acceptable to female workers would lead firms to resort to occupational differentiation by sex. Therefore, neither wage nor occupational discrimination necessarily requires the discriminatory tastes of either employers or co-workers.

Further, in our rents based explanation, firms which do not practice wage and occupational discrimination will make lower profits than firms which do, and firms which employ the non-optimal workers at the lower discriminatory wages will not make higher profits than those which employ the higher paid optimal age workers. Consequently, such discrimination can persist as a long run phenomena. This contrasts with the tastes-based type of discrimination in which firms employing the higher paid workers will not be maximizing profits and will not survive under competition in the long run.[2] Given the long run persistence of extensive discrimination against women across very many different societies and cultures, a rent-based explanation for it seems more viable than a tastes-based one.

An interesting feature of the rents based theory of discrimination is that it explains why a profit maximizing firm will pay lower wages to a female worker with a lower expected employment period than to a male one even when both the female and male workers have the same qualifications, the same years of experience, and have identical productivity on the given job. The explanation lies in the firm's expectation that the female worker will leave the job earlier than the male one and thus will impose the cost on the firm of replacing her by an inexperienced worker. The replacement female worker will, of course, be paid less because of her lower productivity due to her lesser experience; but the replaced female worker also has to bear the cost, through lower wages, of the lost *potential* for further skill accumulation because of her shorter stay on the job. Under this reasoning, the firm will not be willing to pay the male and female workers with identical skills, training and productivity, an identical wage or be indifferent between them in hiring. Calls for equal wages for equal skills, or calls for comparable worth, miss this force making for discrimination. So do most empirical studies which test for discrimination after adjusting for productivity differences: in our theory, equal current productivity is not a sufficient basis for equal pay or indifference in hiring.

Chapter 4 also showed that the extent of wage discrimination will be less in occupations which are not totally segregated - that is, ones in which the firms can and do hire both female and male workers into the same types of jobs. The extent of wage discrimination will be higher in those occupations which are totally segregated - that is, ones in which a female worker will always by followed by another female worker. The expected shorter duration of the employment of the current female worker imposes a lesser potential cost on the firm in the former case than in the latter case. Consequently, the so-called 'women's professions' in which men could not be hired, effectively had lower wages for equal comparable worth than female wages in unsegregated professions.

The rents based theory of discrimination further explains why discrimination against female workers decreases in jobs and occupations with lesser firm-specific skills - and in which there are no special disadvantages for women in terms of physical strength. Women are then found in larger proportions in casual jobs in which long term job attachment on an expected basis is not a condition in hiring. As against this, the tastes based theories cannot explain why 'female occupations' are mainly of the casual type.

The lower wages and occupational segregation implied for women by

218

the rents based theory of discrimination has, of course, the usual re-inforcing supply-side effects: lowered women's job commitment and investment in education and training. These further reduce their wages and make casual jobs the optimal types of jobs for many of them, since a high rate of turnover is by itself not unacceptable in such jobs.

If the rent-based explanation of wage discrimination is correct and the higher expected rate of turnover of females is at the core of such discrimination, the reduction in such discrimination has to come about mainly through reduction in this expected rate of turnover. Assuming a lag in expectations, reductions in the actual rate of turnover will be followed only slowly by the hiring of female workers into career occupations and, therefore, the reduction in discrimination will occur for younger cohorts of female workers and only gradually in the future. Making wage and occupational discrimination illegal may help, for the causes of discrimination can be very diverse, but such legislation by itself must be limited in its achievements, if the female rates of turnover remain significantly higher than those of males.[3]

Discrimination against female workers results in our theory from the firm's expectation that they will leave the firm before the age which is profit-maximizing for the firm. Other groups in the economy may also suffer from a similar expectation about them. These would definitely include groups with high actual rates of turnovers. Black male workers in the United States are often cited as being such a group. Mentally or physically handicapped workers are also likely to be such groups.

Discrimination against female workers is against workers expected to leave before the firm's preferred *retirement* age. Discrimination against hiring older job applicants is because they are older than the firm's preferred *hiring* age. Both impose a cost on the firm through a lower present value of rents generated on jobs with significant firm-specific skills. The profit maximizing firm will only employ the older job applicants in occupations (new or former, if they had already retired) with significant firm-specific characteristics at lower wages than paid to younger workers or will employ them in more casual jobs.

While older male workers suffer from discrimination in hiring by virtue of actually being older than the firm's preferred hiring age, female workers may also suffer from it even when they have the right age at the time of hiring. To illustrate, given a female worker of an age equal to the firm's preferred hiring age, the firm may not hire her into the job positions in which significant firm-specific skills can be acquired because her cohort has a lower expected duration of stay in the job position than required by the

219

firm's preferred retirement age.[4] If she is hired in more casual jobs, and establishes, through her commitment to the firm, an expected stay upto the firm's preferred retirement age, she would already have become older than the firm's preferred hiring age for the firm-specific jobs. She will not then be transferred into such jobs.[5] The female worker is then caught in a cycle of discrimination. To break out of this cycle, female workers as a group may have to first establish the credibility of a long, uninterrupted expected period of employment, starting from the beginning of their career with a firm.[6]

In our analysis, both discrimination against female workers and against hiring older workers occurs in the case of career jobs. They do not occur in the case of casual jobs. We would, therefore, expect both types to be prevalent or absent for particular occupations. Thus, the jobs for which a firm is more likely to avoid hiring women are also ones for which it would tend to reject hiring older male workers.

10.4 The firm's preferred retirement age

On retirement, we used separate analyses to derive the firm's and the worker's preferred retirement age functions and showed that their arguments are quite different. Further, firms find it in their interest to impose mandatory retirement ages at their preferred retirement age while workers would not want mandatory retirement. If the firm is by law barred from imposing such mandatory retirement, profit maximization would imply, depending on the actual context, actuarially fair (that is, probabilistically equivalent), conventional or pattern pension plans.

Considerable attention has been recently paid in the literature to the principal-agent problem and to incentive schemes where the worker's effort and productivity are costly to monitor and enforce. This concern is the basis of the Lazear theory of mandatory retirement which views the worker as having an inherent tendency to shirk on the job. The firm can prevent shirking by paying the worker less than his marginal product during the early years on the job, thereby accumulating a fund owed to the worker. This fund is run down by payments to the worker through wages higher than his marginal product in his later years on the job. As long as the fund exists, the worker stands to lose if he shirks on the job and is fired, since, in that case, the firm will appropriate the fund. This constitutes the penalty and the incentive not to shirk on the job. Since the worker benefits from such a scheme by not shirking and as a result having a higher path of marginal productivity, he will, the incentives theory argues, willingly enter an implicit long term job contract with the firm as a form of self-imposed discipline, with the firm devising the form of the discipline and the pain suffered by the worker for failure. This is in some ways a strange proposition: workers are supposed to put their career, with very few things more important than it in their lives, on the line in a scheme devised by their employer, as a way of disciplining themselves against shirking. It does not sound convincing as typical worker behaviour from psychological and sociological perspectives.

The above story becomes even more unrealistic if we further recognize the temptation that the fund gives to the firm to fire the worker on a spurious claim of shirking and appropriate the fund, thereby increasing its profits. It has been suggested in the literature that the barrier to this is the firm's desire to maintain *its* reputation as a reliable employer. But the firm is not a single, immutable entity. It is a series, over time, of managers. Their perception of the value of the worker and their regard for the 'reputation' of the firm can, and do vary over time. Further, strangely enough in the above story, the worker's desire to maintain *his* reputation as a good reliable worker - checked through references required from previous employers - is not an adequate discipline for him not to cheat/shirk, though a somewhat similar desire by the firm is considered an adequate discipline on the firm/managers not to cheat. Furthermore, while the worker is supposed to be able to trust the firm (as the trustee for his fund), with changing managers over time, the firm cannot trust the worker (not to shirk). The incentives theory thus relies upon asymmetrical behaviour and trust, without adequate justification presented for such an asymmetry. We find it unconvincing as a basis for the relations between numerous firms and their millions of workers, though without denying that it may be applicable in some special cases.

Our rents-based theory of the firm's preferred retirement age is symmetrical: both workers and firms share in firm-specific rents, both stand to lose considerably from a job separation and neither the firm nor the worker need to show inordinate amounts of trust or distrust in the other over long periods. If the worker shirks on the job and is fired, he loses the present value of his share of the rents over a long period in the future, with this amount likely to be greater than any fund accumulated on behalf of the worker with the firm in the incentives theory. This is a strong incentive for the worker not to shirk to an extent such that he will be fired. Correspondingly, if the firm is unreasonable enough in its treatment of the worker to induce him to quit, the firm loses the present value of the rents from his employment. This is an incentive for the firm's managers to behave as good employers in order not to lose a valuable worker. Since both the worker and the firm have an interest in staying together in the presence of firm-specific skills, our theory does not need a bond or fund for ensuring long-term job attachment or for the prevention of shirking on the job. The level of effort that the worker puts on the job is then determined by other factors such as the social norms in the industry, firm and occupation, the particular norms in the work place and the climate of "reciprocity and fairness" in the firm (Rebitzer, 1993, p. 1419).

Note that the incentives theory applies equally well to both casual and career workers. Therefore, its special wage pattern and mandatory retirement implications should be equally valid for both types of workers. As against this, our rents-based theory of retirement implies that firms have a preferred retirement - or job separation - age for career jobs, but not for casual ones. Workers in the latter can leave at a time of their own choosing since the firm does not lose or benefit from replacing them with other workers.

In the case of career jobs, as a worker ages and his abilities decline, a younger replacement worker on the same job will be more efficient and generate higher rents. Similarly, in the case of buildings or dam sites, there comes a time when it is more profitable to replace an ageing structure with a newer one. For both workers and sites, the greater the relative efficiency and productivity of the replacement unit, the earlier will the initial one be replaced. The decision to replace a worker on a job and the efficiency of the incoming generation of workers is thus vital in explaining the firm's preferred retirement age for its existing employees. These factors have generally been ignored in the incentives and other theories of retirement.

10.5 The worker's preferred retirement age

For the analysis of the worker's preferred retirement age, the assumption of the certainty of future wage and asset income is rather a poor one, even though it is generally assumed in most theories of retirement. It implies that the worker can reasonably well predict at the early stages of his career his optimal retirement age. He will then enter into a long-term contract with the firm for a pre-designated retirement age. Since the firm merely implements this contract through its mandatory retirement policy, there is no conflict or resentment by the worker against mandatory retirement.[7]

The analysis of the worker's preferred retirement age under uncertainty destroys this harmonious picture. Given the uncertainty of future wages, the worker cannot early in his career know his optimal retirement age. That must depend, among other things, on his wage (and therefore on what promotions he was given over a long career) and accumulated wealth in the neighbourhood of the retirement age. These are not known early in the worker's career. Consequently, the worker would wish to keep his options on his retirement age open and would not enter into a contract to retire at a definite (non-contingent) age. A mandatory retirement age is, therefore, a unilateral decision of the firm based on its preferred retirement age. The worker, early in his own career, may not show any interest, let alone resentment, against it since he does not know if he will want to retire at it, before it or after it. His interest in this issue will emerge late in his career as he comes to know his wages etc., close to retirement and also comes to know his own optimal retirement age. Therefore, any resentment that he may feel against a mandatory retirement age is likely to emerge late in his career. This is not to say that the worker early in his career would not prefer a job with a higher mandatory age, or with none at all, to a job with a lower one. He would do so since this would yield a greater possibility of retiring at a date of his own choosing and would increase, with other things held equal, his utility.

10.6 Pensions

The preceding arguments show that in the case of career workers, there is a strong likelihood of differences between the firm's and the worker's preferred retirement ages. The firm incurs a loss if its career workers retire at an age earlier or later than its preferred retirement age. Consequently, it would pay the firm to induce the workers to retire at this age. To do so, it may manipulate the present discounted value of pensions to achieve the desired effect. This will result in two different types of inducements. One of these is general, i.e., common to all workers in an occupation. The other is selective to individual workers. The *general* manipulation can result in:

(i) conventional pension plans where the worker is induced to increase his desired retirement age, with an increase in the present discounted value of his pension from doing so.

(ii) pattern pension plans where the worker is induced to decrease his desired retirement age, with a decrease in the present discounted value of his pension if he does not do so.

The *selective* measures are inducements to an individual worker - rather than to his group as a whole - to modify his individual retirement decision. These inducements appear as early retirement bonuses, or, in the opposite case, as special deals to stay longer on the job.

In general, since workers cannot define their preferred retirement ages till late in their careers, any inducements to change their retirement ages would occur later in their careers. Pension plans can then be treated as actuarially fair until late in the workers' career, when the non-fair components may be implemented.

For casual workers, the firm is indifferent as to when they retire. If the firm has a pension plan for them, it will be based on the total compensation due to them out of their productivity and thus be of the actuarially fair variety.

10.7 The rental value of a job position

Akerlof (1984) thought of a job position as a dam site. We extended this analogy to that of a river which can have many dam sites at many locations. For any given river - given the technology of dam building and the demand for the dams' output - there is an optimal number of dam sites and, for each one, some types of dams are more productive than others. Looking at a single dam site, if the technology of dam building and utilization changes, it may even pay the firm owning the site to remove the old dam and replace it by a new one. If the firm owning the site was to rent it to other firms which will build and operate the dam, the firm would want the highest rental value of the site - determined not in isolation for each site but in the overall context of the optimal number of dams on the river - that a competitive bidding would produce.

Another analogy to a job position is that of a land site on which trees are to be commercially planted and harvested. What are the optimal number of trees, the optimal type of tree, the optimal planting age and the optimal harvesting age of the trees? The answers to these are best analyzed as part of a tree replacement model (Clark, 1976). They yield the rental value of the site as the maximum annuity that can be earned, after other costs, from the site.

Job positions can be seen as a scarce resource, created but at some cost, with the firm as the owner of this scarce resource. Both labour and capital go into their creation. Industrial practices enhance or diminish their net worth. The firm, then, can be seen as the owner of job positions, renting them out to workers, just as dam or forest sites are. The most productive users of the job positions would be the workers who are able to pay the highest return or rental value for them, for any given amount of retention from their productivity on the jobs. The highest rental value bid for the job positions will define their actual rental value. The retention will be the wage. The workers able to pay the highest rental value and retain the highest wage would possess particular skills and particular hiring and retirement ages. Other workers, with less appropriate skills or less appropriate hiring and retirement ages, will have to guarantee the firm the same rental value, with lower retention/wage for themselves. The latter would appear as wage discrimination.

This perspective on job positions as being scarce ones, with workers bidding for them, is the dual of the standard perspective on jobs and workers: in the latter, firms bid for workers and to get them, have to pay them the highest rental value - that is, wage - which the workers' skills and hiring and retirement ages can command for them. Both pictures are valid and useful. Focusing on the dual brings to the forefront some elements which often go unnoticed in the standard picture. One of these is the firm's interest in the replacement of workers on the job and in the productivity of the replacement workers. Consequently, the influence of the productivity of the incoming generations of workers - and through it of technical change and of learning - on the hiring, retirement and pension plans of the current generation of workers cannot be ignored. It is at its most visible in industries with rapidly changing skill requirements or where ageing has a strong impact at relatively younger ages, such as physical team sports and fashion modelling, but it is relevant to all firm-specific jobs.

Note that the rental value of a casual job position is not affected by the superior age or other characteristics of the worker. For such job positions, the firm does not have to take into consideration the personal characteristics of the replacement workers. However, the ability to use the capital equipment on the job must remain a requirement.

10.8 The impact of innovations

Technological, social and other changes can alter the firm's share of the rents from its job positions. Such changes are likely to alter the optimal hiring and retirement ages. Chapter 6 showed that such effects would differ if the innovations in rents are identical over all generations, including the present one, than if the innovations are confined to the future generation only or to the present generation only. To illustrate, consider a technical change which increases the productivity and the firm's share of the rents only from the future generations of workers, while leaving those of the current generation unchanged. Such an innovation will lower the optimal retirement age of the current generation of workers. If this decrease was unexpected and the revised optimal age becomes less than the mandatory retirement one - based on the outdated optimal age calculations - firms would find it profit maximizing to retire their current workers earlier through early retirement bonuses and other industrial practices.

Now suppose that the exogenous change was one of improvements in health at older ages, so that the onset of the declines in productivity and the firm's share of the rents will be postponed for several years for all generations of workers. In this case, the firm's optimal retirement age will rise for all generations of workers. However, if there were no such changes in productivity and in rents, but there was increased longevity, the optimal retirement ages set by the firm will not change but the years beyond retirement would increase. If such a pattern was common among firms in the economy, it is likely to cause workers to put greater economic and legal pressure on firms to raise their retirement ages and/or to provide greater income support for the post-retirement years.

Chapter 4 looked briefly at the effects of exogenous changes in the health and longevity on discrimination. It commented on changes which make it feasible for women to work outside the home for periods as long as ones for which men do so. The impact of these on wage and occupational discrimination was analyzed in sections 4.7 and 4.8 of chapter 4. An increase in the health and longevity of the male workers, with an unchanged period of employment expected for the female workers, was shown to increase wage and occupational differentiation. Exogenous changes in fertility rates, in health, in the technology of work in the home and the workplace and other factors have tended to increase the female actual and expected duration of employment with the firm. Such innovations were shown to decrease wage and occupational differentiation. Using a stylized loose interpretation of twentieth century history, the former types of changes were dominant until the 1960s, and the latter were dominant since the 1960s in west European and American industrialized economies. *Ceteris paribus*, our theory then implies that the male-female wage differential would have worsened until the 1960s and improved since then. The effect since the 1960s would be most noticeable in the male-female wage and occupational differentiation of young workers since it is the *expected* duration of employment, with the expectations formulated at the hiring age, that is really relevant. Older workers who were expected to stay with the firm for only a short period but continued for a longer period, would not benefit fully from their longer actual duration of employment.

This book has only considered a few of the types of innovations that can affect the rents retained by firms and the main areas of interest to us. There can clearly be many other types of innovations.

This book has also considered many other issues. Among these are occupational segregation (chapter 4), severance payments (chapter 7), and the vesting of pension funds (chapter 9). We refer the reader to the appropriate chapters for their treatment.

As we have mentioned at other points in the book, we have tried to draw out the common elements among the determinants of the labour market phenomena studied in this book. We believe these elements to be among their major determinants. However, there are likely to be many possible determinants of such phenomena, some of which are likely to be distinctive and isolated to each phenomenon, or to its specific nature in a particular society and economy. The possible existence and relevance of these distinctive elements cannot be ruled out and is not being denied.

FOOTNOTES

1. Rebitzer (1993, p. 1418) has argued that rent-sharing models need to explain why firms would be willing to share the rents with the workers even when the workers do not have strong bargaining power, as for example in the absence of unions. Our explanation of this relies on two sorts of considerations: long run ones through the mobility of workers who want to make *ex ante* choices on joining that firm which promises to pay the highest return to their characteristics, and short run ones based on efficiency wages and notions of fair play and social norms. The latter are often embedded in social practices. (Rebitzer, 1993, p. 1419, fn. 44). Both the long run and the short run factors are reinforced by the emphasis of our model on the replacement of workers on the job and the time required by the replacement worker to acquire firm-specific skills.
2. See Bergmann (1989) for evidence that firms which persistently employ the higher paid male workers when equally qualified and cheaper female workers were available do not suffer relative to other firms which employ the female workers, thus rejecting Becker's tastes-based theory of discrimination (pp. 51-52).
3. Policies that reduce the rate of such turnover and absenteeism on the job can help to reduce discrimination against female workers. Such policies would include better child care and nursery facilities, etc. (For example, see Fuchs, 1989, pp. 38-41).
4. This is, of course, statistical discrimination.
5. Female workers slotted into more casual jobs and then maintained in them have no incentive for job attachment: they can change jobs without a significant wage loss. This will, in turn, induce greater turnover, reinforcing firms' expectations that, on average, female workers do not stay on the job as long as male workers do. There is ample empirical evidence of such

employment patterns and effects (Hamermesh and Rees, 1988, p. 369; Ragan and Smith, 1981).

6. Recent empirical evidence indicates that women's average wages are growing faster than men's, as their uninterrupted stay in the labour force increases and their skills improve. However, there still exist persistent differences in both of these between male and female workers. (see Smith and Ward, 1989; Fuchs, 1989).

7. In this theory, this resentment may emerge late in the worker's career but is really an attempt on his part to renege on a mutually agreed-upon contract entered early in his career. It may be accompanied by bitterness and regret at his own past actions.

Bibliography

Abraham, K.G., and Farber, H.S., "Job Duration, Seniority, and Earnings", Working Paper No. 1819, National Bureau of Economic Research, January 1986. Modified version published in *American Economic Review*, 77, June 1987, pp. 278-97.

Adnett, N., *Labour Market Policy*. London: Longman, 1989.

Aigner, D.J., and Cain, G.G., "Statistical Theories of Discrimination in Labor Markets", *Industrial and Labour Relations Review*, 30, January 1977, pp. 175-87.

Akerlof, G.A., *An Economic Theorist's Book of Tales*. Cambridge: Cambridge University Press, 1984.

Akerlof, G.A., and Yellen, J.L., eds., *Efficiency Wage Models of the Labor Market*. Cambridge: Cambridge University Press, 1986.

Altonji, J. and Shakotko, R.A., "Do Wages Rise with Job Seniority", Working Paper No. 1616, National Bureau of Economic Research, May 1985; Also in: *Review of Economic Studies*, 54, July 1987, pp. 437-59.

Arrow, K., "The Theory of Discrimination", in Ashenfelter, O., and Rees, A., eds., *Discrimination in the Labor Market*. Princeton, N.J.: Princeton University Press, 1973, pp. 3-33.

Ashenfelter, O., and Layard, R., eds., *Handbook of Labor Economics*. Amsterdam: North-Holland, 1986.

Ashenfelter, O., and Rees, A., eds., *Discrimination in the Labor Market*. Princeton, N.J.: Princeton University Press, 1973.

Baily, M.N., "Aging and the ability to Work: Policy Issues and Recent Trends", in Burtless, G., ed., *Work, Health and Income among the Elderly*. Washington, D.C.: Brookings Institution, 1987, pp. 59-97.

Becker, G.S., *The Economics of Discrimination*. Chicago: University of

Chicago Press, 1971.

_____, *Human Capital*. New York: National Bureau of Economic Research, 1975.

_____, "Human Capital, Effort, and the Sexual Division of Labor", *Journal of Labor Economics*, 3, January 1985, pp. S33-58.

Becker, G.S., and Stigler, G.J., "Law Enforcement, Malfeasance and Compensation of Enforcers", *Journal of Legal Studies*, 3, 1974, pp. 1-18.

Bergmann, B.R., "Does the Market for Women's Labor Need Fixing?", *Journal of Economic Perspectives*, 3, Winter 1989, pp. 43-60.

Bernhardt, D., and Timmins, G.C., "Multiperiod Wage Contracts and Productivity Profiles", *Journal of Labor Economics*, 8, October 1990, pp. 529-63.

Blank, R.M., "Review of *Work, Health and Income among the Elderly*", *Journal of Human Resources*, 23, Summer 1988, pp. 397-411.

Blau, F.D., and Ferber, M.A., "Career Plans and Expectations of Young Women and Men: The Earnings Gap and Labor Force Participation", *Journal of Human Resources*, 26, Fall 1991, pp. 581-607.

Blaug, M., "The Empirical Status of Human Capital Theory: A Slightly Jaundiced Survey", *Journal of Economic Literature*, 14, September 1976, pp. 827-55.

Blinder, A.S., *Private Pensions and Public Pensions: Theory and Fact*. Woytinski Lecture No.5, Department of Economics, University of Michigan, December 1981.

Burbidge, J.B., and Robb, A.L. "Pensions and Retirement Behaviour", *Canadian Journal of Economics*, 13, August 1980, pp. 421-37.

Burkhauser, R.V., and Quinn, J.F., "Is Mandatory Retirement Overrated? Evidence from the 1970s", *Journal of Human Resources*, 18, Summer 1983, pp. 337-358.

Burtless, G., ed., *Work, Health and Income among the Elderly*. Washington, D.C.: Brookings Institution, 1987.

Cain, R.G., "The Challenge of Segmented Labor Market Theories to Orthodox Theory: A Survey", *Journal of Economic Literature*, 14, December 1976, pp. 1215-58.

Cannings, K., "The Earnings of Female and Male Middle Managers: A Canadian case Study", *Journal of Human Resources*, 23, Winter 1988, pp. 34-57.

Carmichael, L., "Firm-Specific Human Capital and Promotion Ladders", *Bell Journal of Economics*, 14, Spring 1983, pp. 251-58.

_____, "Self-enforcing Contracts, Shirking, and Life Cycle Incentives", *Journal of Economic Perspectives*, 3, Fall 1989, pp. 65-83.

Clark, C.W., *Mathematical Bioeconomics*. New York: John Wiley & Sons, 1976.

Clark, R., Kreps, J., and Spengler, J., "Economics of Aging: A Survey", *Journal of Economic Literature*, 16, September 1978, pp. 919-62.

Denison, E.F., *The Sources of Economic Growth in the United States and the Alternatives Before Us*. New York: Committee for Economic Development, 1962.

Doeringer, P.B., and Piore, M.J., *Internal Labor Markets and Manpower Analysis*. Lexington, Mass.: D.C. Heath, 1971.

Dow, G.K., "Why Capital hires Labor: A Bargaining Perspective", *American Economic Review*, 83, March 1993, pp. 118-34.

Duesenberry, J.S., *Income, Saving and the Theory of Consumer Behavior*. Cambridge: Harvard University Press, 1949.

Ehrenberg, R.G., and Smith, R.S., *Modern Labour Economics*, 3rd. ed. Glenview, Ill.: Scott, Foresman and Co., 1988.

Elster, J., "Social Norms and Economic Theory", *Journal of Economic Perspectives*, 3, Fall 1989, pp. 99-117.

England, P., "The Failure of Human Capital Theory to Explain Occupational Sex Segregation", *Journal of Human Resources*, 17, Summer 1982, pp. 358-70.

Fama, E.F., "Agency Problems and the Theory of the Firm", *Journal of Political Economy*, 88, April 1980, pp. 288-307.

Fearn, R.M., *Labor Economics: The Emerging Synthesis*. Cambridge, Mass.: 1981.

Fields, G.S., and Mitchell, O.S., *Retirement, Pensions, and Social Security*. Cambridge, Mass.: MIT Press, 1984.

Fields, J., and Wolff, E.N., "The Decline of Sex Segregation and the Wage Gap, 1970-80", *Journal of Human Resources*, 26, Fall 1991, pp. 608-22.

Foster, J.E., and Wan, H.Y. Jnr., "Involuntary Unemployment as a Worker Discipline Device", in Akerlof, G.A., and Yellen, J.L., eds., *Efficiency Wage Models of the Labor Market*. Cambridge: Cambridge University Press, 1986, pp. 57-65.

Fox, H., and Kerpen, M.C., *Corporate Retirement Policy and Practice*. Personnel Policy Study no. 190. New York: National Industrial Conference Board, 1964.

Frank, R.H., "Melding Sociology and Economics: James Coleman's Foundations of Social Theory", *Journal of Economic Literature*, 30, March 1992, pp. 147-70.

Fuchs, V.R., "Women's Quest for Economic Equality", *Journal of Economic*

Perspectives, 3, Winter 1989, pp. 25-41.

Gee, E.M., and McDaniel, S.A., "Pension Politics and Challenges: Retirement Policy Implications", *Canadian Public Policy*, 17, Winter 1991, pp. 456-72.

Gera, S., and Rahman, S.S., "Sectoral Shifts and Canadian Unemployment: Evidence from the Microdata", Paper presented at *Canadian Economic Association Meetings*, Quebec, June 1989.

Gibbons, R., and Murphy, K.J., "optimal Incentive Contracts in the Presence of Career Concerns: Theory and Evidence", *Journal of Political Economy*, 100, June 1992, pp. 468-505.

Gordon, M.S., "The Older Worker and Hiring Policies", *Monthly Labor Review*, 82, November 1959, pp. 1198-1205.

_____, "Older Workers and Retirement Practices", *Monthly Labor Review* 83, June 1960, pp. 577-85.

Gordon, M.S., and Blinder, A.S., "Market Wages, Reservation Wages and Retirement Decisions", *Journal of Public Economics*, 14, October 1980, pp. 277-308.

Groschen, E.L., "The Structure of the Female/Male Wage Differential", *Journal of Human Resources*, 26, Summer 1991, pp. 457-72.

Gunderson, M., "Male-Female Wage Differentials and Policy Responses", *Journal of Economic Literature*, 27, March 1989, pp. 46-72.

Hall, R.E., "Employment Fluctuations and Wage Rigidity", *Brookings Papers on Economic Activity*, 1, 1980, pp. 91-123.

Hamermesh, D.S. and Rees, A., *The Economics of Work and Pay*. New York: Harper and Row, 1988.

Hashimoto, M., "Specific Capital, Employment Contracts, and Wage Rigidity", *Bell Journal of Economics*, 11, Autumn 1980, pp. 536-49.

Hicks, J., *The Crisis in Keynesian Economics*. Oxford: Basil Blackwell, 1974.

Howe, C.W., *Natural Resource Economics*. New York: John Wiley & Sons, 1979.

Hogarth, J.M., "Accepting An Early Retirement Bonus: An Empirical Study", *Journal of Human Resources*, 23, Winter 1988, pp. 21-32.

Hutchens, R.M., "Layoffs and Labor Supply", *International Economic Review*, 24, February 1983, pp. 37-55.

_____, "Delayed Payment Contracts and a Firm's Propensity to Hire Older Workers", *Journal of Labor Economics*, 4, October 1986, pp. 439-57.

_____, "A Test of Lazear's Theory of Delayed Payment Contracts", *Journal of Labor Economics*, 5, October 1987, pp. S153-

70.
_____, "Seniority, Wages and Productivity: A Turbulent Decade", *Journal of Economic Perspectives*, 3, Fall 1989, pp. 49-64.

Jacobson, L.S., Lalonde, R.A., and Sullivan, D.G., "Earnings Losses of Displaced Persons", *American Economic Review*, 83, September 1993, pp. 685-709.

Juhn, C., Murphy, K.M., and Pierce, B., "Wage Inequality and the Rise in Returns to Skill", *Journal of Political Economy*, 101, June 1993, pp. 410-42.

Keynes, J.M., *The General Theory of Employment, Interest, and Money*. London: Macmillan, 1936.

Kleiler, F.M., *Can We Afford Early Retirement*. Baltimore: Johns Hopkins Press, 1978.

Kreps, J., "A Case Study of Variables in Retirement Policy", *Monthly Labour Review*, 84, June 1961, pp. 587-91.

Krueger, A.B., and Summers, L.H., "Reflections on the Inter-industry Wage Structure", in Lang, K., and Leonard, J.S., eds., *Unemployment and the Structure of Labor Markets*. New York: Blackwell, 1987, pp. 17-47.

Lancaster, K.J., "A New Approach to Consumer Theory", *Journal of Political Economy*, 74, April 1966a, pp. 132-57.

_____, "Change and Innovation in the Technology of Consumption", *American Economic Review*, 56, May 1966b, pp. 14-23.

Landes, E.M., "Sex-Differences in Wages and Employment: A Test of the Specific Capital Hypothesis", *Economic Inquiry*, 15, October 1977, pp. 523-38.

Lang, K., and Leonard, J.S., eds., *Unemployment and the Structure of Labor Markets*. New York: Blackwell, 1987.

Lapp, J.S., "Mandatory Retirement as a Clause in an Employment Insurance Contract", *Economic Inquiry*, 23, January 1985, pp. 69-92.

Lazear, E.P., "Why is there Mandatory Retirement", *Journal of Political Economy*, 87, December 1979, pp. 1261-84.

_____, "Agency, Earnings Profiles, Productivity, and Hours Restrictions", *American Economic Review*, 71, September 1981, pp. 606-20.

_____, "Severance Pay, Pensions and Efficient Mobility", Working Paper no.854, National Bureau of Economic Research, February, 1982.

_____, "Symposium on Women in the Labor Market", *Journal of Economic Perspectives*, 3, Winter 1989, pp. 3-7.

Lazear, E.P., and Moore, R.L., "Incentives, Productivity and Labor Contracts", *Quarterly Journal of Economics*, 99, May 1984, pp. 275-296.

Lazear, E.P., and Rosen, S., "Male-Female Wage Differentials in Job Ladders", *Journal of Labor Economics*, 8, January 1990, pp. S106-23.

Leigh, D.E., "Why is there Mandatory Retirement? An Empirical Reexamination", *Journal of Human Resources*, 19, Fall 1984, pp. 512-31.

Lloyd, C.B., Andrews, E.S., and Gilroy, C.L., *Women in the Labour Force*. New York: Columbia University Press, 1979.

Lloyd, C.B., and Niemi, B.T., *The Economics of Sex Differentials*. New York: Columbia University Press, 1979.

Loprest, P.J., "Gender Differences in wage Growth and Job Mobility", *American Economic Review*, 82, May 1992, pp. 526-32.

Machina, M.J., "Dynamic Consistency and Non-Expected Utility Models of Choice under Uncertainty", *Journal of Economic Literature*, 27, December 1989, pp. 1622-68.

Madden, J.F., *The Economics of Sex Discrimination*. Lexington, Mass.: Heath, 1978.

McLaughlin, K.J., "General Productivity Growth in a Theory of Quits and Layoffs", *Journal of Labor Economics*, 8, January 1990, pp. 75-98.

Medoff, J.L., and Abraham, K.G., "Experience, Performance and Earnings", *Quarterly Journal of Economics*, 95, December 1980, pp. 703-36.

_____, "Are Those Paid More Really More Productive?: The Case of Experience", *Journal of Human Resources*, 16, Spring 1981, pp. 186-216.

Mincer, J., "The Distribution of Labor Incomes: A Survey with Special Reference to the Human Capital Approach", *Journal of Economic Literature*, 8, March 1970, pp. 1-26.

_____, *Schooling, Experience and Earnings*. New York: National Bureau of Economic Research, 1974.

Mincer, J., and Polachek, S., "Family Investment in Human Capital: Earnings of Women", *Journal of Political Economy*, 82, March/April 1974, pp. S76-108.

_____, "Women's Earnings Re-examined", Journal of Human *Resources*, 13, Winter 1978,, pp. 118-34.

McLaughlin, K.L., "General Productivity Growth in a Theory of Quits and Layoffs", *Journal of Labor Economics*, 8, January 1990, pp. 75-98.

Munnell, A.C., *The Economics of Private Pensions*. Washington, D.C.: Brookings Institution, 1982.

Murphy, K.M., and Welch, F., "Empirical Age-Earnings Profiles", *Journal of Labor Economics*, 8, April 1990, pp. 202-29.

Neumark, D., "Employers' Discriminatory Behavior and the Estimation of Wage Discrimination", *Journal Of Human Resources*, 23, Summer 1988, pp. 279-95.

Oi, W., "Labor as a Quasi-fixed Factor", *Journal of Political Economy*, 70, December 1962, pp. 538-555.

Okun, A.M., *Prices and Quantities*. Washington, D.C.: Brookings Institution, 1981.

Osberg, L., "Is it Retirement or Unemployment? Induced 'Retirement' and Constrained Labour Supply among Older Workers", Paper prepared for the *Review of Demography*. Ottawa: Health and Welfare, 1988.

Paglin, M., and Rufolo, A.M., "Heterogeneous Human Capital, Occupational Choice, and Male-Female Earnings Differences", *Journal of Labor Economics*, 8, January 1990, pp. 123-24.

Parnes, H.S., ed., *Work and Retirement: A Longitudinal Study of Men*. Cambridge, Mass.: MIT Press, 1981.

Pesando, J.E., and Rea, S.A. Jnr., *Public and Private Pensions in Canada, an Economic Analysis*. Toronto: University of Toronto Press, 1977.

Phelps, E.S., "Okun's Micro-Macro System: A Review", *Journal of Economic Literature*, 19, September 1981, pp. 1065-73.

Polachek, S.W., "Differences in Expected Post-School Investment as a Determinant of Market Wage Differentials", *International Economic Review*, 16, June 1975, pp. 451-70.

_____, "Occupational Self-Selection: A Human Capital Approach to Sex Differences in Occupational Structure", *Review of Economics and Statistics*, 63, February 1981, pp. 60-69.

Poterba, J.M., and Summers, L.H., "Public Policy Implications of Old-Age Mortality", in Burtless, G., ed., *Work, Health and Income among the Elderly*. Washington, D.C.: Brookings Institution, 1987, pp. 19-51.

Pratten, C.F., *Labor Productivity Differentials within International Companies*. Cambridge, Cambridge University Press, 1976.

Ragan, J.F., and Smith, S.P., "The Impact on Differences in Turnover Rates on Male/Female Pay Differentials", *Journal of Human Resources*, 16, Summer 1981, pp. 343-65.

Ragan, J.F., Jr., and Tremblay, C.H., "Testing for Employee Discrimination by Race and Sex", *Journal of Human Resources*, 23, Winter 1988, pp. 123-37.

Quinn, J.E., "Is mandatory Retirement Overrated? Evidence from the 1970s", *Journal of Human Resources*, 18, Summer 1983, pp. 337-58.

Rebitzer, J.B., "Radical Political Economy and the Economics of Labor Markets", *Journal of Economic Literature*, 31, September 1993, pp. 1394-434.

Rima, I.H., "Involuntary Unemployment and the Respecified Labor Supply Curve", *Journal of Post-Keynesian Economics*, 6, Summer 1984, pp. 540-50.

Rosen, S., "Learning and Experience in the Labor Market", *Journal of Human Resources*, 7, Summer 1972, pp. 326-42.

_____, "Implicit Contracts: A Survey", *Journal of Economic Literature*, 23, September 1985, pp. 1144-75.

Salop, S.C., "A Model of the Natural Rate of Unemployment", in Akerlof, G.A., and Yellen, J.L., eds., *Efficiency Wage Models of the Labor Market*. Cambridge: Cambridge University Press, 1986, pp. 93-101.

Sandell, S.H., and Shapiro, D., "An Exchange: The Theory of Human Capital and the Earnings of Women: A Re-examination of the Evidence", *Journal of Human Resources*, 13, Winter 1978, pp. 103-17.

_____, "Work Expectations, Human Capital Accumulation, and the Wages of Young Women", *Journal of Human Resources*, 15, September 1980, pp. 335-53.

Schoemaker, P.J., "The Expected Utility Model: Its Variants, Purposes, Evidence and Limitations", *Journal of Economic Literature*, 20, June 1982, pp. 529-63.

Schultz, T.W., "Investment in Human Capital", *American Economic Review*, 51, March 1961, pp. 1-17.

Shapiro, C., and Stiglitz, J.E., "Equilibrium Unemployment as a Worker Discipline Device", *American Economic Review*, 74, June 1984, pp. 433-44.

Slavick, F., *Compulsory and Flexible Retirement in the American Economy*. Ithaca, N.Y.: Cornell University, 1966.

Sloane, P.J., "Discrimination in the Labour Market", in D. Carline *et al*, *Labour Economics*. London: Longmans, 1985, pp. 78-158.

Smith, J.P., and Ward, M., "Women in the Labor Market and in the Family", *Journal of Economic Perspectives*, 3, Winter 1989, pp. 9-23.

Solow, R.M., "Another Possible Source of Wage Stickiness", in Akerlof, G.A., and Yellen, J.L., eds., *Efficiency Wage Models of the Labor Market*. Cambridge: Cambridge University Press, 1986, pp. 41-4.

Spengler, J.J., "Introductory Comment: Work Requirements and Work Capacity", in Kreps, J.M., *Lifetime Allocation of Work and Income*. Durham, North Carolina: Duke University Press, 1971.

Stern, S., "Promotion and Optimal Retirement", *Journal of Labor Economics*, 5, October 1987, pp. S107-23.

Thurow, L.C., "A Job Competition Model", in Piore, M.J., ed., *Unemployment and Inflation*. White Plains, N.Y.: M.E. Sharpe, 1979.

Topel, R., "Specific Capital, Mobility, and Wages: Wages rise with Job Seniority", *Journal of Political Economy*, 99, February 1991, pp. 145-76.

Viscusi, W.K., "Self-Selection, Learning-Induced Quits and the Optimal Wage Structure", *International Economic Review*, 21, October 1980, pp. 529-46.

Weiss, A.M., "Job Queues and Layoffs in Labor Markets with Flexible Wages", in Akerlof, G.A., and Yellen, J.L., eds., *Efficiency Wage Models of the Labor Market*. Cambridge: Cambridge University Press, 1986, pp. 41-4.

Welford, A.T., *Ageing and Human Skill*. Westport, Conn.: Greenwood Press, 1958.

Wise, D.A., *Pensions and the Labor Market*. Cambridge, Mass.: National Bureau of Economic Research, 1984.

Wolpin, K.I., "The Determinants of Black-White Differences in Early Employment Careers: Search, Layoffs, Quits, and Endogenous Wage Growth", *Journal of Political Economy*, 100, June 1992, pp. 535-60.

Zellner, H., "The Determinants of Occupational Segregation", in Lloyd, C., ed., *Sex, Discrimination and the Division of Labor*. New York, N.Y.: Columbia University Press, 1975.